C000133015

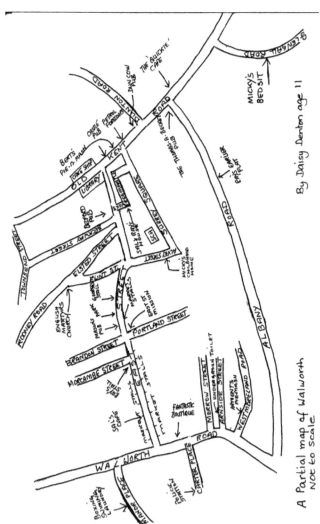

A Partial map of Walworth
Not to scale

By Daisy Denton age 11

Long Live Love

An East Lane Novel

by

Annie B. Brown

Foreword

Walworth is an actual borough of South East London, nestled between Camberwell and the Elephant and Castle. I have drawn on my memories of growing up in Walworth, where I lived until the age of 14.

'Long Live Love,' is a work of fiction, all characters and names are fictitious, with the exception of Tommy Gibbons, a local boxer and one time landlord of The Thomas A Beckett pub.

I have used poetic licence to add shops and stalls to the East Lane market area, that would not have been there during the novels 1969 timeline.

Any mistakes regarding street layouts etcetera are mine entirely. I hope you enjoy my debut novel, and would very much appreciate if you could leave a review. Reviews, especially positive ones, help new writers' immensely.

Walworth. London. 1969

Chapter 1

Ruby smelt him before she saw him. His cloying, musty aftershave, so dense she could taste it. In one swift movement he was on her, giving her no time to react. He jostled her backwards, closer to the shop fronts. Fear stripped her voice and muddled her thinking, giving him greater control, as a nauseous panic turned in her stomach like a flipped coin. With her back pressed into a column of brickwork, he moved his lean body closer. His right hand positioned on the wall to the side of her head. Ruby flinched as her hair snagged in the setting of his gold sovereign ring. The clock above the gentlemen's outfitters directly opposite chimed the hour. Eleven p.m.

'Well, you're a pretty thing, ain't yer? No need to look so scared,' he said, his face within inches of hers. 'Just one measly snog and I'll be on me way. Not too much to ask now, is it?' His lop-sided grin failed to reach his cold, penetrating stare. Unable to escape his foul boozy breath, her focus zeroed in on his gappy teeth. Gappy teeth are lucky teeth, she once heard it said. Ruby knew that if she'd had one ounce of her sister Ellen's courage, the tanked-up Casanova would be choking on those lucky teeth right about now.

His sudden frown lines meant one thing only, he'd spotted the birthmark floating above her right eyebrow. He blew a narrow stream of breath into her fringe, revealing the port wine shape in all its glory. 'Geez, that's one messed up heart tattoo.' He traced the outline with a fingernail. 'Proper amateur job that. I hope you didn't pay the shyster?' He forced a throaty chuckle.

Ruby, frozen by the sickly grin that never left his face, ignored his stale comments. Without warning, his free hand forcibly gripped her outer thigh. Her sharp intake of breath was duly noted. 'Good to see I've got your attention finally,' he leered. Ruby's heart quickened as his fingers rotated deep into her flesh. She quickly closed the gap between her legs.

'Now there's a turn up. Not often I come across a shy one.'

His friend shifted uncomfortably in the car parked at the kerb. With the engine still running he stretched across the passenger seat and wound down the window. 'Give it a rest mate. You can see she's not interested,' he called. 'I'll get pulled by the Old Bill if we don't shift it. You coming or what?'

Drawing breath through thin taut lips, Mickey turned his head. 'Hold your sodding horses. Do yourself a favour, watch and learn,' he sniggered. Before he spoke another word, Ruby had ducked beneath his arm and run full speed along the main street. Checking that he hadn't given chase, and with a safe distance between them, she stopped, caught her breath, and against her better judgement, screamed out, 'Stinking rotten creep!'

His fist, slamming down on the car bonnet made her jump and wish she had kept her mouth firmly shut. She darted swiftly down a side road, where she crawled alongside parked cars, gulping in air and fighting back tears. Resting her cheek against a cold metal bumper, she remained poised, ready to take off again if need be. Her ears pricked at the slightest sound and imagined footsteps set her blood pumping faster still.

When she decided to remain in Walworth alone, she hadn't considered the pitfalls, the dangers linked to those with 'God's gift' stamped on their forehead. In hindsight, she should have snapped up her sister Ellen's offer and moved out to the sticks with the newly-weds. Ellen would have looked out for her, kept her safe.

Hoisting the corded handle of her bag over her shoulder, Ruby straightened up and made her way back to the lengthy Old Kent Road; for all its hazards it remained far safer than the dark and lonely side streets. The main road, hemmed either side with shops, public houses and the occasional petrol forecourt squeezed in-between, was well lit during late evening hours such as now. The pubs were already turning out and Ruby had yet to find a safe haven.

Walking at a steady pace, she kept a discreet eye on the party-goers and skirted round the occasional smooching couple. Saturday nights were reserved for the pleasure-seekers, the fashion gurus and half-cut blokes with dicks like divining rods, honing in on anything remotely female. The Cinderellas in their groovy kitschy prints still managed to dent her dwindling ego. With her lengthy auburn hair partially covering her face, she moved closer to the shop fronts and continued on.

Several yards ahead, a doddery old man shuffled away from a narrow brick outbuilding. He staggered and cussed his craggy hands as they fumbled with his open fly. His greasy grey hair matched the colour of the belt string hanging from his waist. He peered up, side-on and met Ruby's gaze.

'Had a good look, you dirty little cow,' he slurred. 'Piss off home to your mother.'

Her mind ticked over and heart plummeted at the idea taking shape. To walk indefinitely with no bolt hole to aim for filled her with dread. Being fussy was not an option.

With the old man no longer in sight, Ruby pushed back the door of the public toilet and bolted it behind her. Standing in the cramped, tomb-like building, breathing through the filter of her jacket sleeve. she clasped her meagre belongings to her chest and cried. She had promised herself there would be no more tears, but hadn't bargained on the rush of self-pity that swamped her. 'Happy birthday, Watermelon' she mumbled to herself.

The warm draught from the gap below the door grazed her bare ankles. Inch by slender inch she lowered herself to the ground. Lying lengthways across the door for added security would keep late night revellers out. Her possessions, packed in a duffel bag, doubled as a pillow and protected her face from the harshness of the pitted concrete floor. Her feet, wedged to the right of the toilet bowl became an anchor, and with fingers tightly crossed would keep her safe till morning.

Her brother Gary had been right as usual, when, as scraps of kids he had nick-named her Watermelon. She was a cry-baby, petrified of hidden terrors lurking in the darkness, forever present, waiting to pounce. She had good reason too, but some things, no matter how frightening, were best kept to yourself. How many times had Gary told her, *you're always bleeding crying, for gawds sake. If anyone hurts you, just tell me and I'll duff 'em up.* He had promised to protect her, and Ruby, in turn, vowed to stand his corner against any girl who dared to call him four-eyes.

She imagined her mother's voice, its soft and sunny tone relaying the usual yearly message. *Happy birthday, Rube*, she'd say, before handing over a card, heavy with two half-crowns inside, followed by, *hold onto your dreams, girl. They're stacking up out there, somewhere.*

Sixteen years and nothing to mark the occasion, thought Ruby, then quickly berated herself for wasting head space on such trivial shit. Sure, as a little girl she would have been devastated to have her special day slip by unnoticed. But today, here, in the filthy urine sprayed lavatory, with its gag-inducing fumes, it should have been the least of her worries. Besides, in her heart she knew that her precious family would be thinking of her, and there would be an envelope with her name on safe inside her mother's handbag.

The door handle rattled with noisy urgency, tripping her heart into a thunderous gallop. She lay rigid. Her hands clamped tight over her mouth to quieten her breathing. A hefty, well-placed kick to the lower panel reverberated down the length of her spine. Silent tears soaked into the makeshift pillow.

'Get a fucking move on for crying out loud.' The desperate shout echoed in the stillness of the petrol forecourt. 'I'm breaking me bloody neck out 'ere.'

Holding her breath till the cursing faded, Ruby covered her ears as the straggler relieved himself against a nearby dustbin. She imagined her mother's arms wrapped tightly around her; the smell of her lavender fragrance and softness of her hair as it brushed her flushed damp cheek. She fancied she heard her singing a familiar Patsy Cline song, which had soothed Ruby to sleep more times than she could remember. As night drew on and the hum of silence wrapped around her, she finally drifted into a fitful sleep.

A tuneful whistling stirred Ruby. She rubbed her eyes as her face stretched in a yawn. She guessed her father was up and doing, making a start on their early morning tea. The voices in conversation beyond the door puzzled her momentarily. She suddenly twigged and scrambled to her feet, bashing her forehead on the grimy sink in the process. A fractured 'argh' pushed through her clenched teeth. Stepping outside she ignored the curious stares of the pump attendants. She closed the toilet door behind her and walked over to the low wall surrounding the forecourt, where she sat with her face upturned allowing the fine rain to wash away her tiredness.

The younger of the attendants drew close. 'You weren't kipping in there by any chance?' he asked.

'You must be joking!' she said, trying to laugh it off. 'Have you seen the state of that place?'

With no place to go, her thoughts tracked back to the day that she had stood with her family at the bus stop, to the right of the forecourt, however many weeks ago. She had lost all sense of time. One day was much the same as another: long, tiring and achingly empty. She could see them now, huddled together on that July morning. They could have been setting off for a day by the sea, loaded down with bags of goodies. No one would have been any the wiser. Only they knew that there would be no kiss-me-quick hats at the end of their journeys: no sand between their toes or giggles at the saucy postcard stands.

Eleven-year-old Daisy had tried to comfort their little sister, Mary, who'd clung desperately to their mother's coat. Her quivering bottom lip warned of a screaming frenzy should anyone prise her fingers loose. Their brother, Gary, now one of the workforce, had never been known to cry. How he'd made it to his seventeenth birthday without a day's blubbering had to be some kind of miracle. Hiding his pain behind a cheeky grin, in keeping with his tough-boy image, he dashed off towards Darwin Street and the rented room he would share with his buddy.

We best be making tracks, their mother Kate had said, her eyes glazed with tears. *You sure you girls will be all right?* She'd asked for the umpteenth time, ever grateful that her old mate Cecelia had agreed to take in the older two until Kate got herself fixed up. *You do know I'll be back for you as soon as soon as I've found us a place?*

7

Course we do, stop worrying, said Ellen, the eldest, taking charge as usual. *It's all sorted. We'll be fine,* she lied, elbowing Ruby to back her up. The two girls edged away, arms linked tightly for moral support, glancing backwards every few steps. *Smile, make like it's all right,* Ellen urged. *For Mum's sake.*

Ruby's steps were hesitant. To walk away from her mum, not knowing if she would ever see her again, was the hardest thing she had ever been asked to do. Smiling was the last thing on her mind. Part way along the road, Ellen turned left onto Dunton Bridge. Ruby tugged her sister's arm and the girls paused at the corner.

But Cecelia, or whatever she calls herself, lives in Deptford. What're we going round here for? Ruby protested.

If you think I'm staying with that stuck-up mare you've got another think coming. She hates my guts, always has. Ruby's mouth dropped open. As far as she knew everything had been arranged. Ellen attempted to soften the blow.

Look, mum'll get a place in no time and we'll all be back together. I've got mates who will put us up for a while. Come on, she coaxed. *It won't be for long.'*

But how will mum find us?

blurted Ruby, on the verge of tears. *And what about dad?* Knowing their father was cared for in the local hospital was a blessing in disguise, their mother had said. Ruby understood that it was kinder not to let on about the family's predicament, but wondering about his reaction when he returned home to an empty flat had her welling up.

This is Walworth, Rube. You can't even fart here without everyone knowing, Ellen exaggerated, trying to make light of the situation. *Let's just keep walking. Give me time to figure it out.*

What about tonight though? Ruby pressed.

Ellen's silence was answer enough. Ruby watched her mother disappear into the distance. She wanted to run to her; for them to hug until the blood drained from their arms. Yet to do so would open the floodgates. To see her mother cry had been the worst thing in the world. Never, in her young life would she understand how situations could change so quickly.

Yesterday she had a family. Today she was homeless, and tomorrow didn't even bear thinking about.

Chapter 2

A while later, Ruby stood up from the forecourt wall, looped her bag handle over her arm and locked eyes with the curious attendants. She gave a cheeky wave before setting off down East Street, making her way towards the furthest section which housed the market - known locally as The Lane.

The relentless early morning drizzle, an anomaly for an August morning, was cursed by red faced barrow boys, who lugged and positioned their stalls down either side of the market section. A parade of vans followed like battle worn soldiers, inching along the central aisle, searching out their stations, ready to offload.

A voice called out from some distance behind her. 'Oi, Ruby. Where's that brother of yours been hiding out? He bloody well owes me.'

Her so-called absent boyfriend sprang to mind, but was quickly dismissed on remembering that Billy had never met her family. Ruby's stomach churned. It had to be someone from the flats, she decided. Someone best to avoid. With no stomach for random chats with snoops and muckrakers, she shifted nervously on the spot, debating whether to stay put or run. Had she been younger she would have simply closed her eyes to render herself invisible.

Jimmy, her brother Gary's friend, snaked his way between vehicles to reach her. Lifting the peak of his flat cap, he smiled, revealing a chipped front tooth; a trophy from his caped crusader days, swinging from rafters in derelict houses, before the bulldozers came and flattened his dreams of saving the planet.

'You had me rattled there for a minute,' said Ruby. 'Thought you were my boyfriend, Billy, home from the sea.'

The sudden dip of Jimmy's shoulders went unnoticed. 'A sailor boy that rattles you!' He shook his head. 'You might think twice about that?'

'No, I didn't mean - I'm just not looking my best that's all.' She touched a soft fist to his smooth jawline and smiled. 'Anyway, should have known it would be you. What you wearing that thing for?' She flicked the rim of his flat cap. 'You look just like your old man,' she grinned, suddenly thankful that her thoughts had been diverted from herself.

'Don't knock what you can't afford,' said Jimmy, in his usual upbeat manner. 'And anyway, it keeps me brain warm, don't it?'

'If you say so.' For the first time in ages Ruby felt herself relax. She liked Jimmy, a typical Jack the lad, seventeen going on twenty-five, with not a serious bone in his body. No wonder he and her brother were best pals. They were one and the same. Blood brothers they called themselves, after scratching their palms and linking hands like ten-year-old warriors. She had been privy to that ceremony and remembered their pain-filled faces. They had to be the bravest boys she knew!

'So, what've you done with me mate then? Haven't seen him around in yonks.'

Ruby struggled to think on her feet. Once people got a whiff of scandal, they'd tailor the outcome into the worst possible scenario. She never understood why. Maybe it was a ploy to convince themselves that they were personally doing okay, in spite of their own hardships? Jimmy would not be one to set tongues wagging intentionally, but one misplaced word was all it would take. As much as she liked him, she was afraid to open up and let the truth be known.

'Gary's doing okay. Been busy working at the biscuit factory,' she said, avoiding eye contact. 'I'll tell him I've seen you.'

Jimmy turned to leave, hesitated, then spun back on his heels. 'How come you're out so early anyway?'

'Couldn't sleep. Thought I'd grab a tea once this place opens.' She flicked her head back towards the market Cafe behind her.

'Sal won't be here just yet. Tell you what though, you help us set up the stall and I'll let you share me flask, and I'll slip you five bob too! How does that sound?'

Unable to resist the deal of the century, Ruby was about to step out from beneath the shop's canopy, when a small tear in the ageing striped fabric widened, releasing a stream of dirt coloured rainwater directly onto her head. With her long hair dripping in rat's tails, she shuddered. Unsure of what had happened, she froze on the spot and covered her head with her hands.

'Well, don't just stand there you dope.' Jimmy laughed and grabbed her hand to lead her forward. 'That'll teach you to take the mick out of me cap, and serves you bloody right.'

Heading across the street, Ruby recognised the portly, balding figure unpacking various storage crates, as George, Jimmy's father, a familiar face about the market. With the stall half set out and hordes of early birds disrupting his regimental display, he continued to claw items back into position on the dark velvet cover.

'Gis a minute to finish up here girls' and you'll have me undivided, truly you will,' he said, disguising his impatience behind a well-honed punter's smile. The bargain hunters paid no heed.

He glanced sideways across at Jimmy. 'Nice of you to show your face.' The throwaway comment fell on deaf ears.

'You know Gary's sister?' Jimmy said. 'She's come to help us out.'

George clocked the soaked and shivering Ruby with her petal thin jacket plastered to her skin like cellophane. He raised his chin, encouraging his cap to slip further backwards. 'Let's just knuckle down, shall we?' he moaned.

With their heads nit-sharing close, Ruby and Jimmy delved into crates lifting out all manner of tat. She spoke softly behind her hand, 'This is a load of junk. No one in their right mind will want this stuff.'

'Rubbish,' said Jimmy. 'Misplaced heirlooms are what they are, worth a fortune in anyone's books.'

Checking out a tarnished silver candle holder, Ruby became aware of George watching her every move, as though she was about to fleece the old sod. His grouchy mood and arsey character jangled her nerves, so much so that the heirloom slipped through her fingers and hurtled to the ground.

'I didn't mean it. It was an accident. Honest.' Panic-stricken, Ruby lifted the two halves from the gutter and held them together, hoping that somehow they would automatically click into place. Her trembling hands set the metal chinking.

'Don't get yourself in a stew,' said Jimmy, 'Worse things happen at sea. Don't they Pa?'

George sighed like a knackered steam train exhaling its final offering. 'I'll be taking that out of your wage's lad. Now, quit with the larking about and get on with it.'

'Keep your hair on, Pa. I mean, it's not like she did it on purpose.'

George's back straightened. Taking off his donkey jacket, he walked round the stall. His rolled-up shirt sleeves revealed faded tattoos on his leg of mutton forearms. Ruby gasped. In her experience, ticked-off men stripped off their coats for one reason only.

'Look, I'll pay for the damage once I get a job,' she promised, anything to avoid a punch-up between father and son.

The fear in Ruby's eyes stopped George in his tracks. His innocent action had been completely misinterpreted. 'Gordon Bennett girl, I've never hit a woman in me life and I not about to start now.' Ruby watched his lumbering movements as he held the jacket open. 'Here, get that flimsy thing off and put this on before you catch your death.'

Ruby glanced at Jimmy then back to George. 'No, it's okay, I'm all right, really.'

Refusing to take no for an answer, he moved the jacket towards her in stages.

'Please don't make me wear that,' she mumbled behind her hand for Jimmy's benefit.

George shook his head in disbelief. 'Far better you're seen standing girl than stretched out in a box.' Slowly, she slipped her hands into the deep cavernous armholes.

'Looks great. You could start a new trend,' said Jimmy, before looking away to hide the grin that threatened to split his face.' Just fold the sleeves back for gawd's sake.'

She could barely move with the weight of it. Her shoulders, stuck in a slumped position, reminded her of the humped-back old girl who wandered the streets, supported by the handle of a rusty pushchair. Ruby was determined to lose the jacket first chance she got.

'Oi sonny,' said George. 'And I'll have less of your lip in future if you don't mind. I'm off to get a cuppa. You finish up here.'

Ruby watched him disappear into the Cafe. 'Is he always such a misery?'

'Nah, he's a decent bloke normally, you've just caught him on a bad day. He's going through a rough patch at the minute.'

Ruby knew firsthand about those kinds of patches. The ultimate in rough was the nightmare place she had walked away from that morning, and might well be forced back to come nightfall.

'What's up with him then? I won't let on to anyone. Cross me heart.'

'He's in love, Ruby, hook, line and blimming sinker, except she's not interested. She keeps knocking the poor bloke back, and he's really down in the dumps about it.'

'Blimey, I don't ever want to get in that state. So, who is she then? Anyone I know?'

'It's Sal, who runs the Cafe. Word is she's never been married.'

Ruby clicked her tongue. 'People don't have to get married you know. It's not exactly a crime.'

'I know that but - listen here, if you think I'm treating you just to stand there looking like a poser for Dockers Weekly, then you got another think coming.'

Ruby laughed, and tossed the bulky jacket into an empty crate. 'Don't just look like your old man, you sound like him too.' Ruby set to work on finishing the stall. She hadn't noticed the walking stick tied up with string and hanging precariously along the side of the stall, until it clopped her on the nose. One of the bargain hunters winced out loud.

'Felt that one girl, nearly made me own eyes water,' she said, rubbing her face. 'Give it here. I might take it off your hands before it does any more damage.'

'What the hell do you want that for?' asked her companion. 'Don't tell me. It'll keep your old man upright when he staggers out the boozer?'

'Cheeky cow. My Sid's been on the wagon best part of a week, and well you know it.'

'Yeah, but only cos he's too paralytic to climb down off the flipping thing.' She giggled.

Jimmy glanced across at Ruby and smiled. 'You'll be just like them when you're old and grey,' he teased.

'I will not!' she said, feigning offence, while trying to snatch the stick and give him a well-deserved wallop.

With the vans emptied and parked in side roads to make way for the expanding crowd, Jimmy seized the moment with a sudden outpouring of waffle, drawing in the curious and halting Ruby's quest for payback. With an upturned crate as his stage, he started with the banter.

Ruby watched spellbound as he rambled on about local treasures and rare, sought after items. He had the makings of a true showman. His cheeky wit and unexpected antics were real crowd pleasers. Occasionally he would glance across his shoulder at her, give a quick wink, a cocky smile, then back to business. She was struck dumb by his confidence, the way he had the on-lookers nudging forward, clamouring for the best view.

'Bet any one of you would give your eye teeth to get your hands on this beauty!' he said, brandishing the walking stick like a sabre.

'No chance 'ere mate,' called a thin, ashen faced gurner. His grotesque sunken smile sent a ripple of laugher through the gathering.

Ruby noticed George standing back from the crowd, silently nodding his approval. His face glowing with pride. She had read the man completely wrong and felt a jolt of guilt for doing so. She understood, perhaps for the first time, that her struggles were no more or less important than anyone else's.

After suggesting that Charlie Chaplin might have owned the ageing artefact, Jimmy jumped from the crate. With feet pointing at ten to two he gave an impromptu mime of the little tramp, strutting back and forth like a seasoned trouper. Their corner of The Lane came to a standstill. Inquisitive tenants leant out from council block windows, cheering and whistling their support. Jimmy was in his element, a born entertainer, carried away by the excitement of the moment.

With the sky clearing and a welcome ray of sunlight homing in like a spotlight on the Southwark boy, Ruby decided it was time to disappear. As George moved towards the stall, she placed her jacket over her arm and headed off. She felt a pang of guilt for not saying her goodbyes but felt sure they would understand. Besides, there would be other opportunities. She had no plans to flee Walworth. It was where she belonged, after all. Rooting in her pocket for the money that Jimmy had slipped in earlier, Ruby made her way to the Cafe.

Chapter 3

Daisy woke with the sunlight streaming in on her face. For a split second she thought she was back home in Walworth, her sister Ruby's voice still ringing in her ears, *Budge over a bit can't yer? You take up too much bed for a tiddler. I'll be on the floor in a minute!*

With her vibrant blue eyes tightly shut, Daisy covered her face with the bed sheet. She didn't want to be awake, not yet. Her thoughts took her back to the main bedroom of the council flat, where she had snuggled against her sister Ruby for warmth. They lay like spoons in the double bed with its thin grey blankets tucked beneath their chins. Her other sisters, Ellen and little Mary, lay curled in their own space down at the bottom. The wind whistled through the draughty window, like a ghostly presence on nights so cold that patches of ice formed along the lower edge.

Daisy longed to be back there, in that very room, with its cold lino flooring that made her prance like a ballerina whenever she stepped out in the night for a pee. She missed the pillow and pretend fights, the singing and storytelling that had her diving beneath the covers in fear of kid-chomping monsters. She could almost hear her mother thumping on the wall from the sitting room, and calling out, *keep the noise down in there. You'll wake the dead in a minute!* More than anything in the world, Daisy missed having her family around.

Rubbing the sleep from her eyes, she glanced across the room, watching the candlewick bedspread rise and fall in rhythm with her uncle's snoring.

Daisy had never wanted to be in Bromley for one second let alone the remainder of the summer holiday. With no place to go she wasn't brave enough to run away. But one day soon, she would think of somewhere, and when that time came she'd be gone: whipped up faster than candyfloss.

You'll be safer there. The minute I find us a permanent home, I'll come for you, her mother had promised. *Auntie Grace loves you so much.*

But Uncle Tom doesn't, thought Daisy. *He's a moaner and a bully and a sneak.* She'd seen it herself during other school holidays when she'd been there with Ruby. He'd made Ruby miserable, cry even, but Ruby wouldn't talk about it. She did say not to tell mum though, cos mum would get upset. Daisy had promised. Even-so, she didn't like to go there alone, because when she did, he would bully her too!

A promise sworn on her own young life had trapped her. If only she had crossed her fingers behind her back, her words would have counted for nothing and she could tell her mother the truth. A small voice had squeezed through the panic that buzzed like a hive in her head.

My mum's dead clever, a classmate once told her in a game of truth and dare. *She knows what I'm thinking before I even open me gob.*

Daisy had thrown her arms around her mother's tiny waist and clung on desperately. A sudden rush of hope unlocked the youngster's arms and she took a step backwards. She stared, wide-eyed up into her mother's pain creased face, willing her to see beyond the tears.

Kate cupped her daughter's ears in her shaking hands. *I'll come as soon as I can. God's honour.*

Daisy pulled away. *No, you don't understand. Look!* She pointed towards her own face, poking a fingertip into her cheek. *Look harder, see what I'm thinking, she cried. Mum ...*

Daisy crept out to the bathroom, before heading down the stairs to the warm kitchen. She poked her head round the open door, spy-like. She felt sure that her aunt's blindness was put-on. How else could she manage complicated stuff, like knitting and baking? It just didn't make sense. Daisy kept a watchful eye, trying to catch her out. She believed it was only a matter of time.

She grinned at her aunt's sleep squashed hair, flat on one side like a belly-up mushroom, thick, frizzy brown curls on the other.

Grace, seated at the kitchen table, turned her head in the direction of her young niece. Her empty green eyes stared into oblivion, slightly closed under the pressure of a beaming smile.

'Come and sit yourself down then. We don't stand on ceremony in this house, you should know that.'

Daisy scraped a chair backwards across the black and white chequered board floor tiles. 'How did you know I was here then?'

'I picked up your scent.'

'But I don't stink.'

Grace's laughter jiggled her bosom which set the hearing aid box, clipped to her dress, off on its high-pitched whistling racket. Once silenced, her right hand tapped its way along the table in search of the teapot.

'I'm not saying you do. But if you want to sneak about unnoticed, maybe you should ease up with the soap. If I didn't know better, I'd swear you were eating the stuff,' she said, playfully.

Daisy couldn't resist the luxury bars with the creamy, thick lather. It was like washing in flavoured ice-cream.

Of course she wouldn't eat it. She was eleven years old. Only babies did silly things like that.

'I hardly touched it this morning. Cross me heart and hope to wotsit.'

'That's as maybe. But I don't want to be sending you home looking like a skinned sausage now. Do I?'

Daisy sniffed. Adults were a strange lot. Wasn't her mum always going on at her to wash her neck? Yet here, every single speck of dirt was sucked down the plughole. And still they weren't happy. Her shoulder's dropped. She would never get it right. No matter how hard she tried.

Daisy observed her aunt's ageing, hardened finger tips as they recognised and passed over familiar breakfast items with the briefest contact. With a forefinger hooked over the rim of a teacup, her aunt continued to pour the scalding tea.

'Take this up to your uncle, there's a good girl, and I'll pop some toast on for you.'

Daisy gripped the saucer with both hands and moved with small slow steps towards the passage. If she spilt any, she'd get an ear bashing for sure. He was forever moaning about extra cleaning, like he was the only one who did anything. Why did she have to take up his sodding tea? It wasn't fair. The lazy thing should get it himself. *Dad never asked to be waited on, even when he was sick,* she reminded herself. If he was here now, he would scoop her up and take her away. He'd make everything right. She climbed the stairs, each step slower than the last. There was no point to her usual morning prayer of, please let him be asleep. After all, it's not like anyone up there ever listened. Yet the same words rushed around inside her head, just in case.

In any other house it would have been a lovely room, a posh room with fancy perfume bottles arranged on the dressing table, which stood like a show piece between the two front windows. Her little bed, to the right of the door faced the first window. The double bed, in its cramped space, ran alongside the other. Pale silky curtains billowed in the breeze like bridal veils and sunshine bounced off glass fronted photos hanging from chains along the picture rails. She hated it. All of it. Even the stupid box for the blankets, with its daft sounding name. Ottoman. Whoever heard of such a thing?

Daisy crept without sound along the narrow gap between the bed and wall. She noticed a bubble of white, foamy spittle at the corner of his mouth. *Please be asleep*. The beside cabinet was within reach. She carefully placed the saucer onto the white laced cloth. In an instant his eyes opened. He was awake. He was always awake whenever she brought the tea. He tricked her every single time with his games.

He tossed the bed-covers aside, posing like the emperor in his new clothes. His rough and calloused hands moved deftly. Yanking Daisy onto the bed, he positioned her face down on top of him. The stench of his warm, stale morning breath filled the space between them.

She lay there, still as a resting butterfly like she'd done before, silently counting bobbles on the blue nylon pillowcase. She had to put herself in another place. A happier place. She peered across at the Spanish doll centred on the chest of drawers, poised and smiling in a red and black faded costume: layer upon layer of gathered material trailing regally. A fairytale princess from another land. Daisy had dreamt of becoming one herself. Didn't she tell her brother Gary, that one day she would swish up and down the road in a puffed-up dress, with a crown of jewels on her head. How he'd laughed at her fancy ideas and told her not to be so daft. *Kids in council flats never become princesses. And anyway, with only a bag of marbles between them, how were they supposed to buy a crown?* She knew he didn't mean to be so rotten. He was just being a boy.

Uncle Tom's dome shaped stomach pressed painfully into her young flesh. Lying on top of him made no sense at all, other than making it easier for him to grab her bum cheeks. She held her breath, waiting for the game to start. The tickle games she played with Ruby were different. They'd laugh like hyenas as they fought to wiggle their fingers deep into one another's armpits and ribs. Uncle Tom's game had one unbreakable rule: make no sound whatsoever.

'Daisy, your toast is getting cold. What's keeping you?' called Grace from the bottom of the stairwell.

Uncle Tom released his hold and Daisy leapt from the bed and hurried down to the kitchen: her feet barely touching the ground.

Sunday mornings were set in stone. Uncle Tom moved from room to room with his bucket of cleaning rags and favoured tin of beeswax polish. The hose from the cylinder hoover lay curled in the hallway like a comatose snake. The walnut, upright piano, worshipped like a shrine in the front room, had Daisy wondering about its real purpose. No one ever played the stupid thing, and she knew better than to smudge the high wax shine with her so-called grubby fingers. She turned to her uncle.

'Dad would say that's a waste of space. He'd chop it up for firewood, ready for when the gas meter runs out.'

The mirror-like sheen on the piano drew her closer. Her uncle, a short distance behind, stood watching. She could just make out his face as she studied her reflection. His thumbnail dragging back and forth across his scratchy chin, signalled he was close to blowing his top. She knew better than to breathe another word. Daisy felt safer during daylight hours, knowing that her aunt would be somewhere close by;

and safer still when that all important hearing aid was switched on.

'Why don't you go and play? Get out from under my feet,' he grumbled.

'But there's no one around. I already looked.' She peered up briefly and shrugged her shoulders. 'Anyway, it's no fun here without Ruby.'

He placed a firm hand at the nape of her neck and steered her towards the door. 'Well go and see if your aunt needs a hand.'

Weekdays were different, when Tom was off sprucing up houses with a lick of paint. She was never a nuisance when she had her aunt to herself. Daisy revelled in the grown-up role of guiding her aunt around town. Arms linked. Grace's thin white metal stick tap-tapping along the pavement encouraged people to side-step, dance around them. Pats on the head rained down on the little girl, bursting with pride.

Daisy found Grace busily preparing both lunch and the evening meal. She hovered behind her aunt like a misplaced shadow, ever curious. Passing a hand in front of Grace's eyes, she asked, 'Can you tell when it's light or dark?'

'Not really, it's all pretty much the same.'

'Could you ever see? Like when you was little and that?'

'Oh yes, right up until I was a young married woman.'

'So, you know you look a bit like me mum then? Could be that's why you're her favourite sister, cos you look the same I mean.'

'I think you could be right,' she smiled, her hand gliding across the worktop in search of the tea towel.

Daisy plucked the item from a chair back and placed it within reach.

Grace winked, knowingly. 'What would I do without you?'

'S'pect you'll miss me when I'm gone then?'

'Gone? What's all this?' she paused, wrapping her arms around the youngster. 'You haven't been here five minutes. I guess you're feeling lonely without Ruby. Is that it?'

Daisy nodded. 'I am, but I really miss me mum as well.'

'I know you do sweetheart, and in answer to your question,' she paused, and guided by her hands she placed a kiss on the girl's forehead. 'I'll miss you more than you'll ever know. So don't go disappearing off just yet,' she said, wagging a finger. 'We both love you very much. Why, your uncle was only saying yesterday that he wished you were our daughter, then you would never have to leave.'

Daisy stiffened. 'But me mum and dad love me so much!' Her words spilled out in a rush. 'They'd never ever give me away.'

'Come now,' said Grace soothingly. 'We know they wouldn't part with you. It was silly of me to say such a thing. I was trying to explain just how much your uncle and myself love having you here. We'll have to be content with school holiday visits.'

As much as Daisy loved her aunt Grace, she promised herself that once she left this time, there was nothing in the world that would ever bring her back again.

Chapter 4

Part way through the Cafe door, Ruby stepped back, to allow a stony-faced, mumbling customer to exit. Sal, behind the counter, continued slicing through a tray of bread rolls. 'I'll sort it first chance I get, Ray. I'm up to me ears in it and that lazy little so-and-so hasn't turned in again. If I've told her once...'

''Scuse me,' said Ruby, leaning on the counter. 'He's already left.'

Sal placed the bread knife on the worktop and brushed crumbs from her hands onto her patterned pinafore. She tutted, glanced towards the door and back again. 'My giddy aunt,' she said aloud to no one in particular. 'I'd swear that man has the patience of a gnat.' Her brow wrinkled into deep creases.

'You all right, duck?' asked Sal, concerned. 'You're looking a bit peaky if you don't mind my saying. Go sit yourself down and I'll fetch you a nice cuppa.'

Settled in the far corner with her duffel bag tucked beneath the chair, Ruby took in the familiar surroundings. Black and white prints of bygone days hung randomly on magnolia walls. The oversized weeping fig, starved of sunshine and water was slumped in its usual position against the back wall. She had never been in the Cafe so early before, and being partially empty it appeared larger than she remembered. Her finger traced the lined pattern on the yellow Formica table. No tea rings or sticky sugar granules to divert her route. No over-filled ashtrays spilling particles of greyness like tiny insect wings. Everything, spotlessly clean, quiet and eerily unnatural.

A sudden light-headedness together with muffled hearing had Ruby clinging onto the table edge. Unaware of what was happening, she attempted to call Sal but her voice refused to cooperate. Sal nevertheless appeared in front of her. Ruby saw the woman's lips moving, although her words were little more than echoes from some faraway place. Ruby felt herself slipping deeper into a place of darkness. Minutes later, sipping sweetness from the cup that Sal held to her lips, the muzzy headed feeling began to clear. 'When did you last eat something young lady?' Sal demanded, tilting Ruby's chin upwards. The colour gradually returned to her cheeks. 'I knew I recognised you,' Sal continued. 'I've been wracking my brain here. You're Kate's girl, from the flats. Am I right or what?'

'You're right,' Ruby nodded, determined to say as little as possible.

'Does she know you're out and about so early? Come to think of it, haven't seen your mum about lately either.' She placed a hand on Ruby's shoulder. 'Is everything OK? I mean, nothing's happened has it, duck?'

'Everything's fine, really.'

'Glad to hear it,' said Sal, unconvinced. She slid the plate of toast across the table. 'Well get that down yourself, every last bit of it mind.'

Ruby happily did as she was told, chewing each delicious mouthful until there was practically nothing left to swallow.

'You sorted those rolls yet, girl?' boomed a voice from the doorway. 'I'm that starved. Me stomach thinks me throat's been slit!'

Sal sighed with exasperation. 'Give us a flaming minute, Ray. Soon as Pam turns up...'

'Speak of the devil.' Ray ushered in the hired help with a bow and a sweeping wave of a hand. 'Maybe now I'll get me some nosh? You know where I am when it's ready.' Slamming the door shut, Ray returned to his stall.

'Do us a favour Pam, sort him out with a couple of bacon rolls, he's driving me barmy.'

'Is that before or after I dump my bag in the cupboard?' she answered, reaching to switch on the radio.

'Just get on with the doings, there's a girl.' Sal never took umbrage at Pam's attempts at sarcasm, although it did remind her of what her old dad mentioned about it being the lowest form of wit.

'It's all set up there,' Sal pointed. 'I just haven't had time. I don't suppose you clocked that Mandy on your travels? I gave strict instructions for her to be here early and get that fridge sorted.'

Pam gave a you've-got-to-be-kidding snigger, as she removed the lid from the butter dish. 'Saw her down The Lord Wellington last night, bet she's nursing a hangover.'

Sal shook her head in disbelief. 'I'll give her hangover when she shows her face.'

Ruby watched the browsers and passers-by through the plate glass window, every one of them with a purpose, a place to go and more than likely a home to return to. She wondered about the handful of women with huge rollers escaping from silk head scarves, the old girls with dainty hats held fast with gaudy pins, and the flat cap brigade, all over the place like a cheap suit. People watching filled her time. She scanned every passing face, knowing in her heart that someday she would happen upon a smile she recognised, maybe even her mother's.

Finishing the last mouthful of tea, she peered up over the cup. The face stuck fast to the window, blowing silent raspberries, had Ruby close to choking. She laughed out loud and a startled Sal followed Ruby's gaze to the source.

'I might have known it. Off with yer.' Sal gestured with a back-handed wave. 'You steer clear of him, duck. Got the cheek of the devil that one.'

Jimmy strolled across to Ruby's table, pulled out a chair opposite and sat down. 'So, what made you scarper then? Oh, I know, my little routine back there embarrassed yer.' He chuckled. 'You could have told me instead of legging it.'

Ruby ran a fingertip round the rim of her teacup. 'Surprised you even noticed.' She teased. 'I just got stuff to do that's all.'

'I can see that! You wait till the South London Press gets a hold of it. Young entrepreneur given elbow in favour of a cup of rosie and a slice of toast!' he said, removing a crumb from the corner of her mouth.

'What's an entrepre thing?' she asked.

'No idea, heard it on the radio this morning. Sounds good though, don't it? Anyway listen, tell Gary I'll pop up tonight around seven.'

Ruby could feel her toast threatening to re-surface. 'You can't. I mean, he won't be in. We're not there anymore,' she panicked, completely unaware that Sal had one ear cocked.

'He got himself banged up, has he?' Jimmy asked.

'No, course he hasn't. Why would you say such a thing? Besides, I already told you he's working at the factory.'

'So how come you're not at the flat then?'

Ruby could feel herself getting flustered. She wanted to open up to him, explain the situation, but could she deal with the aftermath and his inevitable questions?

Did she know him well enough to rely on his discretion? The last thing she needed was to fall out with Jimmy. Mates were hard to come by, and ones that go to extremes just to hear you laugh were rarer still. Snatching her bag from the floor, she headed out back to the yard. 'We moved,' she called over her shoulder. 'To Camberwell if you really must know.'

'I don't understand. Why would you go there? Ruby! Ruby!'

Escaping into the yard, she closed the door behind her and rested against the smaller of the outbuildings. She unzipped the side pocket of her bag and took out the small collection of photographs she had taken from the flat. She stroked the images on the stained and creased prints. Her mother and father in Christmas cracker hats, their cheeks so rounded with laughter she could almost hear them. Another print revealed her beautiful sisters, Ellen, Daisy and Mary, with a face-pulling Gary immersed up to their necks in a hop-picking bin, made her ache inside. Smiling down at the scene, she gulped back a sob.

If she could start her life over from one of those happier, early years, she promised herself she would be a different Ruby. One who would never whinge or sulk her way through the hungry days. She would attend school, forcing the truant officer to pound a different door to off-load his summonses. And, if that wasn't enough, she would try her hardest not to be terrorised by the darkness and the memory of the uncle who had stripped away her childhood.

Opening the door closest to hand, she poked her head inside the narrow brick-built store, home to a pile of nibbled cardboard boxes, a grey metal pail and a worn broom head. A wealth of abandoned cobwebs, like threadbare lace, hung heavy with dirt and carcasses from the ceiling and walls.

The toilet, with its high reaching rusted cistern and string pulley, was housed behind the second door and used only by the brave or desperate.

With a plan forming, Ruby hurried to the back gate. She pulled the bolt back just enough to appear still locked and returned to the Cafe, by which time Jimmy had left.

'Here you are lovey,' said Sal. Had me worried for a minute, beginning to think you'd fallen down the hole,' she chuckled. 'Sit yourself down a minute; I'd like a quiet word.'

Ruby liked Sal. She reminded her of aunt Grace, her mum's sister. They had a similar round mumsy shape and ready smile. Sal's silver-streaked hair mingling with her brownish curls aged her slightly, although she quashed any 'old girl' teasing from her customers with her favourite quip: *I'll have you know that these here highlights are the latest fashion and cost me a sodding fortune. I'm more up-to-date than her Majesty. God bless her.'*

Sal kept her voice low, ensuring that the table of workmen waiting on their fry-up were out of earshot. 'Listen duck, I'm not one to pry into other people's business, but I know something's up. Now you don't have to tell me, it's entirely your choice, but if you need help then you've only got to ask.'

Ruby smiled. No one would ever call Sal a nosy parker. She had no interest in pumping people for titbits; not that she had to! Folk lined up to dump their worries on the poor woman. Any gap between queuing customers and they seized her, like a shoal of piranha claiming their ounce of flesh. Sal never repeated stuff, unlike the gossip-mongers in their little cliques, balancing ample breasts on folded arms and holding court around a crowded doorstep.

Leaning forward, Ruby dared to hug Sal, mainly for just being there, but also to stop her from saying anything else. If she had learnt one thing, it was that kind words from well-meaning people turned her into a blubbering wreck.

'Bless your cotton socks,' said Sal, easing the words through the tightness in her throat.

Ruby pulled back. 'I'm not a kid any more Sal. I'm working age now.'

'Oh, take no notice of my silly expressions; I'm a daft bat at the best of times.'

The Cafe grew noisier as more customers filed in. Ruby decided to leave and made her excuses.

'Thanks for everything, Sal. I'll try not to conk out next time I'm here,' she smiled.

'You take care of yourself now. Oh, and remember me to your mum.'

'I will. I promise.'

To avoid bumping into Jimmy again, Ruby made her way to Merrow Street, from where she could cut through the back turnings to the main road. She had traipsed the same streets day in and day out searching for her parents. Her black open-toe sling-backs were fast wearing out.

You'll cripple yourself in those things, her mother had previously warned. *You see if I'm not right.* Every few steps had Ruby reaching down to yank the straps back up over her heels, often losing balance in the process. If the painful blistering from scrunching her toes failed to render her disabled, then it was only a matter of time before the sideways stooping would. Her mother's warning remained as clear as Fox's glacier mints.

Chapter 5

The Old Kent Road was buzzing with its usual throng of traffic, buses, black cabs and risk-taking pedestrians all clamouring for space. Standing briefly outside Bert's, the pie 'n' mash shop, Ruby noticed the net curtain twitching in The Castle pub opposite. She spotted a shadow behind the upstairs window, closed to the grime and noxious fumes. The landlady, a friend of the family, eventually showed her face and gave a hesitant wave. Ruby forced a smile in return. That had been their room, hers and her sister Ellen's, for two wonderful weeks, during which time Ellen had left for a new start in Kent.

Ruby could still feel the softness of those chunky Witney blankets tucked up under her chin. She wrongly assumed that the little hideaway would be hers for as long as needed. She hadn't reckoned on being turned out in favour of a stranger with a bulging wallet. How never to take things for granted was a hard lesson and one that she wouldn't forget in a hurry.

The sweetshop nearby, with its tall glass jars lining the walls, tempted Ruby to break into one of her half crowns.

'Get a lid on them milk chews fast,' the shopkeeper shouted to his wife. 'Our friendly neighbourhood tea-leaf is back in town.'

The woman tutted. 'Give it a rest. You're embarrassing the poor girl.'

Ruby would never live down her act of daring at the four-a-penny section, when, knee high, she had squirrelled a milk chew up the sleeve of her crocheted cardigan. The white wrapper glaring through the cherry red wool resulted in a ticking off and a threatened visit from the local bobby. She vowed never to touch another sweet without there being a penny in her pocket.

'She knows I'm only playing,' said the shopkeeper, handing over a measure of candy twists and giving Ruby's hand a friendly squeeze.

With the afternoon spent between the library and the Elephant and Castle shopping centre, it was well after closing time before Ruby found herself back in East Street.

She crept quietly along the alley behind the shops, careful not to let the clip-clopping of worn heels give her away. She quickly scanned the area for would be blabbermouths before opening the yard gate behind the Cafe, just enough to slip through and secure the bolt.

The storeroom had definite possibilities and was far safer than the petrol forecourt. She settled in the corner on a length of cardboard, her knees drawn to her chest. It reminded her of the pram sheds adjoining the council flats. She recalled the opening of The Secret Seven club, the brainchild of local kids, bursting with self-importance, locked in their cosy den, with orange box seats, candles, and a square of mat taken from the bomb site.

The minute Ruby heard the footsteps, her thoughts changed and body tensed. Her shallow breathing, quiet as the mouse sniffing at her ankle, almost gave out completely when the toilet cistern flushed. Ruby thrashed about in the darkness, desperate to dislodge a mouse that shot up her trouser leg. She sent the pail crashing against the wall. Scrambling on all fours, Ruby cowered behind a shield of cardboard. Her heart thumping, she swallowed hard to stop the swell of vomit rising from her stomach. She stared unblinkingly, waiting for the door to open and to suffer the consequences, whatever they might be.

'Don't you give me any trouble now,' called Sal, in a firm, don't-mess-with-me, manner, attempting to override the fear that would otherwise have her running onto the street. 'This is your last warning before I phone the police.' She pressed her ear against the door. Nothing. 'Suit yourself. But you leave me no choice. The way I see it is, you either get out now or I lock you in and let the coppers deal with you.'

A stillness hung in the air, like smoke from a spent cigarette as each of them silently counted down the seconds. Sal turned the handle and the door creaked open. Ruby followed the beam from Sal's torch as it darted about the walls, before coming to rest in her glazed and squinting eyes.

Sal screamed and stumbled backwards as the torch fell through her fingers and died a noisy death on the concrete path. 'Heaven's above!' she cried, with one hand placed at her throat, trying desperately to steady her breathing.

Frightening Sal was furthest from Ruby's thoughts. She wanted to stand up, show herself, but the only movement her body allowed was the visible pulsing in her stomach from the deep quiet sobbing. If she curled herself up small enough, maybe she would just disappear? Then she wouldn't have to justify her actions. This growing up lark was hard, and certain situations were even harder to wangle out of. Ruby doubted she would ever get the hang of it, or even wanted to. Slowly pushing the shield away, she eased herself up onto her feet.

'Oh Ruby, what on earth are you doing in there? You nearly gave me a heart attack, girl.' Sal stepped inside the storeroom, took a hold of her hand and coaxed her out into the yard.

'I didn't mean to scare you, Sal,' she said, tears streaming down her face.

'What were you thinking of? Haven't you got no home to go to?' Sal knew the answer to that before she had even finished speaking. 'Here, stop your grizzling, duck.' She passed Ruby the clean handkerchief she kept tucked in the sleeve of her cardigan. Sal wanted to turn the situation around, make light of it somehow. After all, there was no real harm done and her breathing apparatus no longer gulped in air like a hungry newfangled hoover.

Sal's parental impulses had rarely surfaced throughout her barren years, apart from the odd cooing and overly exaggerated baby talk to a pram strapped nipper. Sal had clearly become attached to the girl who, for reasons unclear had camped out in her storeroom. Sal ushered Ruby into the cafe.

'Well, it's a good job I stayed on to sort that fridge out, else you could have been a goner by morning. We had rats out there a couple of weeks back. Big as cats they were,' she demonstrated with her hands.

Part way through mopping up the mess that had become her face, Ruby froze.

'Lucky for you the council got shot of 'em, quick smart,' continued Sal.

Ruby searched Sal's face for a smidgen of truth, but her blank, plaster cast stare gave nothing away. Unable to continue the ruse for much longer, Sal's face cracked and she laughed.

'I'm pulling your leg you daft ha'porth.'

Ruby's jaw dropped. 'I can't believe you did that! You frightened the wits out of me.'

'No, duck, just that snivelling lark.' She grinned. 'See, now you're back to normal, you won't be so bothered when I tell you about the mice.'

'I know already!' Ruby blurted, eyes bulging with revelation. 'One got stuck up me bell bottoms.'

'Get away with yer.'

'It's the truth. I swear on me life.'

'Yeah, and I'm Marilyn Monroe. Now get yourself over to that kettle,' she pointed, 'and sort us out with some tea. You've got some explaining to do young lady.'

With the kettle chugging into life, Ruby leaned her elbows on the counter. Her face, cupped in her palms, rested within an inch of the radio. 'You can turn it up you know,' said Sal, 'I'm partial to some of them pop songs myself.'

'Songs remind you of all sorts, don't they?' said Ruby. 'This one's me sister's favourite, Ellen was always singing it. We'd have *Daydream Believer* busting our eardrums in the mornings and every spare minute up until we crawled back to our beds. Least that's how it seemed. Drove us nuts,' she remembered. 'I really miss her.'

Sal knew better than to push her luck, but she had to, if she was to get to the bottom of things. 'Where's your sister now?' she asked, taking the tray of tea and biscuits over to a table. With a flick of her head, she encouraged Ruby to join her.

'We'd stayed together when the family,' Ruby paused. 'They chucked us out.'

'Good heavens. Who did? I don't understand. Look, sit yourself down, you're making me nervous.'

Ruby dragged out a chair and flopped into it. 'Mum got a letter from the council, an eviction notice. She couldn't afford to pay the rent with Dad being ill for so long and no wages coming in. She tried to find another place for us all but no one wants kids on their premises, so we had to split up till Mum sorted something out.' The words tumbled out and would have continued if Sal hadn't pitched in.

'Didn't she go to the welfare?'

'No, Mum would never do that! She was so ashamed, like it was her fault, but it wasn't.' Ellen and me were doing okay together, then she upped and married a boy from Catford. Love at first sight she reckoned.'

'It does happen, the love thing,' said Sal, knowingly. 'So, where's Ellen living now?'

'She moved to Chatham in Kent. Her hubby's a carpenter, got a job at the dockyard. They begged me to go with 'em, but I knew it wouldn't be right. Besides, I need to be around here.'

'What about your mum and dad? If I know Kate, she'll be climbing the walls wondering where you are.'

'Dad was in hospital at the time. I've phoned 'em since but he's been discharged, and I've no idea where Mum is either.' Ruby could feel herself welling up. 'I can't find anyone Sal. I don't know where to look next. The soggy, over-dunked piece of digestive biscuit sank to the bottom of Ruby's cup. She agitated the pulp with her spoon, which separated into tiny sand-like globules. 'I've searched everywhere, Sal.'

'And Camberwell? I heard you mention it to Jimmy.'

'We're not really there. I think it's best that people don't know our business.'

'But we're not just any people Ruby, we're friends. You should at least give us a chance to help.'

Sal reached across to fuss with Ruby's wayward fringe when she noticed the swelling. 'What all this?' she asked, careful not to touch the fresh bruising.

Using her fingers as a comb, Ruby adjusted her hair. 'It's nothing. I had an argument with a sink, that's all.'

Sal squirmed in her seat, unable to cope with the loneliness staring back at her through red-rimmed eyes. She leapt to her feet and cleared the table. With no mind to avoid breakages, the dirty crockery clattered into the sink. 'Right, that's it, my mind's made up.'

Ruby was at Sal's side in the white tiled alcove faster than a sneeze. 'Please don't dob me into the welfare.'

'Would I heck as like! What do you take me for? Besides, there's no need since I got a spare room going. So, you're coming home with me and that's all there is to it.'

Chapter 6

Uncle Tom's afternoon chores spilled outdoors along with Daisy. The postage stamp lawn, framed either side with weed free borders, was edged with a low white painted scalloped wall. Miniature apple trees lorded it over a wealth of snapdragons and petunias, all lavishly tended like new-borns. The idyllic scene reeked of boredom for the eleven-year-old. She didn't want to sit in the deckchair, centred and sun-facing on the crew-cut grass. She wanted to scream and shout and laugh, split the silence and have fun pour through the gap like colourful bubble-gums from a penny machine, bringing chaos to his stupid garden.

The youngster picked a lone daisy poking through the neighbouring chain link fence, plucking each white petal in turn. 'He loves me, he loves me not, he loves me. Me mum likes flowers,' she said, thinking aloud. 'She had some pretend ones in a little plastic vase, pinned to the wall in the front room. Me and Ruby wanted to buy some real ones for her birthday, but didn't have enough money.' Daisy and her uncle made eye contact. He acknowledged the youngsters rambling with a brief nod, but made no comment.

'We got a small Vienna loaf instead,' she continued. 'All wrapped up in tissue paper it was. Mum got upset and cried. I think she had her heart set on flowers.'

Snatching a leaf from an overhanging branch, Daisy inched towards the deckchair. With nail-biting precision, she stripped away the greenery, revealing a fan shape of skeletal fingers, which she crushed and flicked into the air. Sundays were like sleeping with your eyes open. She hated them as much as nit lotions and soggy cornflakes.

Thoughts of Ruby crept in, and how different things had been in previous school holidays. Days sped by like the hand-holding sisters, roller skating for miles on smooth unbroken pavements. Or bike riding like daredevils on spruced up rust-buckets, charging round the sleepy cul-de-sac, and being ticked off by snooty neighbours for squealing far too loud and disturbing their peace. And those mealtimes - when so much as a glance at each other had them crying in a fit of the giggles. Together they were stronger, their confidence and daring unmatched. Alone, as now, with her spirit barely intact, and cheekiness bubbling away beneath the surface, she knew she could never be the model child her uncle insisted on. A sudden shout put paid to her daydreaming.

'Get that blasted finger out of your nose, right now. How many times have I told you? Go on,' her uncle sneered through yellow stained teeth. 'Get inside and wash those filthy hands.'

Daisy sulked off towards the back door that led into the kitchen. 'Can't do anything in this stupid place,' she mumbled to herself.

'And we'll have less of the backchat. You're not at home now young lady, in case you've forgotten?'

Daisy would never forget, ever. Home was the best place in the world. Just because they lived in London, it didn't mean they were a bad lot, far from it. Any backchat earned her a telling off, and if she swore indoors, she could wave goodbye to her friends for a day or two. Home was a safe place. There was never any danger of a fat uncle crawling beneath her blankets in the middle of the night, or slipping his hand up her skirt whenever the fancy took him. She also knew that if her dad ever found out about her uncle, he would turn him into mincemeat and chuck him down the chute with the rest of the rubbish.

A pot of oxtail stew simmered on the old electric cooker. Daisy allowed the warm, moist air to drift up into her face. She could almost taste the pearl barley, bobbing up and down like mini eyeballs. At the far end of the kitchen her aunt was gathering ingredients for a trifle. Wiping her face dry with the edge of her cardigan, Daisy moved swiftly across the room.

'Is this for our pudding?' she asked.

'Good grief, no.' She smiled. 'It won't be ready in time. Besides, you'll have no space left after the stew.'

'Bet I would.' she muttered beneath her breath. 'Mum says that being in the countryside gives you a good appetite.'

The blue free-standing larder with its pull-down worktop was littered with pieces of broken sponge. A glass bowl housing cubes of strawberry jelly sat close-by on the matching table. Unable to resist the sweet stickiness, Daisy popped a square into her mouth, mere seconds before the remainder was doused in boiling water. Taking a spoon from the cutlery drawer, Daisy swirled those liquefying ruby gems until they disappeared.

'Do you want me to drop the sponge bits in now?' she asked, desperate to sneak a crumb or two beforehand.

'OK, but you best rinse your hands off first though?'

Daisy was glad that she didn't live in Bromley permanently. Covering herself in silky scented lather twice a day was OK, but hand washing every five minutes was a pain in the neck, and clearly something only posh people did. She tickled the surface of the soapy water already in the sink, wiped her hands down her dress and set to work.

'So, what's your uncle up to out there?' asked Grace, in her usual sweet as home-made toffee tone. Daisy loved the way her aunt's cheeks bulged upwards when she smiled, making the thin skin beneath her eyes appear cracked like fine china. She was beautiful and Daisy loved her. Everyone did. Except uncle Tom.

'He's digging dirt and picking his bleeding nose again.'

A rasping sound escaped from her aunt's throat, followed quickly by bouts of wheezy coughing. Daisy gave a nervous giggle, trying to determine whether her aunt was putting it on or having a fit. She'd heard about fits from a classmate, who told her that people bit their own tongues clean off. With no blood dribbling from her aunt's mouth, Daisy breathed a little easier. She decided that a simple 'bleeding', could not have set her aunt off. Cursing and swearing were forbidden, she knew that, but some words spilled out by accident. She could hardly be blamed. And anyway, the 'bleeding' word wasn't proper swearing. Daisy heard her uncle's footsteps approaching the back door. In fear of a hiding, she tugged on her aunt's sleeve. 'He wasn't really picking it. Honest. I was only joking.'

Her aunt nodded. 'It's OK, I've only myself to blame. I shouldn't have sneaked a taste of that dry sponge.'

Daisy sighed knowingly. 'Mum reckons when you gobble food quickly it can end up down the wrong hole. Is that what happened to you?'

'Yes, I expect so,' said Grace, filling a glass with water. 'That will teach me not to nibble between meals.'

Daisy remained quiet. Her fingers curled around the extra piece of sponge she'd placed in her trouser pocket for later.

Mealtimes were usually silent affairs. Daisy ate her evening meal slowly, careful not to make slurping or other noises that jangled her uncle's nerves. She fished out the barley from her plate, one delicious piece at a time.

'Stop playing with your food, and eat it properly,' her uncle barked, before picking slivers of oxtail from his teeth with a matchstick.

Daisy peered up. 'Ruby always says to eat the best bits first, cos if you pop your clogs before you finish, at least you won't have missed the good stuff,' she explained quietly.

Completely unaware of her husband's disapproving glance, Grace covered her mouth with a hand to hide her broadening grin.

'And of course, you always do what Ruby tells you?' he replied.

A short silence stretched between them like well chewed gum. With her head down and voice barely audible, Daisy dared to answer. 'No, but I do like barley.' A deafening buzz filled the air. She lifted her head just enough to peer up and gauge her uncle's reaction. She could tell by the smirk on his face that she would be across his lap later, having her backside smacked as punishment for her so-called lip.

Aware of the rising tension, Grace quickly stepped in. 'So, when are you back at school then?' she asked.

'A couple of weeks, but I'll have to go home soon though to see me mates and to get things ready.'

The oxtail bone held fast between Tom's fingers had been stripped clean of meat and sucked dry of marrow. Slowly, he licked the gravy from his fingers. 'What's to get ready?'

'Mum got a grant for my new uniform. We have to go to Peckham to sort it out.'

'Well, that won't take more than a morning; you can do that on the Saturday beforehand. It's a bit selfish, you wanting to go back early. Your mum deserves a break too you know.'

'I have to go,' she answered abruptly. 'It was Mum that said so.' She quickly bowed her head to avoid his cold staring eyes that unnerved the youngster even more than his words. As wicked as she knew it to be, Daisy wished he would drop down dead that very minute. But wishes, like prayers, were a waste of time.

A gentle rapid sniffing prompted her aunt to reach out a calming hand. 'Come on now, finish up your dinner. There's a good girl.'

Daisy emptied a reluctant spoonful into her mouth. Her throat felt tight, swollen. She couldn't swallow. The sobs in her belly were unrelenting and snot trickled from her nose and settled on her top lip. She sniffed harder. Panicked by a sudden gagging motion she dashed to the sink and heaved. Dragging the sleeve of her cardigan across her face, her sobs broke through in pitiful bursts. She ran from the kitchen and up to the bedroom, where she threw herself onto the bed and hid her face beneath the pillow.

'Leave it to me Tom, I'll sort it out. Something is obviously bothering her,' said Grace leaving the room.

'You mollycoddle her, that's the trouble. She's got you wrapped around her finger.'

Grace coaxed her niece into a sitting position, her legs dangling off the bed. With her face cushioned on her aunt's chest, and her body secured by arms that hugged and rocked her, she felt momentarily safe and loved.

'So, what's brought this on then? Can't have been the stew, surely? I even put in extra barley since I know it's your favourite.'

The corners of Daisy's mouth inched slightly upwards. She snuggled closer, breathing in the familiar flowery perfume. If she could share a secret with anyone, it would be her aunt. She had come so close, more than once. It was only by curling her lips inwards and holding them clenched between her teeth that she stopped the words from tumbling out.

Daisy knew that if her uncle found out that she had no home to return to, or worse still, had no clue as to where her family were, he would claim her and hold her prisoner, forever. With the new school term close to starting, she would go as planned. She had promised herself, the moment she thought of somewhere safer, she would pack her bag and leave. That time had come.

'Nothing's wrong really, I just miss me family that's all. And your stew's lovely, just like Mum's.'

'Well, I'm glad to hear it, about the stew that is, because I've saved what's left of yours for breakfast,' she said jokingly.

The following morning, Daisy heard the milk float stop and start around the cul-de-sac. She peered across the room to find the double bed already made. The hands on the brass alarm clock had just touched on seven. Her uncle had already left for work. She had the morning and Auntie Grace all to herself, and time enough to pack her few belongings for the lunchtime bus. The butterflies dancing in her empty belly would soon calm down once she'd filled the gap with porridge.

Daisy couldn't wait to leave, knowing she would never have to see her uncle again. She would return to Walworth, find a new home with a real coal fire to toast her bread on, like she used to do with her sisters and brother Gary. She would stop being a grizzle gut, as Gary annoyingly called her. She would show him, show everyone, just how brave she could be.

Daisy delved into the brown paper carrier bag she had retrieved from the bottom drawer of the dressing table. Inside, wrapped in a garment of clothing, lay a small envelope. She prised it open, careful not to prick her fingers and draw blood. Going across to her uncle's side of the bed, she pulled back the covers and sprinkled her collection of rose thorns, snapped off from his precious bushes. A triumphant smile spread across her face. 'See how you like that, fatso.' Easing the covers back into a tidy position, Daisy skipped her way through the house and into the warm kitchen, where a delicious bowl of creamy porridge was waiting.

Chapter 7

A sliver of daylight peeking through a gap in the dark curtains had Ruby guessing at the time. The tiny back room, no bigger than an oversized cupboard, barely had space for the bed let alone the chest of drawers and the white painted kitchen chair squeezed in at the foot. Easing the curtains back along the wire she lifted the sash cord window just enough to let in some air. Birds singing from roofs and chimney tops broke the silence of daybreak. She peered along the gardens below. A forgotten item of washing draped over a line some four houses up, hung corpse-like in the weak morning sunlight.

A sudden shout forced Ruby round with a jolt. Catching her knee on the metal bed frame unbalanced her, cursing beneath her breath she tumbled clumsily onto the bed. She stretched across, snatched up her clothes from the chair and dressed in record time. With the door slightly ajar, she stood side-on and listened to the heated discussion below. One of her mother's old sayings interrupted her concentration. *People who eavesdrop never hear good of themselves.* She couldn't waste time on analysing words of wisdom, any-more than she could prise herself away from the door. She had to know what was going on. Ruby recognised the voice sounding off in the kitchen as the grumpy, demanding character from the Cafe. Her breathing quietened.

'Frigging hell Sal, you taken leave of your senses or what? You're too bloody soft for your own good, that's your trouble.'

'She's a good kid Ray. Just down on her luck at the minute.'

'What, like the conniving little mare you took under your wing last year? Robbed us blind, and in our own home too, let me remind you.'

'This is different. It's Kate's girl, from the flats.'

'And that makes it all right, does it? Well not in my book.'

'Shh, keep your voice down,' she pleaded. 'You'll wake the poor thing upstairs in a minute, not to mention the neighbours.'

'To hell with the lot of 'em. You just make sure she's not left in this house on her own.' he bellowed, slamming the street door behind him.

Ruby tip-toed down the stairs and through the living room. She stopped at the open kitchen door. 'Is it safe to come in?'

'Course, duck,' come on in.' Sal prised off the whistling cap from the gas kettle. 'Sit yourself down there,' she pointed through to an armchair angled by the hearth, 'and I'll fetch you a drink. Must seem strange being back here, after what you said last night about knowing my Mum.'

Memories of being a youngster in that very room led Ruby back to a happier time. The china spaniel dogs sitting either end of the tiled mantelshelf and the cottage style suite with its chintzy covers remained in the same position. She could still envisage the old lady with the wispy silver hair, her smiles and patience as she explained the workings of junior crossword puzzles to a hungry young mind. Ruby's gaze lingered on the painting above the fireplace. Lightning Logan, the retired greyhound with doleful, downcast eyes, was the sole reason she tore from the school building the instant that home bell sounded. She would traipse the streets with her four-legged friend, her head held high and near bursting with Queen-like importance.

'He was a lovely old thing,' said Sal, placing the cups on the coffee table. 'So, you were one of the walkers then that Mum kept on about? She often joked about the kids wearing the door knocker out, not to mention her old knees, back and forth along the passage.'

Ruby sipped her tea. 'Sal, about earlier, I heard,' she hesitated.

'Now don't go worrying yourself over that. Ray's all right really, just takes a bit of getting used to. He'll come round; you'll see. Meanwhile, you can help out at the Cafe, and maybe on the stall when his lordship calms down. We'll pay a wage, not a fortune, mind.'

'Oh Sal, maybe I should try and find somewhere else,' Ruby offered.

'I'll not hear of it. You finish your tea,' she said, draping her pinny over a chair. 'Then we best be making a move. We'll grab something to eat at the Cafe, OK?'

Freemantle Street, with its bay fronted houses had always been a quiet, well kept turning tucked discreetly between Surrey Square and East Street. A market trader's lorry, bulging with fruit and vegetables, was often parked overnight by the back entrance to the school. Kids from nearby flats mooched about in the darkness, arms extended beneath the tarpaulin, rooting around for a juicy pomegranate, or something else worth risking a thick ear for. Sal and Ruby turned the corner into East Street. Ruby's thoughts kept returning to George, Jimmy's lovesick father. Any sadness she felt for him was far outweighed by Sal's own situation, living in the same house as that loud-mouthed oaf. She deserved better. Everyone could see that, except Sal herself. George and Jimmy would already know of the weird set-up, surely?

'You're not still thinking about earlier, are you?' asked Sal.

Ruby nodded. 'Kind of. If it wasn't for me, he'd have no reason to be shouting at you like that. I'm causing trouble for you, Sal.'

'Bless your little heart,' Sal gushed. They stood a while on the corner outside the funeral parlour. 'Listen to me. Ray's a good sort, harmless enough. He lets his mouth run away with him sometimes, but he doesn't mean nothing by it. His heart's in the right place. You'll see, once you get to know him better,' she added reassuringly.

Ruby had doubts that she would be around long enough to glimpse a nicer Ray. He would probably have her packed up and shipped out before the week was through.

'When I'm older I'll get my own place, a bedsit in New Cross. And I won't have no old man telling me what to do either.'

'Good for you girl.' Sal took the youngster's arm. 'Now let's get a move on, else they'll be bashing the door down and helping themselves.'

*

Ray made his way through The Lane to his lock up. Joe, his regular barrow boy and general dogsbody, loitered patiently on the corner, scoring his initials into the brickwork with his new penknife. Ray, like other regular traders, left their barrows fully stocked overnight ready to be hauled into position the following morning. Casual traders would take their pick from the stalls stored nearby in an open yard. The ones with the ragged tarpaulin already strapped in place and often sagging with a measure of rain were snapped up first. A moment's lapse in concentration saw wheels dipping in and out of potholes while bleary eyed barrow boys hollered and cursed as rainwater streamed down the length of their backs.

It was close to lunchtime when Mickey Loughty made an appearance at the stall. Checking that his collar remained up-turned, he flicked a spot of lint from his mohair suit. 'So, how's it going, Ray? You made your fortune yet?' he asked, momentarily distracted by a leggy blonde in a mini skirt. He gave a low whistle. 'Would you look at that? Geez, any higher and you'd call it a belt. Not that I'm complaining mind.'

'Dream on sunshine,' said Ray, shaking his head. 'And if you're here for another handout, you can think again. 'Bout time you got yourself a job. Talking of which, how do you fancy helping me out tomorrow?'

'All depends on what you've got in mind.'

'Thing is, me old mate in Dagenham is calling it quits. He's offered me his stock, but I need to get over there pronto before the fly boys' get wind of it.'

'So, what're you saying then, you want me to drag along?'

'No, dipstick.' His eyes disappeared upwards. 'I need you to man the stall, help out Joe here till I get back.'

Mickey peered across at the lanky school leaver, busily fussing with the display. 'You having a laugh or what?' He grinned. 'I'm not cut out to be working no stall. Now, if you give me the keys to your Bedford, I'll nip over and bring the gear back. Can't say fairer than that.'

'Come on, use your loaf. What if you get caught without a licence?' Ray ran a hand back through his head, rubbing the residue of Brylcream onto his jeans. 'Nah, too risky. One small favour is all I'm asking. It's not like I won't line your pocket.'

A doddery old girl in a moth-eaten fur jacket brushed against Mickey's arm as she squeezed through a narrow opening between the sea of bodies.

'Here darling, watch the goods,' he moaned, vigorously brushing off a clump of stray fibres. 'Quality like this don't come cheap you know.'

Ray eyed him quizzically. 'Where you getting that kind of dough from?'

'Oh you know, bit of this, that, the other,' he said, laughing at his own joke.

'Give me strength,' Ray sighed. 'Listen up pal. If you're still shifting them dodgy Vespas for those pikies, you need your bloody head examined.'

'Pays a good wack and then some.' Mickey tapped the side of his nose.

Ray shook his head in disbelief. The kid was on the fiddle, taking more than his due. The silly git truly considered himself untouchable, swanning about like Mr fucking Big and listening to no bugger. One of these days he would come unstuck and Ray would be left to pick up the pieces.

'So, like I was saying, what about Saturday then?'

Mickey would not be swayed. 'Look, you know I'd help you out if it was anything else. But, to be honest mate, I'd rather snog me old gran than flog handbags. No offence like,' he said, realising immediately the consequences of his words.

*

The mere mention of the deceased woman, even in jest, guaranteed that Mickey would battle to clear her image from his mind's eye. Her final days had terrified the boy he once was, causing him to wake at night in cold and sodden pyjamas. She lurked tormentingly behind his closed eyelids. He would never be free of her

53

shrivelled and gasping form. Those wisps of damp wire wool hair sprouting from a shrunken head. Her face, a waxy canvas stretched to buggery over a bony frame and those damn teeth! Protruding headstones rising up from a gaping black hole. The stuff of boyhood nightmares. His parents dismissed his protests, his fears of planting his mouth anywhere near that sweat drenched phoney passing herself off as Gran. He remembered her breath, that God-damn smell of rotting fish; the throwing up in the outside bog and his tainted lips, scrubbed raw. He belched loudly to suppress the dry heaving. 'Fuck it,' he said out loud, knowing he had just taken a sledge-hammer to what promised to be a good day.

*

There were times when Ray had to literally hold himself back from giving the wide boy a swipe round the ear. Mickey's constant jokey manner and half-cocked grin irritated him no end, and yet there was something about the lad that reminded Ray of himself. He too had been a bit of a smart-alec in his day, often on the take and giving little or nothing in return. Ray had no qualms in promising to look out for the lad, when his old pal John succumbed to the big C, like his good lady wife before him. Yet he never felt he had the right to chastise him, and now, at twenty-one, Mickey was his own man, making mistakes at every turn and learning nothing.

'Here, string bean,' he called out to Joe. 'How many times have I told you? Don't stack the bags like that; it's not a sodding jumble sale.'

Ray had been on the same path as Mickey all those years back, but a brief spell in borstal helped to quell his downward spiral. As a young man, he'd been a bit of a flash-harry too, convinced that he was destined for bigger things, he remembered. A life in which locals nodded in passing by way of respect, coupled with a tinge of fear, for the tough self-made man.

Everything had changed for Ray on a December morning, when the snow lay thick on the ground and the street lamps were capped in bright white bonnets. Closing the door on his bedsit, he ventured out into the deserted tree lined street. Yesterday's bare branches were dressed with dazzling garlands that had him squinting at their sun touched brilliance. Everything seemed strangely different somehow. But standing there alone, looking down the empty stillness of Albany Road, was like seeing through someone else's eyes.

A few chimneys offered up the first wisps of smoke into a rare blue sky and Ray found himself consciously taking stock for the first time in his life. Sure, he wanted it all, but without the sad, has-been ending, catching glimpses of life from behind a cell door. A feeling of anticipation rose in his gut as a battle flared inside his head. Panicked by the thought of going soft in the head and turning into some form of nancy-boy, his footsteps quickened, kicking out at the snow like a pissed off schoolboy.

A sudden, unexpected movement in the distance encouraged Ray over to the far sided pavement. His pace slowed and heart rate increased as he drew closer to the dark, shifting bundle. A slim stockinged ankle appeared from beneath the coat fabric. Without a second thought, Ray dashed across the road and helped the young woman to her feet. Decrying the wretched snow and her mother's smoking habit, the young woman retrieved the cigarette packet from the ground and hobbled a few painful steps. Ray scooped her up in his arms and carried her the hundred yards or so to her home, with no idea of the detrimental effect his kindly act would have upon his life.

Chapter 8

The heat in the Cafe was stifling. The front windows were clouded with condensation plus a few smiley faces drawn by a bored child with a jam coated finger. The rising cigarette smoke and constant heat from the kitchen had Ruby wondering how long she could stomach working in such a place. Remaining partly hidden in the alcove, she cursed the dirty crockery, stacked hazardously on a trolley by an overly zealous waitress. Perspiration trickled down from beneath her heavy fringe, blurring her vision. Towards the end of the morning chaos, Ruby and Sal nipped out to the yard for a quick break.

'Keep an eye on the counter for us love,' Sal instructed Mandy, hopeful that the girl would up her game having received a final warning. 'We're just out in the yard, so give a shout if you need help.' With backs to the wall they sipped at their tea, enjoying the cool breeze on their faces.

'This place is like a flipping mad house,' said Ruby, running the back of her forearm across her face.

'Just the way I like it,' beamed Sal.

Ruby and Sal's bond strengthened by the day. Ruby adored the woman and would be forever grateful to be living in safety beneath her wing. Things could have turned out so differently had Sal not stepped in. The last thing Ruby wanted was to upset her by repeating idle gossip. She decided she had little choice. Sal had a right to know what was being bandied about. During a lull in the conversation, Ruby took a breath. 'Sal, I've been meaning to say,' she stopped to re-jig her words.

'Spit it out, lovey. We'll be dragged back inside any blessed minute.'

'It's just that, well, I heard someone say that Ray had a daughter. I know it's none of my business and I don't normally repeat stuff, but I thought you should know.' Ruby immediately hung her head, worried sick that she'd just made the biggest mistake of her life.

Sal's focus remained on the empty beer bottles that had been tossed over the gate the previous evening. Presently, she turned to face Ruby. 'Now I'm only telling you this so you get a better understanding of Ray, since you'll be around for a while, and it'll help you see the poor sod in a different light. What you've heard is true.' She sipped her tea. 'He went through a bad time some years back. Got himself mixed up with a young woman from Wells Way. She worked at the Union Jack Club, you know, down Waterloo, in the library of all places. Real prim and proper she was, least that's the impression she gave. Everyone sang her praises but there was something about her that didn't sit right. I could feel it in my bones.' Sal paused to pluck a tiny insect from her teacup.

'You really don't need to explain. Like I said, it's none of my business. I just thought it best you knew.'

'You're a good girl, looking out for me. Bless yer. Now, where was I? Yes, the sad thing is that most folk believe Ray was born a misery. If they knew what he'd been through they'd soon change their tune. The poor man's been eaten up with grief half his life. I see you as family now duck, so I trust you'll keep to yourself what I'm about to say. Anyway, they couldn't have been together more than a couple of years, when she upped and left. No warning. Nothing. Turns out the little madam had been seeing someone behind his back. She'd buggered off with one of them American soldiers from the Union Jack Club. Took their nipper too!'

'Blimey,' said Ruby, imagining the fallout from such a situation.

'Spitting feathers he was, and who could blame him? He doted on the kiddie, and would have been a brilliant dad if he'd been given a chance. Poor little dot barely made her third birthday, whooping cough apparently. He took his anger out at the boxing ring down Manor Place. Had a few fights and teamed up for a while with Stan, another local boy making a name for himself. I've seen men turn to drink for less than what Ray went through. Broke his heart it did and mine too, I don't mind admitting.'

Ruby felt a measure of pity for the loud-mouth sod, but it didn't change the fact that he acted like a complete basket case at times. 'My dad did a bit of boxing when he was younger too,' she said, trying to soften the mood. 'He didn't get famous like Ray though.'

Sal threw the dregs from her cup into the drain. 'No, Ray wasn't famous, well not for boxing any way,' she grinned, easing down the door handle. 'If I had a penny for every time Ray's mouth was compared to Blackwall Tunnel, I'd be in clover. After a broken nose or two he took up at the market. Figured he'd make a go of that till something better came along. Been there ever since. Mind you, he never got close to another woman after that. Reckons they can't be trusted, none of them.'

As young as she was, Ruby knew there were two sides to every story, and that it wasn't her place to offer an opinion. She couldn't understand though why Sal would allow herself to be treated like dirt by a known bully, too big for his own damned boots.

As if reading Ruby's thoughts, Sal continued. 'There's nowt as queer as folk and besides, he's the only family I have left. In spite of everything, I would rather have my brother around than not.'

'Brother?' Ruby's jaw dropped. 'But I thought you two were...'

Sal guffawed. 'I'd guessed as much. Lesson one, young lady, never judge a book an' all that. And before you ask, Ray gave up his bedsit and moved back home. Made more sense, moneywise.'

Sal wiped her feet on the coconut mat and pushed the door open. The blast of heat forced them back a step. Crooking her index finger, she beckoned Ruby closer. 'Don't let on that I mentioned any of this, about his wife and all. It doesn't do to drag things up.'

'My lips are sealed.' Ruby drew her thumb and forefinger across her closed mouth. To remind Ray about his past life would likely result in a premature end to her own. Naive she might be, but stupid? No way. She remembered her mum's words about dreams stacking up. If keeping schtum meant one day having them realised, then that's exactly what she intended to do.

Chapter 9

Jimmy maintained his usual upbeat presence, drawing in the customers with his effervescent quips and knock down offers of dubious antiquities. However, his father George was quick to notice that all was not shipshape in the Jimmy fan club. His boy had become all too easily distracted, from the moment that girl appeared on the scene. More so now, with her working within spitting distance.

He likened his boy's attention span to a fart in a colander: up, down, and all over the place. George would never belittle the lad's so-called love interest; after all, he knew first-hand how consuming his thoughts of Sal could be, and if given a free rein they would undoubtedly drive him barmy too. But business was business, and he would need to have words to keep his boy on track. 'What d'you keep craning your neck like that for?' he asked 'You're liable to do yourself an injury if you're not careful.'

Jimmy grinned, totally unaware of his so-called tic. 'Just keeping an eye out for me mates. No law against it.'

'Not saying there is, son, but with your head stuck in the clouds, you won't have noticed the light-fingered Herbert who just made off with the pocket watch!'

Jimmy's face drained of colour and the amplified sound of his heart pounding in his ears caused his head to swim. He glared down at the obvious space on the velvet cover. 'Holy shit,' he muttered, his mouth dry as a sand pit. Shamefaced, he turned to his father.

George remained quiet. Dipping into his trouser pocket he produced the watch, and holding it at arm's length set it swinging like a pendulum. Jimmy shook his head in disbelief.

'Rotten git comes to mind. What'd you do that for? I nearly messed me bloody self.'

'Just making a point son, and watch your language in front of the ladies. They don't like to hear that stuff, and it's not good for business neither.' Placing one arm around his boy's shoulders, George pulled him down into a friendly head-lock and ruffled his hair.

The pair fell into a light-hearted sparring when a pint-size pensioner, jumping to the wrong conclusion, dealt George a blow to his back with her handbag. Not backward in coming forward, she let him have it, both barrels.

'Pick on someone your own size. You spiteful fucker.' Egged on by the shoppers, she continued. 'There's a word for people like you, and if I could remember what the bleeding thing was, I'd be saying it to your face.'

Aware that Jimmy was bent double with laughter, George threw his hands in the air to ward off further attack. In an attempt to dodge the crazed woman, George's fancy footwork propelled him into the stall's frame. The whack to his arthritic knee brought the shenanigans to an abrupt halt. Agitated and wincing with pain, he faced the old girl.

'Now ease up darling, for gawd's sake. We were just mucking about.'

Flustered by her obvious mistake, she stepped aside. 'Well, that's all right then. I suppose?' Her wizened mouth twitched at the corners. 'I thought I was doing right by the young 'un.'

George brought his face down to hers. 'To be honest love it's not all right. You shouldn't be swearing like that in front of the boy. Sets a bad example.'

George had a good relationship with Jimmy. He never set out to be the boy's best pal; that bonus happened along the way. His primary role was to guide him, bring him up properly in a way that his late wife, Dolly would have been proud of.

Jimmy was like his mother in many ways. They shared an easy-going nature and smiling hazel eyes. Sometimes George caught a glimpse of Dolly in the boy's mannerisms, and it often pained him to the point of looking away. It was soon after Jimmy's birth that his wife contracted TB. She didn't stand a chance, so slight in build she had nothing to fight with. He vowed he would never marry again; no one could fill her shoes. But as the years passed his loneliness grew. He knew in his heart that Dolly wouldn't want him to struggle on alone, yet he felt that to bring another woman into their home would be disrespectful.

Then out of the blue came Sal. Like Dolly, she had that same caring heart. He'd never once seen Sal as partner material. They'd been friends since the year dot; practically grown up together. Then one day his feelings changed, knocking him clean off his feet. He wanted to be with her, to share the happiest of days and those long lonely nights.

'One last thing, son. I hear Ruby's knocking about with a sailor? You'd better watch yourself there. You know what them buggers are like, a girl in every port and that. He'll be dipping his wick whenever he gets the chance, make no mistake and there's no telling what sort of souvenir he might bring her back.'

Jimmy couldn't believe his ears. He felt totally affronted that his own dad would talk about Ruby in such a way. 'But she's not like that.'

'I hope not, for your sake. I'm just warning you to be careful, that's all. Wouldn't be doing me duty by you otherwise.' He paused. 'Look, son, I know you're sweet on the girl. It's as plain as flour, but she's spoken for. Best steer clear is all I'm saying.' He lifted a ten-shilling note from the takings. 'That's it. I've said my piece. You'll not hear another word from me on the subject. I'm nipping to Sal's for a sarnie. Hold the fort for us. Won't be more than half hour.'

*

Asking advice from his dad came easy to Jimmy; there'd been times he needed it too. But being spoon-fed on what to do, what to say, and how to feel was taking the biscuit. He had never come up short in the common-sense department. He could work things out himself, in his own time. He and Ruby were mates, first and foremost. His dad was right on one count though, his feelings towards Ruby had changed. Quite when that had happened left him puzzled, since there was no one defining moment. In the scheme of things, it hardly mattered now. He'd been too slow to recognise the shift. His own stupidity had forced him to the side-lines, where he'd no choice but to accept that Ruby's sights were set on someone else.

A chorus of whistles cut short Jimmy's thoughts. He could hardly ignore the sailor, strutting by with a mini harem dripping off his arms like exotic leeches. A wry smile crept across Jimmy's face as the trio gathered admiring glances. He never understood why a uniform turned girls into would-be groupies. As they drew level with his pitch, Jimmy's heart sank. He had never been friends with Billy Beaufoy, although he recognised him immediately. He knew him as the toe-rag from his final year at school; the bloke with more tickets on himself than the clippies at Peckham bus station. A feeling of dread tightened his gut, as his thoughts returned to Ruby and the spectacle now heading her way.

Beaufoy had to be the one she went on about, after-all, sailors were a pretty rare breed in Walworth. If only he'd realised that Beaufoy was the absent boyfriend, he could have warned her. Chances are she wouldn't welcome his interference. Yet he couldn't stand by and see her hurt. It might well backfire, he told himself. Even so, he had to say something, try and get her to see sense, whatever the cost to himself. He would bide his time, voice his concerns at the earliest opportunity.

Chapter 10

East Street, for best part of the week, saw less human traffic than Brenchley Gardens, the local cemetery. With its kerbsides cleared of mountainous packaging and rotting vegetation, the rats from the old tenements in Blendon Row and mangy stray dogs sought rich pickings elsewhere. Save for a token gesture of stalls turning out on Tuesdays, nearby residents wallowed in the calm before the bedlam that ensued from Friday through Sunday. With the Cafe barely ticking over, Sal earmarked the quieter periods for cleaning, leaving Ruby free to re-visit her mother's old haunts.

Ruby's appointment with Mr Collins, the probation officer, had completely slipped her mind. To turn up a week late was unheard of and could place her future in jeopardy. She had some fast talking and grovelling to do in order to divert any plans he might have of visiting the flat. If he got wind of the eviction, he would almost certainly need to get the welfare onboard. As probation officers go, she could not have wished for a more decent character. Given their job was to keep criminals on the straight and narrow, she often wondered at his reaction when being allocated a teenager with a police record, for skipping school.

Even so, she always found reasons not to drag herself around Newington Butts and into the posh offices down Renfrew Road. *A touch of lazyitis*, her mother had called it, when Ruby sulked her way out of the tedious route-march. With a short time left on her two-year order, it was more important than ever that she made an effort. It seemed ironic that she should be punished for truancy, when, on the occasions she did show her face in the playground, she suffered a worse fate at the hands of bullies.

'You were lucky to catch me. I'm normally up in court today.' He pulled her file from the tall metal cabinet. 'I expect you'll be pleased to see the last of me,' he smiled.

When lost for words, as now, Ruby would focus on the photograph of his two sons, framed in silver filigree to the right of the giant blotting pad on the desk. She guessed he was a proud, loving dad. One who had always found time to play those daft masked hero games that her brother Gary had loved so much. Mr Collins was a kind, softly spoken man, who never once raised his voice to get a point across. His light grey suit matched his thinning hair, and his smile, a permanent feature of his slightly gaunt appearance, was genuinely warm.

Ruby liked him, even though the majority of people considered it traitorous to have any time for the Old Bill or their counterparts. Given that she had no choice in the matter she was just grateful she hadn't been landed with one of the others who, rumour had it, were so inflated with self-importance, that one rip-roaring fart would shoot them into infinity. He shuffled through the paperwork in front of him. 'I see you're due to finish school next Easter. Any idea what you might like to do?'

'I already left,' said Ruby, pushing forward in her seat. 'Glad to see the back of that place.' Her face brightened. 'I'm working now though, down The Lane in a cafe and sometimes on a stall, selling smashing handbags. But I've decided to be me own boss one day, design my own clothes and that, like Mary Quant. Open up a dress shop and all sorts.' Ruby's words skipped with enthusiasm.

Mr Collins rested backwards into the heavily buttoned leather chair. With his fingertips steepled beneath his chin, he grinned like the proverbial cat.

Ruby stared back, straight-faced, wondering what the hell she had said that had tickled his funny bone. Sure, she got carried away with the Quant thing especially since she didn't have a clue about designing. But it didn't mean she wasn't interested or incapable of learning. According to her mother, she could do anything she wanted if she put her mind to it. Maybe he wasn't so different from his colleagues after all. Her confidence around him had certainly grown over the past year, and although she felt at ease speaking her mind, she needed to remind herself not to overstep the boundaries. Remaining calm, she spoke her thoughts in a restrained yet firm manner. 'Are my ideas that funny? D'you think I'll end up in a factory like everyone else. Is that it? Just cos I live in the flats doesn't mean I haven't got dreams you know.'

'Far from it,' he quickly cut in. 'You've a good head on your shoulders and I've no doubt you could be very successful if you applied yourself. I smiled because I was pleased. Nothing derogatory was meant by it at all.' He paused. 'I was actually thinking how refreshing it was to see you so enthused for once. Our aspirations are as important as life itself.'

Ruby was momentarily tongue tied. She hadn't expected that reaction. It definitely beat the usual 'what will be will be' nonsense response she normally garnered from oldies in general.

'Well, I'll let you know when I'm famous then,' she said, giving a nervous chuckle.

He flipped through his diary. 'Meanwhile, tell your mum that I'll stop by to see her the minute I get a chance.'

Ruby jumped in. 'There's no point. Mum has a job too, so she's unlikely to be home. But I'll tell her you said hello.'

'Maybe another time then?' He stood up and reached out to shake Ruby's hand. 'You've come a long way Ruby, and I wish you and your family well for the future.'

She rose to her feet. Her hand settled in his. There had been no mention of him retiring, old as he was. 'I don't understand?'

'Two years are up,' he smiled. 'You're free at last. Don't tell me you haven't been counting down the days?'

Ruby's fingers tightened around his. She leant towards him and planted a kiss on his cheek. With all the upheaval of the past weeks she had completely forgotten that this would be their final meeting. She wanted to sing out with joy but decided it inappropriate. 'Seems daft but I'll miss seeing you,' she said shyly. The man stepped up during times of crisis. He'd made a difference to the family and she would always be grateful for that.

Stepping out onto the pavement, Ruby headed home. She prided herself on a job well done. As amenable as he was, Mr Collins was no pushover. She knew she'd be kidding herself if she thought otherwise. Her convincing performance didn't guarantee that he wouldn't suddenly show up at the flats and discover the truth. Her only consolation was the fact that the council never hurried itself in redecorating and letting to new tenants. With the net curtains still hung at the windows he would be none the wiser. And he wouldn't lower himself to the rent man's standards by spying through the letterbox to catch them out. And besides, he'd have no reason to since she was no longer on his books. The man had said so himself.

Ruby, back home, and with bread toasting beneath the grill, quickly adjusted the gas when a sudden pounding on the street door threw her into a panic. She raced along the hall and threw open the street door. A grubby four foot nothing, with knees hanging out of his trousers leant breathlessly against the wall. 'You Ruby?' he asked, puffing like a chain smoker.

'Depends on what you want?'

'Ray needs you to watch the stall.'

'I don't believe it' she huffed, eyebrows disappearing beneath her fringe. 'All right, tell him I'll be there soon as I can.'

The boy was slow to walk away. The sole of his shoe, detached from the upper, made a distinct flapping sound. Fishing in the pocket of her jacket hanging from a hook in the hall, she pulled out some loose change. 'Here,' she called, handing the lad a handful of pennies.'

'Cor, thanks, Ruby.' He stared at the coins centred in his palm. His face bright with wonder, as though Christmas had come early and no sod had bothered to tell him.

On returning to the kitchen, the burnt toast hit the bottom of the bin with a clunk. Ruby snatched up a couple of biscuits from the barrel on the side and mad her way to The Lane.

Joe, not bothering to show his face, had Ray fuming. Rather than risk a tongue-lashing, Ruby made no mention of the boy. She watched the stall while Ray nipped back and forth to the betting office, his mood fluctuating like the odds on his chosen fillies. In between time she griped about the disgusting smell wafting from the wet fish shop not three feet away. Its high-sided tray out front, alive with black shiny eels slithering about in slime, turned her stomach.

The sound of laughter and loud excited chatter drew a curious Ruby into the central aisle. With hands plunged into her money belt, she watched intently as a group of hippies made their way through to the main road. Their psychedelic garb and fringed jerkins held her gaze, right down to the beaded bands pulled tightly across their foreheads. Everything about them radiated a happiness that she hadn't glimpsed in the longest time. She felt decidedly scruffy in comparison. Her worn bell-bottom trousers and plain jumper, chosen only for their warmth, would hardly set a new trend. Although brimming with envy, she couldn't undo the smile that touched her lips as she captured a taste of their free spirit.

A dreamer, her mother had called her. Ruby savoured the moment. Her mother knew her far better than she knew herself. Her dreams, though too many to count, were the only constant in her life. They gave her the strength to plough through the drawbacks mounting at every turn. One day, she too would wrap herself in a rainbow of swirls and paisley patterns and grab some of those happy vibes for herself.

Chapter 11

Returning to the stall, Ray positioned an upturned crate at the kerb's edge and parked his ample backside. With a copy of the daily paper folded to a quarter of its size, he studied the form at Kempton Park, circling possibilities with the stub of pencil plucked from behind his ear.

With a sudden flurry of potential customers, Ruby kept a careful watch as they pawed the goods on display. While pushing paper stuffing back inside a handbag she became aware of two figures, stock-still, watching her. She raised her head and the blood immediately drained from her face. Uncle Tom and Aunt Grace stood grinning like exhibits from Madam Tussauds. A feeling of dread knotted Ruby's insides as she battled to gain control of her thoughts. She could have kicked herself for staring him out, mouth gaping like an idiot, with not a single word crossing her lips.

She had to get a grip, somehow calm the panic that forced her hands to tremble. Her heart bashed against her ribs. She had to be careful. One wrong move would give the game away. She couldn't let that happen, not now. With hands at her sides, she gripped the wooden framework, her knuckles threatening to burst the skin.

Ray shifted position. A sudden spasm in his gut made him sit up and take notice. His newspaper became a prop. He couldn't focus. His concentration had been disturbed by the waxy faced porker blocking his stall.

There was something about the bloke. He couldn't put his finger on it, but he knew bad news when he saw it.

Unfurling her fingers, Ruby moved towards the main walkway. She clasped her aunt's outstretched hand and kissed her cheek. Her vision blurred with unshed tears as she melted into the warmth of those welcoming arms. She didn't want to be released, not now, not ever.

Presently, moving apart, Grace's fingers gently traced the contours of the young face. 'Well, look at you! All grown up and as tall as me too.'

'Yeah, all of five foot nothing,' said Ruby, tightening the grip on Grace's hand.

'Well, what a lovely surprise to bump into you. We didn't know you worked the market, did we, Tom?' Grace upped the dial on her hearing aid box and waited for his response that never came. 'We nipped up the flat,' continued Grace, 'but there's no one home. I expect your mum's out shopping.'

'Enough of the chit-chat woman. Give someone else a look in,' moaned Tom, elbowing Grace out of the way. 'So, what about a hug for your uncle then?' His arms opened in readiness.

Ruby cringed at his smarmy grin. The thought of him touching her sent shivers through her body. She dragged her feet. Tom stepped forward, reached out and pulled her in. He tightened his hold, reminding her of his strength. The heat from his body heightened the sickly scent of his sweat. She held her breath, turned her head side-on and sucked air back into her lungs.

Ray glanced up from his paper. The look on the kids face spoke volumes. He could turn a blind eye and sod off back to the turf accountant's or he could intervene. 'Oi, Ruby, this ain't a bleeding social. There's customers' waiting. Get yourself back round this side.'

Begrudgingly, Tom released his hold. Looking down at Ray on his makeshift chair, the men glared at each other before Tom looked away and shared the reason for their visit.

'We thought we'd take Daisy back for a few days,' he said, in a feigned, jolly manner as if doing the child a favour.

'No, you can't,' Ruby exclaimed, walking back behind the barrow. The words blurted out in a moment of panic. With no idea where Daisy was, she searched desperately for a good enough excuse. Remembering that schools had returned after the summer break would be explanation enough. 'The school board man will have a fit.' She lied.

'We'll have her back home by Sunday. I'm sure your mum can sort it out?'

'No, Mum won't allow it; she's already in trouble for Daisy hopping-the-wag.' She felt safer with the stall between them. She knew she had pissed him off when he dragged his thumb nail across his dimpled chin.

Stretching across the stall, Tom handed Ruby a slip of paper. She prised her hand from his damp palm. 'That's our phone number, in case your mum's forgotten it. Give it to her. She might change her mind. We can always nip back tomorrow if need be.'

Ruby wanted to rip the paper to shreds and chuck it back at him. Her aunt's ever smiling face changed her mind. Knowing Grace would be the one to suffer his foul mood on the bus journey home, Ruby stuffed it in her pocket. As much as she despised him, she didn't want to be the cause of her aunt's inevitable tears.

Grace linked her arm through Tom's as they headed back towards the Old Kent Road. Aware of Ray's curious gaze, Ruby straightened display items in a bid to look busy. She made no attempt to secure her hair back behind her ears when it tumbled down, partly obscuring her face. She sensed that Ray was itching to stick his nose in and satisfy his curiosity. Well, he was about to come unstuck. He could dig around as much as he wanted but she would never confide in him. Ever.

'No love lost there then,' he muttered, popping a Victory V sweet in his mouth. His disinterested tone didn't fool Ruby. She had met his kind before. She refused to be drawn in.

'So, what's the story between you two then? Oh, don't tell me, it's another of your little secrets?'

Ray knew nothing about her past apart from her immediate situation. Spending time in a remand home was a secret known only to her family. And as for her uncle, Ray was baiting her. It was nothing but a game to him, a cruel game in-keeping with his bully-boy tactics. She refused to turn and face him. The reddening rims of her eyes would only add to his amusement. Ruby shrugged it off. 'Don't know what you mean.'

'Sure you do. I wasn't born yesterday you know. The porker had perve written all over him. Never trust a bloke with beady eyes is what I say.' The words were out. He could hardly take them back. The way the girl's body visibly tensed made him feel like scum. What the hell had got into him? His runaway gob would attract a bullet one of these days. And he would only have himself to blame. He wanted to say something, make it right, but he couldn't trust that he wouldn't make matters worse. Instead, he turned on his heels and headed back to the betting shop.

*

Ruby's mind drifted to the time spent in the remand home with Daisy. Those two long weeks in a house filled with female strangers brought the worried sisters closer still. Their days, punctuated with 'what ifs' and feeble excuses for their truancy.

That judge woman won't really send us to boarding school, will she? Daisy had asked. Her saucer-like eyes pleading for Ruby to come up with the right answer.

Nah, think she wanted to scare us, that's all. Anyway, remember what dad always says, don't worry worry, till worry worries you.

Daisy had looked bemused. *That's proper cobblers, and you know it.*

Shh. Ruby placed a finger to her lips. *Don't use that language here.*

Why not? It's not swearing. I heard Nan tell someone that dad looked like the dog's, you know what, when he got a job at Claridge's. And Nan never swears!

Ruby remembered looking out onto the back garden, watching the stream trickling by in the distance. How different things were in Croydon. The closest they'd come to a garden had been a flower pot out on the landing by the street door, which someone pinched within the first week.

So, why'd they send us here then? It's all that school board man's fault. They'll lock us up for good cos of him?

No they won't. Don't be silly, said Ruby, gently teasing the tangles from her sister's hair with their moulded plastic brush. *We're here for medical reports, remember? We told the judge that we weren't well and that's why we couldn't go to school?*

But we're not really sick?

Course we're not. But maybe we should practise some faces before the doc shows up?

What, you mean like this? Daisy forced her eyes towards her nose and lopped her tongue out.

You daft sod. Ruby had laughed, giving her sister a playful shove. *I meant sick-looking not loopy.* They tumbled onto to the bed, arms around each other. Apart from an occasional hiccup escaping Daisy's throat, the girls lay in silence, with nothing on the white painted walls to distract their thoughts.

On the day of court hearing Ruby continued her upbeat charade, for Daisy's benefit. She could only hope that the Jesus she knew, from her younger Sunday school days, would remember her as a good kid, and prompt the judge to be lenient. When the two-year probation order was read out, she raised her eyes to the ceiling and mouthed a silent thank you.

Chapter 12

Ray's return from the betting office snapped Ruby back to the present. Close to packing up time and with customers few and far between, he sat counting his winnings. Ruby stood listlessly with her nose pressed against the pawn shop window situated directly behind their pitch. With no real interest in jewellery, her eyes flitted from one item to the next. Apart from helping to while away the minutes, it saddened her to know that the well-stocked window was solely due to local families being down on their luck.

A gold wedding band with tiny crescent moons running along its edges kept drawing her back. The moment she saw the small embedded red stone, her suspicions were confirmed. A memory of her mother's tear-stained face sprang to mind. She had lost her ring's solitary, minute diamond, which her father had promptly replaced with a garnet. Ruby's heart fluttered. She had been in the shop several times over the years, watching as the ring was handed over and the cash used to relieve the sting of hungry bellies.

As she pushed open the door, the familiar sound of the doorbell jangling above, summoned the elderly shop owner from his cubby hole. The musty interior with its brown paintwork and tobacco-stained ceiling reminded her of Old Jack's second-hand shop. The only difference was that Jack's was packed solid at all times with locals often coming to blows for the cast-offs. Ruby kept her voice low, secretive, as deemed customary in such places.

Ray stood ready to pounce the moment she stepped out onto the pavement. With his attention drawn between Ruby and the lone customer, removing the cellophane wrapping from nigh on every wallet on display, he asked edgily. 'What business you got in there then? Flogging off the family silver or what?'

The reasoning behind his questions was obvious to anyone with a brain cell. Under different circumstances Ruby would have tried to string him along, rattle him with innuendos. Wounded as she felt, her mood was such that she ignored his daft game. 'It's me mum's ring,' she pointed. 'He's selling it on. Won't even put it by for me. Said its cash up front or nothing.'

Satisfied that his belongings were safe, Ray's interest quickly waned. He had more pressing things to worry about, like the old bird turning his display into a war zone. Stepping back behind the stall, he spoke his mind while making good the mess the biddy had left behind. 'And where's that leave him when you change your mind.' He chuckled, cynically. 'Got bills to pay like the rest of us. Can't live off fresh air you know.'

'But I gave him my word!'

Ray's scornful glance riled her. Her sister Ellen would have treated him to a fat lip for less. 'According to the ticket, mum brought it in a few weeks ago.'

'Well, she couldn't have been that bothered is all I can say?'

Ruby glowered at him in disbelief.

'What?' he snapped, eyes goggling and shoulders lifting in complete denial that anything he'd said warranted the daggers flying his way.

'You don't care about anyone except yourself. Do you?' she blurted. 'I bet you've never gone without in your entire life.' She could feel the tears pricking her eyes. She never understood why anger made her cry. It made her look pathetic, a weakling in the eyes of others.

Ray snapped back. 'You watch your mouth, girl, or else.'

'Else what?' she pushed.

'You'll be out on your ear for starters.'

A sudden image of the lavatory at the garage forced her to swallow her pending words, already lined up like poison darts. She muttered beneath her breath instead. 'Oh, do what you like. I couldn't care less.'

Ruby sloped off to the Cafe. 'You'll change your tune when the probation officer finds out,' he called.

The revelation stopped her in her tracks. She turned slowly and matched him stare for stare.

'Not so cocky now, eh? You think I don't know your little secrets?' He'd hit a raw nerve. The panic in the kid's eyes threw him off course. He hadn't meant to take it that far. Threatening kids who didn't know when to shut their trap wasn't his thing at all. Regardless, he wasn't about to be bad-mouthed, not by anyone. 'Bring us back a mug of tea when you're done in there,' he said. 'And don't think about gobbing in it neither.'

Grimacing, with face damp as a dewy morning, Ruby slammed into the Cafe.

Chapter 13

With Ray off to Dagenham to bag some cheap merchandise, it was left to Ruby and Joe to run the stall. Ray's regular barrow boy, Joe, an older lad from nearby flats, jumped at the offer of manning the stall with Ruby. They rubbed along nicely as part-time mates. Their connection being, Joe's past ill-fated crush on Ruby's sister Ellen.

The youngsters laughed their way through a hectic morning. Saturdays were always busiest and the teenagers were under no illusion that Ray would leave them a minute longer than necessary.

The mood in The Lane was electrifying, almost palpable. Jocular traders tempted punters with their gift of the gab, each striving for top-dog position. The record dealer, a few stalls up belted out the latest upbeat offerings back-to-back, while Ruby drooled over the fringed fashions displayed along shop front exteriors. The lukewarm sun shone down on the growing hordes vying for space in the carnival-like atmosphere. The day had started well. The duo revelled in their grown-up roles as stock moved faster than a landslide.

The ambience changed the moment Mickey Loughty reared his head and, lying through his gappy teeth, introduced himself as Ray's overseer.

Ruby recognised him immediately and swiftly turned away. Fear unravelled like string throughout her body and knotted each muscle in a rapid sequence. She felt trapped in her own skin. Those long minutes of when he'd pinned her against the wall played out in their entirety. She prayed that the man's memory was as lousy as his character.

'Clowning around won't go down well with the boss,' he warned. 'How much you sold then?' Mickey's lecherous gaze on Ruby's rounded breasts filled her with dread. She slid her hands protectively into the canvas money belt tied around her waist.

'Some.'

'Some? What the fuck is some? Got any notes in there?' Aware that Joe was clocking his every move, Mickey got shot of him in a trice. 'Hey, gormless, make yourself useful, get us one of them sarsaparillas,' he demanded, tossing a coin through the air. He detested the hot, berry flavoured drink. 'But when needs must,' he muttered to himself.

Pushing his way around to the pavement area, Mickey sidled up to Ruby and draped his arm across her shoulders. With his back to the shoppers, he plucked a stray hair from the scooped neckline of her top.

'So, you're the little orphan Ray's got kipping under his roof. He's a sly dog that one.' Droplets of spittle escaped Mickey's mouth as he forced a mocking chuckle. 'I wouldn't send you packing either.'

'I'm not an orphan.' Ruby wiped the spit from her chin.

'Ah, is that right? Wormed your way in on a lie then. Figures. But what the boss man don't know can't hurt him, right? I'm with you on that one darling.'

'I'm not your darling either.' Although her words lacked conviction, she braced herself for the backlash. His twisted grin sealed his mouth shut, but the menace in those eyes forced her to look away.

A blast of warm air tousled Ruby's fringe. A quick flip of the head returned the dishevelled hair to its usual tidy position, but not in time to screen the birthmark.

Mickey's jaw hardened. He took a long, slow breath. 'Well, who'd have thought it,' he sniggered. 'The mouthy little cow who thinks she's a cut above. Let me tell you something for nothing, darling,' he said, bringing his face close to hers. 'No one calls me creep and gets away with it. You comprende? So, let me give you the heads up. Being kinder to me in future is how this pans out. Ain't that right?'

The stale odour from his cigarette breath filled her nostrils. She tried to shrug him off, put some distance between them. He dug his fingers into her young flesh and yanked her against him. Delving into the money belt, his hand rested gratuitously against her lower belly, before grabbing a handful of notes and stuffing them in his pocket. 'So, what's the deal today then? You offering after sales service?' He laughed out loud. 'And by the way, I wouldn't go blabbing to Ray if you value your bed and board. The minute he gets wind of you creaming off his profits you'll be gone, back under the arches or wherever the hell you came from.'

Ruby's face dropped. 'I would never steal his...'

'Your word against mine? No chance. Think on it. I'll be seeing you soon for more of the same.' He slapped her backside and sauntered off towards the local pub.

Ruby's eyes clouded over. She was as mouthy as the next with her mates, but alone, she was the same scared kid she had always been and dealing with a scumbag like Mickey was never going to happen. He reminded her of the uncle who preyed on the young. They were loathsome gits, one and the same. They had it coming, and with luck on her side she would be around to bear witness. Strong as her thoughts were, she never had the pluck to voice them. Ellen and Gary loomed large in her head. Where were they when she needed them? Their streetwise bravado was clearly not a trait she'd inherited. They wouldn't be standing there bricking it, like their yellow-bellied sister. Their razor-sharp words alone would have annihilated the likes of Mickey. Ruby vowed that one day she'd have a backbone, embrace her fearsome shadow and above all else, make her family proud.

Ruby and Joe shared the fruit drink between them. 'That bloke who just nabbed yer,' said Joe. 'I reckon he's a homo. You never see him with a girl.'

Ruby's head snapped up, her attention well and truly hooked. She stepped closer. 'Blimey, where'd that come from?' she quizzed. 'You don't half come out with some stuff.'

'Mum cleans for our neighbour. He's one. Throws his weight around too. All mouth and trousers she calls him. She says it's just a front, a cover up.'

Ruby held her tongue. Mickey Loughty might be many things, but she wouldn't bet money on him being a fairy.

'They call him Backdoor Billy; my neighbour that is,' continued Joe, in the same matter-of-fact tone.

'Here, watch it.' Ruby nudged him. 'That's me boyfriend's name and he's no homo.'

'Course not. From what I hear your feller's a sailor and them lot, well, we know what they're like. And anyway, how come I've never clocked him?'

People doubted her claim regarding Billy. She'd seen it written in their faces, and as much as she wanted to erase the false impression she'd created, she lacked the nerve to do so. To refer to Billy as a boyfriend was not in itself a falsehood. They had paired up during school trips. They'd been friends for heaven's sake, up until the time she almost drowned in saliva when he'd kissed her. To have a boyfriend in name only, worked. It saved her from unwanted attention.

'Might have something to do with him being at sea?'

'If you say so. Look, don't go letting on, but I've been offered a job at the cheese factory down Tooley Street.'

'Oh, you lucky thing. My sister worked there. They have music playing through the tannoy all day long, and no more frost bite!' Ruby stretched out her arms. 'But you'll miss this carnival though.' She smiled.

'Yeah, right. Why not come with me. They got lots of vacancies.'

'Can't. It's complicated.'

Joe shrugged. 'Your loss.'

'Maybe.'

Shortly after lunch, arriving back at the market from a successful trip, Ray pushed his way through the gathering. A shrieking, banshee of a woman swiftly waylaid him.

'What the hell's going on?' he demanded.

'Getting rich at my expense. Diddling me is what she's doing, robbing little mare.'

'She reckons she gave me a quid when it was only a ten-bob note,' Ruby blurted. 'I'm good with money, you know I am.'

Aware of the bodies edging nearer, baying for blood, Ray cursed beneath his breath. 'Might have known that cowbag would have something to do with it.'

'And what's that supposed to mean? I've a good mind to get myself over to Carter Street right now, see what the Old Bill have to say about it.'

'Give her the money,' said Ray.

Ruby stood dumbfounded.

'Just give her the bloody money and be done with it.'

Ruby placed the coins begrudgingly into the woman's hand.

'She's known for pulling a fast one. Must have seen you as an easy target.'

'But you've made me look like the thief.'

'A bit of advice for the future: always keep the money in your hand before you give the change. Those new fifty pence coins coming in will soon put a stop to her game.'

Ruby would never do people out of their hard-earned cash. She had been shown up, made to look dishonest in front of everyone. She wouldn't put up with it, not for a minute longer. She tossed the money bag onto the stall and stormed off towards the park area adjacent The Mason Arms.

'Where do you think you're going? Oi, Ruby, get yourself back here right now.'

She ignored him completely. He could poke his job as far as she was concerned.

Within minutes of moping on a nearby bench, Ray was at her side, having left Joe to fight off the customers single-handedly. 'You can be a right stroppy mare at times. What the hell's got into you?'

With hands in her lap, Ruby twiddled her thumbs. 'I'm not feeling great - having a bad day if you really must know.' In truth, it was on the tip of her tongue to say, your precious friend, Mickey, is a pervert and a thief and he's robbing you blind except you can't see for looking.

*

Ray cringed. He wasn't stupid. Women got moody at a certain time in the month, he knew that, but stone the crows, he wasn't about to be having a conflab about it. Admittedly, she wasn't the worst kid in the world, not shy of grafting neither but, when all's said and done, if she wanted to shove off then so be it. There were plenty more willing to take her place. 'Look, I don't need staff that push off every time they get their ear chewed.' He stood up to walk away. 'Up to you, take it or leave it. And, just so as you know, I wasn't accusing you of anything, but it's the only way to handle situations like that.' Ray moved off, content in the knowledge that Ruby trailed a few steps behind.

Chapter 14

With the market stall secure in the lock-up, Ruby nipped into the Cafe. Sal quickly bolted the door as the last customer left, before tramping her way back to the deep enamel sink. 'Don't know about you, duck,' she said, wringing out a hot soapy dishcloth, 'but I'm just about all in.' Sal washed down the tables while Ruby followed behind buffing them to a deep shine. Something bothered Ruby; her unfocused gaze and redundant tongue were dead giveaways to Sal, who recognised the girl's foibles better than her own. 'Come on then, out with it,' coaxed Sal, fully expecting her brother to be at the crux of the matter. 'What's he said now?'

Ruby shook her head. 'Oh, it's nothing to do with Ray.'

Sal's eyebrows raised, dislodging beads of perspiration that trickled down and clouded her vision. Rubbing her eyes with her free hand, she replied, 'Well that's a first, if ever there was.'

'It's just, I've been thinking.'

Sal jumped in. 'Oh Lordy, you need to quit with that lark. No good will come of it,' she chuckled at her own silliness. It had little impact on Ruby's glum expression. 'Don't mind me, lovey. I'm just excited about putting me feet up later, and turning this head off.' She tapped her temple. 'The day I've had! The things I've heard. You would not credit. I'd swear my brain's softened from the weight of it all, like a great dollop of scrambled egg I shouldn't wonder. Anyway, you were saying?'

The buffing cloth passed back and forth through Ruby's hands. 'Sal, If I got myself a proper job, could I still stay with you and pay rent?'

'A proper job indeed!' exclaimed Sal, hands pressed firmly on her hips as her pinafore soaked up the moisture from the dishcloth. 'You mean to say that these past years I've been kidding myself that I'm providing a worthwhile service?' Her stunned tone had Ruby backtracking fast.

'Oh, I didn't mean it to sound like that. Everyone knows you do an amazing job.'

'Yeah, all right, enough of the eye-wash,' she grinned, throwing the dishcloth into the empty sink. 'Damn thing's only soaked through to me drawers,' she mumbled to herself. Her focus shifted back to Ruby. 'I was just playing. Don't look so worried, you daft ha'porth. So, what's brought this on? You sure Ray's not been breathing down your neck again?'

'A bit, but that's not what it's about,' she replied. 'It's just, well, I've been thinking about working in one of them boutiques, like the new one round the corner. '*Fantastic*' it's called and the clothes are just gorgeous. You should see them, Sal. Some days I can't prise me nose off the window.' Ruby rambled on, eyes sparkling like cut glass. 'I might get clothes at bargain rates and you never know, if I work hard, I could be manageress one day. Wouldn't that be something?'

Not normally lost for words, Sal found herself struggling. 'I don't quite know what to say. You've obviously given it a lot of thought. Is this '*Fantastic*' place looking for staff then?'

Ruby sighed. 'I don't think so,' she said dejectedly, only to become animated again with the next breath. 'They'll put a card in the window, like they did before. I could be first through the door. Be in with a chance. Oh, Sal, I love you to bits, and nothing will change that, but to work in that shop would be a dream come true. It really would!'

Sal's heart-strings were firmly tugged by the girl's passion. As much as she would miss Ruby during the working day, the undeniable guilt of hampering the girl's dreams would be a far worse option. 'Leave it with me. I'll have a word with his nibs. See if we can work something out.'

Ruby, stretching up on tip-toes, wrapped her arms around Sal's neck. They turned in unison as Ray rapped on the window.

'What's going on in there? You having a funny turn or what?' He walked off in a huff the minute he saw them both giggling, in that silly girly way that left men completely stumped.

'Before you go,' said Sal, 'Everything OK with you and Jimmy? I haven't seen hide nor hair of him these past days.'

'He's probably busy Sal, that's all.'

'You haven't had a falling out then?'

'Not exactly.' Ruby knew that Sal wouldn't pry further, and even if she did, there was nothing to tell. She hadn't exactly argued with Jimmy. Although his words, his obvious dislike of Billy, had riled her, she'd reacted calmly with a few comments of her own. Did he honestly believe she was gripped by some silly schoolgirl crush? Billy Beaufoy had served a purpose, in name only.

*

Later, with the night drawing in and her feet aching after another hectic day, the last thing Sal needed was to drag herself along to the pub. But she had promised George, and broken promises had no place in her life.

Lowering her feet into a bowl of water, softened with soda crystals, was nothing short of bliss. With a towel close to hand, she eased herself backwards and sighed with contentment as the stresses of the day melted away. Ruby's earlier words had triggered Sal's memory. With both Ray and Ruby out for the evening, she allowed her eyes to close and her thoughts to drift to a time long gone.

The scene played out like a film once viewed. August 1940. A glorious balmy afternoon. The sun danced in her hair, picking out the auburn tones while the warm breeze teased the gathers of her lemon floral dress. She had never felt more beautiful or wanted as she did in those moments. She walked hand in hand with James, her fiancé. Their grip tightened and pace slowed as Waterloo station came into view. People stared at the young soldier clad in new army issue. Men tipped their hats in salute. James's zeal equalled that of the other young men, filing up the steps to the main concourse, like a wave of khaki buoyant with pride.

Standing alongside the train carriage, James drew her into his arms. Her heart hammered as the station master's whistle continued its piercing shrill. She tried desperately to remain strong, but those blessed tears she'd promised not to cry now streamed down her face. Boarding the train, and with hands tightly held through the open window, James leant out and kissed her trembling mouth. *I love you to bits, Sal,* he'd said as the engine fired up. *Promise you'll wait for me?*

I'll be here. The moment you return, she had promised. Her hands gradually slipped from his grasp. Seconds later he was gone.

Sal's eyes opened and she brushed the dampness from her face with her sleeve. Her toes, resembling bleached prunes, were quickly dried before racing upstairs and throwing on an ensemble of glad-rags.

Awhile later, pushing open the door to The Masons, a blast of heat and opaque smoke caught Sal full in the face. She gave a polite cough and smiled her way around the maze of chairs and groups of regulars all striving to be heard above the din. George waved her over to a table close to the jukebox, before disappearing to get the drinks in. With her coat folded beside her, Sal grinned and bobbed her head in reply to the silent greetings coming her way.

She was glad she'd made the effort, especially since George had saved her a seat on the comfy buttoned-back bench. He had no qualms with the loud, thumping music. Neither did Sal after the first ten minutes, once she'd been rendered deaf by The Beatles and The Stones. Come Fridays, with the working week behind them, locals often hurried to their preferred pub early to secure seats. One minute after eight and pickings were slim. Sal was grateful to George, offering to drag out on her behalf.

She watched as he moved steadily away from the bar, easing his way through the throng of bodies. She did have feelings for the gentle giant. He was a good sort, a diamond even, never failing to lift her spirits. But could she handle the demands a union would bring? A sudden memory made her cheeks glow, her embarrassment quickly veiled by a handkerchief from her clip-top handbag. No one had ever seen her unmentionables before, not even old Dr Clarkson down at the surgery. An image of her mother's garish nylon bloomers drying on the fireguard brought tears of laughter to Sal's eyes. She was fast losing the plot.

Go on, laugh all you like, her mother had scolded. *But it would do a blind man good to see them, and that's a fact*. Sal's light covering of foundation had been stripped away by the damp handkerchief. She had to pull herself together before George returned, or risk being carted off to the funny farm.

He handed Sal her advocaat and lemonade and she popped the customary cherry from the cocktail stick into her mouth. George sat opposite on the curved back chair and sipped the froth from his beer. Wiping the remains from his top lip with the back of his hand, he beamed across at Sal. 'What's tickled you then, mate?'

Drying her eyes, Sal managed to compose herself. 'Believe me George, you're better off not knowing.'

'I trust your decision, Sal. Wouldn't do for us both to start bawling. After-all, I have a pint to protect. Can't be doing with watered down beer.'

'You're a daft lump, George, and no mistake.'

'I am, when I'm around you Sal.'

Her gaze shifted briefly to the regular ancient eccentric, holding court and regaling those close by with farfetched tales, made more believable with a shifty of his homemade elixir. 'I'm guessing you've sampled his latest concoction?' Sal joshed.

'Not so much as a sniff. Scouts honour. It's lethal stuff girl. Couldn't feel me damn legs for two days solid last time.'

As the evening wore on, couples jigged about to selected records, well-oiled voices grew louder, while dense, cigarette smoke, drifted like ghostly figures around the heads of the whole caboodle. The seafood man entered, along with a welcomed corridor of clear, cool air. His tray of local favourites, suspended from heavy duty shoulder straps. emptied within seconds. Sal tucked into her small tub of cockles while George's jaw worked overtime with his portion of whelks. 'Puts you in mind of the seaside, doesn't it?'

George nodded. 'It does that. Talking of which, I saw Ray's name was down for the Beano. Did he make it this year?'

'Does he ever? He always says he's going, rarely turns up though. Reckon he's feeling his age now. What about you? Did you go?'

Pushing the empty fish carton aside, George tapped the end of a roll-up on his silver tobacco tin, and shook his head. 'Nah, bit old for that game now. It's a break from routine I'll give you that, but Southend's nothing like it used to be. It's jam-packed with youngsters, pissed out their heads and brewing for a punch-up. Who needs it?'

'Anyway, on a different note, what about you and me going to the pictures? We might catch one of them Carry-On films at the Odeon. What d' you reckon girl. Fancy it?'

Sal warmed to the idea. She liked a good comedy and they didn't come better than the Carry-On crew. 'OK, you've twisted my arm. Sort something out and let me know.' The time bell rang for last orders. Sal was first up on her feet. With her camel coat on and buttoned, and the handles of her bag nestled in the crook of her arm, she eased her way around the table to George. Bending down, she stared a still-seated George straight in the eye. He puckered up. Clamping his lips firmly together between her fingers and thumb, Sal informed him, 'And we won't be sitting in no back row neither, so don't go getting any funny ideas.'

George took hold of her hand, emptied the last mouthful of beer down his throat, and stood up. 'Thought never even entered my head. I'm a gentleman, Sal, one of a dying breed. You'll be safe as houses with me,' he said, with a twinkle in his eye that near dazzled her. There was no denying he was a lovable old rogue. What's more, he made her laugh, and that counted for so much in her books. 'So, you walking me home then, George?'

'Surprised you even have to ask,' he patted her hand as she rested her arm through his. George puffed out his chest with pride. Sal had given him a glimmer of hope and turned him into a rich man. After all, he was one hundred percent up on what he had yesterday.

Chapter 15

Saturday arrived with a bleary-eyed Daisy huffing warm breath onto the windowpane of the first floor flat. She wrote her initials, DD. The grey skies and fine drizzle created a ghostly mist in the empty streets below. The swing park with its high black painted railings, jutting out from behind the council flats opposite, had a trio of wooden seats hanging still and sodden from heavy chains. She could almost smell the damp rustiness of the chunky links on her hands. An array of shrubs and roses surrounding the estate had passed their best, and pink petals littered the grass like oversized confetti. A dark figure spotted in the distance moved slowly into view. Mopping the moisture from the window with her forearm, Daisy pushed her face against the cold glass.

'You haven't seen me fags have you?' asked Mrs Brinton, breezing into the room, busily upturning old newspapers and clothing left strewn across the settee. Reaching down into the hearth, she switched on the electric fire. 'I'm sure my Julie hides them you know.' The thinly built woman with sunken features and short peroxide hair moved faster than a whippet. Anything not bolted down was re-positioned in a flash. 'What you doing up so early anyway?' she asked, moving across to Daisy. She flicked back the curtains to check the windowsill, her eyes in perpetual motion scanning the room. 'She's a real fidget my Julie,' said Mrs Brinton, pausing for breath. 'Arms and legs all over the shop.

She's clopped me on the nose before now. Maybe you'll be best off sleeping on the settee?'

'Nah, she's all right. I just needed a pee. That's all.'

Daisy and Julie had become almost inseparable from day one at the local school. They shared everything, from chicken pox and nits to sweets and crayons. Mrs Brinton had a soft spot for the cheeky blonde kid with the butter-wouldn't-melt smile, but in truth, the last thing she needed was another mouth to feed. Bringing up her own daughter was difficult enough, on scant wages earned from her cleaning jobs. Yet, within seconds of that door knocker echoing down the empty passageway, the homeless youngster was warming her toes round the fire.

A sudden sneezing fit had Mrs Brinton delving blindly in her deep overall pockets for a handkerchief. Her dull, watering eyes brightened as her hand touched on the cigarette packet. 'Would you believe it? They were here all the time,' she said in dry, croaky spurts. 'Thank gawd I don't have to drag to the paper shop.' She peered through the window. 'I mean, look at it! That fine stuff soaks through to your bones.'

Daisy looked up and smiled, trying to draw the woman's attention away from the window. 'How come it only ever rains at weekends? asked Daisy.

'It just seems that way,' said Mrs Brinton. 'In any case, a drop of rain has never stopped you kids playing out.'

The lone figure, now stationary on the grassed area below, peered up into their faces. A motherly hand tilted Daisy's chin. 'Now you listen to me little one. I've told you before, he mustn't keep showing up like this.' Her words were soft, apologetic. 'The neighbours are already talking, not to mention what it's doing to you. It just not right sweetheart. How did he even know you were here?'

'Cos I told him!' Daisy held back the sobs, trapped them inside as she'd seen her mother do. Her bottom lip quivered as tears pooled in her lower lids. 'He's me dad. He's all I've got left.'

Breathing through the tightness of her throat, Mrs Brinton answered. 'I'm sure he'll get himself sorted, once he knows how much it's upsetting you.'

'But I'm not upset,' cried Daisy. 'I'm happy. Look!' She demonstrated by forcing her biggest smile.

The pain in the girl's face gnawed at the woman's heart. She needed to remove herself before breaking down. 'I'm off to stick the kettle on.' She headed towards the door. 'Come away now, there's a good girl. You've got that new school to be thinking about. Come Monday you'll be knee deep in new friends.'

Daisy turned back to the window. Placing her hand on the glass, she positioned it just so; make-believing she could touch the unshaven cheek of the man with the saddest eyes ever. When he smiled up at her, she felt a deep hurt inside, a growing ache, so tight that she expected her skin to split under the pressure. She tapped a forefinger onto the outside of her wrist, before placing both palms against the windowpane. Her fingers splayed to breaking point, indicating minutes, to which her father gave a nod of understanding.

*

Charlie had never felt so lost. With shoulders slumped and head slightly bowed, he straightened his cap before making his way slowly across the slippery grass to the far wall of the flats. His ex-security officer suit had been a Godsend. The thick black serge, worn and shiny in places, helped ease the sting of bitter winds that threatened to strip away his thin flesh. But when soaked through, as now, it became a curse, clinging to his bones and making each step more difficult than the last.

Charlie could not fathom what had happened. He'd racked his brain every waking moment searching for an answer. Just two short months ago he had a wife, a family and a home. Life had been tough, there was no denying it, and even more-so when the doctor threw him on the scrap heap, declaring him unfit for work. People resorted to all sorts out of desperation, he knew that, had seen it with his own eyes. Moonlight flits were something others did to escape their debts, but not him, and certainly not his Kate. Had he not been in and out of hospital, suffering the curse of emphysema, his family would still be together, and laughter would still ring out from the rooms of the council flat. He had struggled up those stairs to that second-floor landing, umpteen times in the past week, his ear jammed in the opened letterbox, listening intently to the echoes of his children.

With his back against the brickwork for support, Charlie's mind momentarily switched off. He stared vacantly at the young woman hurrying along the pavement, battling to knot a headscarf of swirling colours beneath her chin. Slowly, he lifted a hand; a hint of recognition teased a corner of his mouth. His Kate had found him. He always knew she would come looking. The woman scurried past, giving the loner a wide berth, before her clip clopping heels disappeared around the corner and faded into the distance.

His legs buckled and he dropped to his knees. He cradled his head in his hands as a low piteous wail escaped his throat. His heart and life were now on equal footing. Broken. The end of the road loomed ever closer, and for the life of him he could see no way past the misery that lay ahead.

*

Mrs Brinton had one last gulp of her tea, snatched her cigarette packet from the worktop, and flew out through the street door like a windstorm. 'If I'm late again so help me, they'll have my guts for garters,' she called, her voice trailing off along the landing. Money earned from cleaning the local funeral parlour and nearby pub and put food on the table, making life a sight easier for the widow. It made no odds that she often smelt like a brewery by the end of a shift and without so much as a drop passing her parched lips.

Daisy emptied the last dregs of sterilised milk into a cup, rinsed out the long-necked bottle and filled it with water. She spread a thick layer of lemon curd between two slices of bread, buttoned her coat over her nightdress, and she too was off and running.

Arriving at the usual meeting place she poked her head round the corner. Her smile fell away, as she rushed to kneel beside the crumpled figure on the paving slabs. 'What you doing down there? Did you fall over or something?' Daisy asked. 'You'll catch pneumonia you know,' she added, remembering her mother's warning about sitting on damp concrete.

Charlie stared into the child's face. Her cool blue eyes, rounded with unanswered questions. That little turned up nose, sniffing in a formed dewdrop, and her skin, so smooth and pale as milk, just like an angel's. His angel. Suddenly, gripped by shame, that his little girl was carrying the weight of a grown man, his resolve hardened. He made a promise to himself there and then. He would turn things around, if it was the last thing he did. If not for himself then he would do it for Daisy. 'It's me ankle, girl, gave way on me that's all. Nothing to worry your pretty little head about. So, what we got here then?' He pointed at the sandwich with a big surprise-like grin on his face. Daisy considered herself too grown up to play those baby games.

'You know it's lemon curd,' she tutted. 'Same as always.'

'Did I tell you that curd was my absolute favourite?' he said, before taking a bite.

'No, cos it not. Everyone knows you love beef dripping best.' She reached over and wiped a tear from his cheek. 'You been crying again?'

'Again? What do you mean, again? You cheeky rascal.' He tweaked her nose between the knuckles of two icy bent fingers. 'It's this damn cold wind, girl. You know how it makes me eyes stream.' He took a sip of the water. 'I'll give myself a nice shave later. Got the necessaries right here in me jacket.'

Charlie guarded his shaving gear as closely as his tobacco tin, even though both, much like himself, had been pretty redundant of late. He had allowed his standards to slip, and although he was armed with all manner of excuses for his so-called decline, he needed a kick up the backside, and quick. He would cut through the back turnings to the underground toilets in Arnside Street. Grab himself a proper wash and shave and stop by the tea shop opposite. Kate was known to drop in there when mooching about, window shopping.

He had passed many sleepless hours, wondering what the striking young woman had seen in him all those years ago. Ten years his junior, her slim, shapely build and beautiful smiling face could turn more heads than a day at the races. She could have had the pick of the bunch, and yet she'd chosen him, making him the proudest man on earth. She had loved him, relied on him, and like a fool he'd let her down.

Thoughts of Kate filled him with renewed strength and determination. He would find her, and when he did, she would see that despite everything he had taken care of himself, and would do his damnedest to provide for his family once more. He would not stand before her, the rag-bag of a man he'd become today. He would hold his head high, and pray that she would trust him enough to put things right.

'Well, best I get a move on,' he decided, his voice laced with urgency. 'Things to do, places to go and all that. Help your old man up, there's a good girl.' Daisy's hands locked together beneath his elbow and she pushed upwards with all her might. 'That's got it.' He straightened himself against the wall. Brushing off gravel from the seat of his trousers, he continued, 'Now, if I'm not about in the morning don't you go worrying yourself, OK?'

Daisy peered up at him. A look of panic swept across her face.

'I'll get word to you as soon as I'm sorted. I promise.' Charlie leant over and placed a kiss on the youngster's cheek. 'Everything will be OK, you'll see. Now get yourself back indoors, before you get that pneumonia your mum's always harping on about.'

Chapter 16

Mid-way through the morning, a summons from the Cafe, delivered by an impatient errand boy, ignited Ray's fuse. 'No way. You tell 'em Ruby's busy. Can't spare her.'

'Not doing that,' the boy answered. 'If she doesn't come now, I won't get my shilling.'

'A shilling!' Ray eyes popped. 'For crossing the road? It's daylight bloody robbery, if you ask me.'

'I'm not,' said the boy, 'asking you that is. And I'm not budging either, mister. Not till she does.' The boy stood defiant: arms folded, nose in the air, and a scowl so comically fierce that it softened the edges of Ray's irritation.

'Get going Rube, and take that ginger bandit with you. I'll expect you back in five,' said Ray, tapping his watch.

The lad moved faster than a souped-up dodgem car, zipping full pelt around slow-moving human traffic. After losing him in the crush, Ruby caught a flash of red hair as he stopped outside the Cafe. She watched the exchange. Several coins dropped slowly into the boy's eager, outstretched hand, not by Sal, as expected, but by Mickey.

Ruby, on automatic pilot, lifted a handful of notes from her money belt and slipped them down the neck of her jumper, and into her bra. She could return to the stall or give Mickey the handout he now waited for.

Either decision would put her immediate future in danger. She moved towards him.

'Took your bleeding time,' sneered Mickey.

'Can't just drop everything you know.'

'Sure you can. If you know what's good for you. So, hand it over.'

Ruby stalled. She peered through the cafe window. To meet in clear view of Sal made no sense; unless he wanted to be seen. But why would he put himself at risk? 'You're supposed to be Ray's friend.'

'I'm everyone's friend, darling.'

Ruby pulled the two remaining notes from her belt. 'That's all there is.' Ray's taken most of it already.' A knot of dread tightened in the pit of her stomach. Their eyes locked. Realising she had forgotten to breathe, Ruby looked away and sucked in a breath.

'Don't go playing me for an idiot.'

Her words rang out. 'I'm not. I'm just saying...'

His raised hand cut her short. Ruby flinched, anticipating a slap. 'Shush,' he sounded. Pipe down.' He smiled for the benefit of all within earshot. Ruby recoiled from his touch. A slap would have been preferred to him pawing her hair. With added space between them, Mickey leant in. 'If you let me down again, I'll be having words with the boss man. And we don't want that now. Do we?'

*

Sal did a double take on seeing Mickey ahead in the queue. Her suspicions roused. Never, in all her years had he graced the premises. He ordered a tea. 'Could have sworn I saw you out front talking to our Ruby?'

'Yeah, not so lucky me, eh?'

'Meaning?'

'Oh, you don't wanna hear my problems, Sal.'

She didn't. That was strictly Ray's department. From the titbits her brother had shared over the years, she'd decided from the off to keep her distance. But if Mickey was messing with Ruby, that was a different matter entirely. Aware of the subtle glances cast towards him, Sal asked, 'What you all togged up for then? You been to court?'

Mickey slid his thumbs beneath the lapels of his grey suit jacket. 'Leave it out, Sal. It's called taking pride, looking the business. It singles you out from...' He grinned at the two seated young women with eyes trained on him. 'I rest my case.'

Sal harrumphed, and began to pour the tea, wondering how pristine the work-shy man would look after a day's hard slog. 'As I was saying, you and Ruby?'

'That's exactly my point. There is no me and Ruby. The girl's obsessed, Sal. Won't leave me alone.'

The tea quickly overflowed the mug and spread across the counter before Sal recovered her senses. 'Now look what you made me do.' Using a handful of tea towels from the shelf below, she mopped up the surface. 'You and your wild ideas. Had me going there for a minute.'

'Nothing wild about it. The girl's a right pain; always nagging me to take her out. Even cadges dough! What's a man supposed to do?'

'Give your sodding tongue a rest for starters,' barked an irate queuing customer. 'There're people waiting 'ere, dying of thirst.'

Sal flushed and pointed Mickey to a near-by table. 'I won't be five ticks,' she told him. 'So don't move a muscle.'

With her concentration in tatters, Sal bumbled through until customers' orders became muddled or forgotten. In fear of a lynching, she called for Pam to take over. By the time Sal had reached Mickey's table, armed with a mountain of questions, he'd disappeared. His tea remained untouched.

Sal puzzled over what to do with the information Mickey saw fit to impart. She drifted across to the window and stared out vacantly. He had never sought her out before, aside from hurried 'hellos' in passing, even those she could count on one hand. Ray was his go-to person, always had been. So why her? Why now? It made no sense. As for Ruby falling for his dubious charms, the very idea was ludicrous.

Sal knew Mickey to be a troubled soul, unstable. She'd picked up that much from Ray. There were rumours too; rumours she dare not repeat. Her fingertips rotated deep into her right temple to ease the beginnings of a headache.

'You OK over there?' called Pam.

'Never better,' answered Sal. 'Just taking a moment,' she added, silently praying that whatever was lurking in the wings, didn't make its entrance until she had a clearer idea of what was going on.

Jimmy's grinning face on the other side of the glass brought Sal back to the present. Nudging the door with his shoulder, he stepped inside. 'If you're touting for business, Sal, you'd do better ditching the frown.' He laughed, and instantly ducked to dodge the playful slap aimed at his ear.

'Saucy beggar. This lunchtime was chocker block, like Picca-frigging-dilly. Why're you so late anyway?' she asked, her fingers moving a stray damp curl back from her cheek. 'There's not much left. Those builders from the new estate practically cleared me out.' Sal joined Pam back behind the counter, and dropped fresh teabags into the empty pot. The hissing from the hot water spout encouraged Jimmy to speak louder than usual.

'I know. Dad said. He popped by earlier, but queues are not his favourite pastime.'

Sal nodded, flipped up the lever to the water supply, stirred the pot and secured the lid. 'Ham rolls and bread pudding it is then. How does that suit?'

'Fine by me.'

'Sit your bum down a minute while Pam sorts the order. I'd like a quick word.' Sal deduced that Jimmy, more than anyone, would understand her concerns. 'I'm not one to pry, you know that, but I'm worried about Ruby. Something's amiss. I'm sure of it.' Sal fussed with the condiments, repositioning them continually, until Jimmy put his hand over hers and stalled the flow of movement. Sal looked up. 'It's difficult with Ruby, her being a bit of a closed shop an' all. I thought you'd likely know if there was anything troubling her?'

'You're asking the wrong person Sal.' He shook his head. 'She barely speaks to me now.'

Sal straightened up. 'I'd no idea. What's brought this about?'

'I tried to protect her. Warned her about Billy Beaufoy and she threw it back at me. Reckons I was making it up. I love the girl, Sal. I wouldn't hurt her for the world.'

'Good Lord, it's worse than I thought. All things considered, could she have taken a shine to Mickey? Only I saw them out front earlier.'

Jimmy laughed. 'Mickey? You mean that walking coat hanger who poses for the Freemans catalogue?'

'He never does?' said Sal, surprised.

'No, just kidding, but I reckon he gets his clobber from them. Wears it once then sends it back. One of our customers, an agent, mentioned all the tricks used to get out of paying. You were saying? Yeah, Ruby and Mickey, not a chance Sal. Told me herself, weeks back, that she can't abide the bloke.'

'But I spoke with him, not ten minutes ago, and he says she borrows money off him.'

'Order's ready,' interrupted Pam, pressing keys on the cash register.

Jimmy stood up, paid his bill and tucked the bagged-up rolls beneath his arm. With a mug of tea in both hands he moved closer to the door.

'He's having you on Sal. Ruby wants nothing to do with him. If he is bothering her, I'll have words with him myself.'

Sal stood by the open door. 'No don't do that. It's just, well I did see money changing hands.'

'Then best you ask Ruby. That Mickey geezers got a reputation Sal, and it's not for helping old dears off the bus. You might do better having a word with your Ray. Oh, and do us a favour Sal, next time you see Ruby, put a good word in for me. I really miss her.'

'Bless your heart lovey. I'll have words. I promise.'

With her mind made up, Sal's mood lifted. She would talk to Ruby, pin the girl down, if need be, to learn the truth of the Mickey situation. Only then, and if absolutely necessary, would she involve her brother.

Chapter 17

A month into the school term found Daisy hanging about nervously by the main gate. Groups of girls in smart grey and mauve uniforms filed noisily through. She was none too fussed about attending school, but given a choice she would have opted for Trinity Girls for one reason alone: the grass covered hill beyond the perimeter wall that she fancied formed part of the playground. She had seen it many times from the upper deck of the number 63 bus. It reminded her of sunny days, clambering up hills at Greenwich Park with her mates, and rolling down again at frightening speeds, screaming and yelling at the top of their lungs.

Dressed in a hand-me-down cotton frock and an oversized cardigan, Daisy stood out a mile. She hated the constant attention, the gawping and snide remarks. It was hardly her fault that the grant applied for by Mrs Brinton hadn't arrived. Within minutes of the bell sounding the majority of girls had entered the building, leaving a couple of stragglers puffing furiously on the last of their cigarettes. Fidgeting on the spot, Daisy argued the toss inside her head: stay or leave. She skulked off towards the indoor shopping centre.

'And where do you think you've been?' Mrs Brinton bellowed the instant Daisy arrived back at the flat later that afternoon. Daisy looked over at Julie, sprawled out on the settee thumbing her way through a dog-eared copy of her Bunty comic. Julie's eyes widened with caution.

'It's no good looking at her. It's you I'm asking,' Mrs Brinton ranted, arms folded across her flat chest.

'You know where I've been,' spoke Daisy, quietly. 'School. Where else?'

'So, how come you weren't there when I turned up at lunchtime then?'

'I, I nipped to the shop, for some sweets.'

'Do you think I was born yesterday? They didn't even have your name in the register. So, what you got to say about that then?'

Daisy shrugged her shoulders. She knew it was only a matter of time before she got found out. 'I'm not going back there again.' she blurted. 'They're always picking on me. I'll go somewhere else.'

Mrs Brinton shook her head. 'But there isn't anywhere else, love. You were lucky to get a place there. They'll be carting you off to boarding school if you don't pull your socks up.'

Daisy plonked herself down in the cream vinyl armchair and lapsed into a sulk. 'What d'you go there for, anyway?' she asked.

'You forgot your lunch.'

The youngster fiddled with a length of cotton hanging from the hem of her frock. She opened her mouth to speak, but decided against it.

'Look, I've not got time for this now, I'm already late for my shift. Don't either of you set foot outside this door till I get back.'

With the coast clear, Daisy made a bee-line for the kitchen and the bread packet. Her friend hovered close by. 'Mum'll go bananas if she catches you fibbing again.'

Daisy pounded the block of margarine with the knife handle. 'This stuffs like a bullet.' She mashed a marble of fat into one of the bread slices, before reaching for the sticky jar in the cupboard. 'Well, it's not exactly lying, is it? I didn't say I wouldn't see me dad. Did I?' She spread a thick layer of yellow sweetness, licked the excess from the knife, and popped the near empty jar back on its shelf.

'I s'pose,' said Julie. 'Won't make no difference though, we'll still be in for it.'

Daisy's rendezvous in Townsend Street had gone unnoticed by all except her friend, who was sworn to secrecy. It was only by chance and a moment's eavesdropping that Daisy had learned of the abandoned car with its new occupant. Mrs Brinton had been caught by the neighbouring gossip on the stairwell, know-all Nelly, bearer of bad tidings and just about anything worthy of a gasp or two. 'What your mum don't know can't upset her. Can it?'

'No, but she's bound to find out, and when she does, I'll be the one who gets a clout, not you!'

Daisy placed the holey sandwiches into a brown paper bag and walked to the street door. 'It's only for a little while, then he'll have a proper place with a bed and everything.' Her words skipped with excitement. 'He told me so himself.'

'Well, he better be telling the truth, as I'm fed up with him golloping all me lemon curd.'

Beckway Street with its mix of terraced housing and council flats provided the quickest route to Townsend Street. A sharp left turn at the far corner, where the old Crossways mission had been razed to the ground, would lead her directly to the battered Cortina blocking the pavement. A shout from the so-called sacred bomb-site stopped Daisy in her tracks. The large rubble strewn area housed several flimsy homemade camps, fashioned into teepees with rusted corrugated tin, where boys held their pow-wows and coughed their way through pilfered cigarettes.

Daisy's heart momentarily skipped as a trio of local kids piled through the gap in the mesh fencing. She recognised the older boy as Rob, one time friend of her brother Gary. Rob's disciples, the light-fingered Finley twins, lived a stone's throw from the grocers in Rodney Road, who had no choice but to bar them, or put the shutters up for good. Singularly they were bearable but together they were demonic. Rumour was they'd turned their mother's hair grey overnight.

'Here, slow down short-arse,' called Rob, 'What's the big hurry? You been caught doing something you shouldn't?' He sniggered.

'No I haven't!' Daisy answered crossly. 'If you must know, I'm on an errand for me mum.' Her hand tightened around the little brown parcel.

'So where you going then? We'll drag along if yer like?'

'No thanks. I'm only going up the road. 'Sides, I have to be back home for me tea in a minute.'

Frankie Finley's prattling in his twin sister's ear unnerved Daisy. Within seconds, Fran had snatched the bag from the unsuspecting youngster's grasp. Daisy looked on helplessly as each of the twins bit a chunk from the sandwich, before tossing the remainder in the gutter. Daisy welled up but refused to cry. A sudden surge of terrifying thoughts exploded inside her head. *Kick 'em in the goolies. Punch 'em in the gob,* her brother had told her many times over. The idea of sticking up for herself terrified the girl more than the thought of a beating. Daisy held her breath. She didn't know how to fight.

'Leave it out you two,' said Rob, turning his attention to Daisy. 'Why don't you hang about with us?' he suggested, nudging her with his shoulder. 'We're off to have fun with the old man dossing in the banger,' he pointed.

The trio made off towards the old car. 'You coming then?' asked Rob.

Daisy made no answer. She had to stop them, somehow. Her feet inched slowly forward. Each hesitant step became longer and faster, till she found herself running. Daring to barge between them, she stopped abruptly and turned to face their questioning stares.

Frankie sniggered. 'Changed your mind then?'

Daisy struggled with her thoughts. 'Yeah. I mean no.'

'Well, what is it? We're not hanging round here all day.'

She swallowed hard. Her hands, partly hidden by the folds in her dress, curled into tight fists. She felt the pain of jagged, nails digging deep into her palms. 'Leave him alone. He's done nothing to yous.' The words boomed out far louder than she intended, and would likely cost her a black eye.

'Hark at her! Mouth almighty.' piped in Fran.

Frankie took a step in Daisy's direction. His fixed smirk pushed his cheeks up like misplaced plums. 'What you getting your knickers in a twist over? He your boyfriend or what?' He chuckled, while looking to the others for approval.

Rob remained silent, watchful. At fifteen, a school leaver, he was the oldest by far. He liked Daisy, and if any harm came to her, he would have Gary to answer to. The twins edged closer. Daisy raised her arms, barring their way. 'I'm not letting you pass. Just leave us alone,' she shouted. 'He's not me boyfriend, if you must know. He's me dad.'

Frankie's hand shot forward to shove Daisy backwards, but the girl's outstretched arm swung round at speed. The boy hadn't a hope of dodging it. Daisy's clenched fist landed heavily into the side of his nose. If she remembered one thing that Gary had taught her, it was, *never pull your punches.*

Frankie's startled expression remained unchanged, in spite of his sister's plaguing that he'd been beaten by a squirt.

'I'll get you for this, you spiteful little cow,' he called, as they made their back towards Beckway Street.

Twelve short steps later, Daisy peered in through the car window at her father and sobbed uncontrollably. Startled by the unexpected outpouring, a sleepy-eyed Charlie forced himself upright. His head spun with confusion as he tried to make sense of the situation.

'Why've you got to sleep here? Why haven't you got a proper place like you said?' Her sobs were unrelenting. He managed to ease open the rust eaten door just enough to angle his aching body through. 'It's all your fault. It's all your fault,' she cried, tugging on his jacket. Charlie held her tear stained face in his hands.

'What's happened? What did I do to get you in such a state?' he pleaded, trying to keep his emotions in check. He bent down and kissed her forehead. 'Tell your old dad, please. I'll make it better. I promise.'

'I didn't mean to do it,' She pointed down at her plimsolls and the puddle of steaming liquid meandering its way to the kerbs edge. Charlie's dull eyes closed as his lungs emptied with one seamless sigh. Wrapping his arms tightly around the shivering mite, he pulled her close. With her damp rosy cheeks buried in the warmth of his waistcoat, Daisy's breathing began to settle and her tears finally petered out.

'Forgive me, angel. I'm trying to make things better. Honest I am.' Charlie crouched down. With their faces inches apart, he added, 'I swear on my life, girl, cross my heart and hope to die.'

The following morning, on the pretence of going to school, Daisy fastened the toggles on her duffel coat and left the flat. Mrs Brinton watched from the balcony, smiling and encouraging the youngster on her way, satisfied in knowing that her patience had finally paid off. 'You'll be back before you know it,' she called. Daisy returned the smile before zigzagging her way along the street, dodging lines and cracks in the pavement.

The dark, heavy clouds had fused together, covering the whole of Walworth in a blanket of grey. A heavenly rumble in the far distance forced her pace to quicken and her concentration to slip. Her foot dipped into broken paving. To break her fall, Daisy launched herself into the closest soft target, a startled Rob and his mother. Shrieking and cursing, the woman pushed Daisy aside and rushed forward.

'I'll catch you up mum,' shouted Tom. Turning back to Daisy, he asked, 'You off to see your dad?'

She nodded, slowly, troubled by the look on his face. She drew breath. 'You better not have hurt him or I'll get me brother after you, and he'll punch your rotten face in.'

'Look, I've done nothing all right, but he's not there. That's what I'm trying to tell you. Jesus, give your mouth a rest.'

'What d'you mean he's not there? Where's he gone then?'

'The council towed the old banger away this morning. Mum told me. She saw 'em from the balcony.'

Daisy shook her head. 'You're a liar, just trying to get me back cos of yesterday.' Rain-soaked, she started to run towards the top of the road.

'You're wasting your time. The car's gone I tell you.'

As Daisy spun round, her dripping hair lashed her face, catching the corner of her eye. She soothed the smarting with the heel of her hand. Her steps continued slowly backwards. She called out, 'Where is it then? Where is it?'

'The bloody knacker's yard. Where do you think?'

Minutes later, Daisy stood alone in Townsend Street. She picked up a shard of glass from the roadside and examined it closely, before allowing it to fall through her fingers. Children's voices sang out from the school's assembly hall, several yards away to her left. With no thoughts of her own, she allowed the voices to fill the gap inside her head. As she stared blankly towards the terraced houses opposite.

A downstairs window, straining against the sash cords, juddered upwards. An inquisitive woman with poppy red lips and a head full of huge prickly rollers leant out. 'What you hanging about here for? You'll catch your death of cold.'

Daisy focused on the woman's lipstick as thoughts of her mother filtered through. Any day now, she crossed her fingers, they would be back together. They'd snuggle round a coal fire just like they used to and everything would be back the way it was.

'I've gone and lost me dad,' Daisy sniffled. 'D'you know where the knacker's yard is lady?'

Chapter 18

Ray's ears were deceiving him, surely? Mickey, blackmailing Ruby, a minor with no means to protect herself. Why hadn't she come to him for help instead of Sal? He already knew the answer of course. The poor thing was scared he'd believe Mickey over her. Sal did good to put him in the picture. He'd suspected something underhand, since takings were down, while pre-Christmas sales boomed. Someone was dipping their grubby mitts into his pie, and his suspicions wrongly rested with Ruby.

Ray's anger surged and heart thumped with fury. He slammed his fist into the bathroom door, feeling the impact reverberate through his arm. The pain in his knuckles was nothing compared to the betrayal he felt. After all the handouts, the sacrifices he'd made for Mickey over the years, how could the good-for-nothing steal from him?

On hearing the loud explosion upstairs, Sal coughed out her mouthful of tea and rushed along the hallway. 'Good grief, are you OK up there?' she called. 'Has the roof caved in, or what?'

'Calm down woman. No need for hysterics. I fell against the door is all. That chippy chap up the road will soon have it sorted.'

Sal caught sight of herself in the hall mirror. A tea stain, resembling a misshapen globe, sat centre stage on her lemon quilted housecoat. 'Look at the state he's got me in,' she mumbled to herself, heading back to her armchair.

Ray's grazed and bloodied knuckles began to sting. He uncapped the TCP from the bathroom cabinet and poured directly onto his hand. 'Sodding Norah,' he winced. The stench alone stole his breath.

Later that afternoon Ray made his way along Glengall Road. Mickey emerged, as if on cue, from the three-story house where he lodged in a room at the top. The high wall at the beginning of the row became the perfect screen for Ray. With streetlamps few and widely spaced he remained in the shadows. As Mickey's footsteps approached, Ray stepped out.

'Geez, Ray. What the fuck!' Mickey lurched sideways, lost his footing and landed with a thud.

'Off to pay back my money? You thieving little git.' Ray held off from yanking Mickey up by his paisley cravat. 'I'm here to save you the bother. Hand it over.'

Mickey dragged himself upright and brushed a layer of grit from his Crombie. 'A pittance for Christ's sake, that's all I borrowed. Hardly worth breaking a sweat over.' He smoothed back his hair. 'And if that bitch has told you otherwise, then she's talking bollocks. She's the one playing you. Not me.'

A sudden move from Ray saw Mickey cower, his hands raised to protect his face. His words, designed to be heard by the strolling couple opposite, rang out. 'I'll pay you back. I promise. Please don't hit me.'

Stepping back, Ray sniggered. Disregarding the evil stares burning into his skull, he applauded Mickey's tactics. The twenty-two-year-old wastrel, playacting at being a man, deserved an Oscar for his performance. Ray knew, onlookers or not, if he'd wanted to lump the kid one, he would; despite his split knuckles. How many times had he backed off already? Done the decent thing and walked away. Times when the veins, plump in his arms, and fists, tighter than a miser's purse, ached for release.

Enough is enough, time to cut the ties. 'Listen up, you smarmy, fucking cowson. You and me, we're done. Kaput. Get it? Take my advice, don't come sniffing round me or mine again.' Ray turned and began walking away when Mickey darted ahead, keeping distance between them. He thrust two fingers up at Ray, while his cocky laughter resonated through the street. Ray shook his head in wonder at the juvenile action, smiled to himself and continued on. He had no doubts that Mickey's downfall would be of his own making. The kid didn't need his input. He was doing a sterling job all by himself.

Chapter 19

Uncle Tom decided on a leisurely route to work. His bicycle clips, close fitting round his thick set ankles, were pushed into place. Fastening the heavy wool jacket on top of paint-stained overalls, he set off. A worn leather knapsack housing tools of the trade, brushes, cheese sandwiches and a stash of sweets nestled snugly against his back. The roads were often deserted early morning. He could pootle along without breaking a sweat. Being a self-employed odd-jobber, certainly had its perks. With customers supplying the main materials, he could turn up at a time convenient to himself, armed with a winning smile and bucket loads of flannel. What could be easier?

He cursed those precious years wasted in the factories. That clocking on lark in a whinging adult environment stifled his desire for something better, something more stimulating. But with rent to find and bills to pay, those red-letter demands had trapped him, held him prisoner. He shifted his bulk on the saddle. As for her indoors, he'd tip-toed around Grace throughout his best years. Become a slave to the housekeeping, those endless bloody chores. Granted, it wasn't her fault the surgeons botched the surgery: her sight damaged beyond repair. It still rankled though, how her eyes wandered unfocussed whenever he spoke. She became less attentive too and that cut deeper still. Her fumbling groping ways were hardly passion inducing. Truth be told, it chilled him to the core. A lesser man would have walked away, but not him. No, he did right by her. Stuck it out, sacrificed his life in the process.

His foot slipped from the pedal and the bike wavered. His attempts to gain control were thwarted by a shout from inside a passing vehicle. 'Get off and milk it, granddad,' the passenger yelled. 'Be a lot safer for everyone.'

The single mums were the most sympathetic. Wives too, coping alone with their offspring while the old man worked away. He won them over, every single one. Gullible deluded fools. They all loved a sob story. Poor hard done by Tom, in need of a bit of chivvying. He could see it all, written in their faces. He favoured the little girls, always had done. Their gleeful faces bright with wonder as he bounced them on his knees. *More, more*, they'd shout, unaware of the hand slipping beneath their bottom. Cost him a small fortune in sherbet dib-dabs. Those unexpected bonuses made it worth the while. He laughed to himself. Seizing the moment is what it's all about. Another string to his bow, another opportunity. 'Could life get any sweeter?' he asked himself. He knew how the young mums loved shopping and the occasional evening down the pub, broke as they were. He'd be some kind of git to deny them a break.

He'd never take their money, wouldn't dream of it. They were scratching a living like everyone else, in spite of the newspapers' insistence that the whole damn world was better off than ever. Bathing his charges or tucking them in for the night was no hardship. It nourished his soul to help out where he could, made him feel useful, wanted. They loved their Uncle Tom and his tickling games. He loved them too, in his own way.

Stopping at the crossroads, he watched the same mud splattered Vauxhall as earlier run a red light. The two occupants jeered as they sailed by.

'Still upright then, pops?' A two fingered salute shot through the open window.

Tom shook his head. What happened to respect? Bring back National Service, that'll sort the buggers out. Early mornings were Tom's favourite time of day. He enjoyed the calmness, trundling along, taking in the sights. The sparrows, pecking through gold topped bottles on painted doorsteps; they had it sussed, the cunning blighters. Taking just enough cream before moving onto the next. Thinking time, that's what mornings allowed.

He hawked the mucus from his throat onto the road. Wasn't her blindness enough to contend with, without the deafness too? That wretched control box clipped to her neckline, crackling, whistling, like an un-tuned radio, drawing unwanted attention.

The woman he faced at the altar had long gone, replaced by a shapeless, dowdy effigy with a perpetual smile that shredded his nerves. Like all was hunky-fucking-dory in her world. Well, it wasn't hunky-fucking-dory in his. He alone suffered the piss-takers when her lipstick went way above the lip line, or caked her teeth like blobs of damp candyfloss. He caught himself grinning. Come evening time though, with that control box switched off he would vent his frustrations. Blast her with profanities. Tell her exactly what a noose she'd become, knowing the only downside would be – that bloody smile.

He turned into the country lane, flanked either side by a mishmash of trees and far-reaching hedgerows. The gaps in the crisp decaying foliage allowed the watery sunlight to filter through and touch his face. Today was a good day. The new job sounded promising. Nothing like a recommendation to bolster a flagging ego; it would keep him ticking along nicely. Thank you very much. Needs it done yesterday, she'd emphasised, her voice barely registering above an excitable brood. Another single mum struggling to make ends meet. He'd be some sort of prat not to help out.

The vehicle, a fair distance ahead, appeared stationary; a likely breakdown, he decided. There was no urgency on his part. What he knew about engines could be written on a thumb nail. With the gap between them closing, his inkling became a reality. There was no mistaking the car. The toerags who'd given him grief earlier sat patiently inside, waiting on some do-gooder to put things right. They wouldn't have bargained on him! He'd give them granddad; show them a thing or two about respect. Salivating, he licked his lips in anticipation of the humble pie coming his way.

The sudden roar of the engine, the continual deafening revs, had Tom confused. He applied the brake lever, removed his feet from the pedals, and with a foot to the ground shifted his weight. Meanwhile, the car tyres screeched as the clutch fully engaged, corrupting an otherwise clear sky with a cloudy haze of blue. Momentarily gripped by a bilious wave flooding his system, Tom's thoughts raced in competition with the car speeding towards him. His initial reaction was to turn tail and get the hell out of there. His increasing anger dictated otherwise. He wouldn't satisfy their warped humour by bolting. He'd face them head on, play their pathetic game.

Climbing back on the saddle, he set the wheels in motion. With a known passing place within reach, he could veer off if need be. They would hit the brakes any second. They couldn't hold out much longer, wouldn't dare. His heart thrashed against his ribs. Still they came, ever closer. Sweat oozed from his pores, trickling down from his forehead. His vision distorted. He had to swerve, now, while he still had a chance. Lifting his backside, he pushed down hard on the pedals, yanked the handlebars into position and prayed he had not miscalculated. The impact on the near side ripped into his leg and spun him like a top.

With the speedometer unchanged, the driver checked the rear-view mirror. The crumpled figure, face down on the tarmac, fast became little more than a grey contorted splotch, interrupting an otherwise idyllic scene.

Chapter 20

Apart from one elderly neighbour scrubbing her doorstep, Freemantle Street stood empty. The woman's turban style headscarf reminded Ruby of her mother, on days when she had cleaned the stairs in the council block. With her head already tilted to her shoulder, Ruby's body arched at the waist, determined to glimpse the face of the woman concentrating on the doorstep, that curved at its centre from years of boot leather traffic. Aware of being watched the woman raised her head; blocking the sunlight with her free hand, she met Ruby's gaze. 'Did you want something?'

'Not really. Ruby smiled. 'I was just thinking that you looked like my mum, with your headscarf an' all.'

'That's nice dear,' she grumbled, plunging the brush back into the bucket of grimy water and continuing the job in hand.

Below the cheekbones the woman's skin hung in slender folds. The jowls drooped like saggy burst balloons, dragging her mouth into an unnatural, weary looking position. Ruby moved on, visualising her own mother's face. Her beautiful smooth as butter complexion that had dad forever boasting about being the luckiest man alive. It had been weeks since Ruby had set eyes on her parents. She continued to walk the streets on her days off. Her new shoes, courtesy of Sal, were so comfortable she kept glancing down to ensure they were still attached. Earlier, as she strolled by the stall, Ray had shouted for her to, *follow the yellow brick road*. She felt chuffed to bits that he'd even noticed. But then nothing ever got past Ray.

Ruby unlocked the door to Sal's house, stepped across the threshold and elbowed the door towards its closed position. The speed of the hand that clamped her mouth threw her mind into a confused state. The wild, staring eyes, boring into her own, spoke their own familiar language. Mickey's intentions were clear. With arms flailing and her dragging feet ruching up the flimsy hallway runner. He forced Ruby along the passage and into the back room. Slamming her against the far wall, he warned, 'One sound and you're fucking dead. You get it?'

Satisfied that his words had hit home he slid his hand down from her mouth and applied pressure beneath her chin, forcing her face upwards and her neck to stretch beyond reason. Ruby's tears counted for nothing. He seemed to get off on them in some perverse way. Her brother Gary's voice dominated her thoughts. *Bring your knee up. Use your feet. Anything. But don't just stand there.* He'd taught his sister to defend herself, in times such as now. He'd drummed it into her over and over, but still she couldn't do it. Any of it. Her voice mocked her, yet still she remained petrified. Why did no one mention that fear could also paralyse? Mickey's hand covered her breast in a grabbing, squeezing frenzy. She could hear his rapid breaths over the muffled sobs trapped in her throat; his endless, demeaning words, laced with hatred.

'You're nothing but a prick tease like the rest of the slags, and grassing me up to the boss man was one bad move. No one messes with me and gets away with it. You hear me? You fucking hearing me?' he shouted.

Ruby's eyes closed. A slave to her weakness. A woman's lot, she'd heard it said. There was no mistaking the cries of neighbours as sozzled husbands set about wives with closed fists. Ruby swore that one day she would fight back. And when that day came, the likes of Mickey Loughty had better watch their step.

With no let up on the pressure beneath Ruby's chin, she peered through damp lashes. A figure, quiet as a floating feather, emerged in the doorway. From the corner of her eye, she watched Ray place a finger to his lips as he crept forward. In one swift movement he grabbed Mickey's shoulders, yanked him round and slammed his fist into the pretty boy's face. Mickey lay sprawled across the armchair, legs dangling like a disused puppet. He spat out the warm sticky blood that oozed from his nose and into his mouth. His face twisted with rage as he struggled to his feet.

'Oh, I get it,' he jeered. 'All making sense now. You're keeping her for yourself.'

'What the fucks got into you? She's a kid for gawd's sake.'

Mickey charged towards Ray, growling like a rabid dog, intent on a head butt to the stomach. Ray quickly side-stepped and with a swift heel-boot to Mickey's backside sent him flying down the passage. Moving quickly after him, Ray yanked him up by the scruff of the neck and threw him out onto the street. Tripping over his own feet, Mickey landed face down in the gutter.

'If you ever show your face around here again, you moron, I swear I'll do for you,' Ray warned.

Mickey stared unblinkingly at the tough guy who had just pulverised his ego. He cuffed the blood still dripping from his nose and taunted lamely, 'You and whose army pal?'

Ray threw his head back in amusement. 'Do yourself a favour and get lost. There's a good lad.'

Mickey moved hesitantly along the empty street. His rigid frame and stop-start pacing convinced Ruby that he was far from done. Each loud crack of his tight fist hitting his open palm had Ruby flinching and curious neighbours tweaking curtains for a clearer view. Mickey clocked the subtle movements in his peripheral vision and laughed insanely. He glanced from window to window, as his voice boomed out in the tiny upmarket street. 'Had a fucking good nose have yer?' Losing all sense of reality, he threw up his arms and turned on the spot like a manic preacher. 'You wanna signed photo or what?' Glaring back across his shoulder at Ray, he pointed accusingly, 'I'll have you for this, you see if I don't. You best watch your back from now on. I'm coming for you.'

Back inside the house, Ruby sat trembling on the settee, biting the remains of her nails. She rushed at Ray when he entered the room, and resting her head on his chest she wailed like a baby. Ray was uncomfortable with such a show of emotion and unsure of how to handle the situation. His arms hung aimlessly at his side. Gradually, in fits and starts he lifted a hand and placed it on the girls back and within seconds found himself applying a gentle patting motion. As her tears began to subside, he suggested she washed her face and gave her the option of staying indoors.

'I don't want to be here on my own.'

Ray gave a nod of understanding. 'OK. Look, there's no hurry. I've got Joe minding the stall. More fool me,' he added. 'When you're ready we'll head back to the market. And don't start that worrying lark that you women are prone to. If the blokes got an ounce of sense, he'll be keeping his distance from now on.' Ray smiled, as an idea quickly formed. 'Tell you what, help Sal out for the afternoon, she can always use an extra pair of hands. I'll have a word if you like? Let her know what's gone on.'

Ruby stopped abruptly. 'No, please don't.'

*

Ray's decision to palm Ruby off on Sal had been an act of desperation rather than any degree of nicety on his part. Sal was more equipped to deal with the fallout. He couldn't be party to all that emotional stuff; after-all, what the hell did he know about teenage girls, other than what he'd seen at the market? The cocky little show-offs with their command of obscenities that would paralyse a naval fleet, and the others who whinged and sulked and bled their parents dry in the name of fashion. Kids were a complicated business. He was better off keeping his distance.

The second he'd spotted Mickey trailing a vulnerable Ruby, his gut instinct, which he trusted implicitly, kicked in. He had done what he had to, full stop. He would manage the guilt as best he could for battering his old pal's son, and as for Ruby, a measure of resentment guided his thoughts. He would never turn a blind eye to anyone being treated in that manner, let alone a young girl, but the fact remained, that having her live under his own roof irritated him beyond words. The sooner she found her mother the better it would be for everyone. Maybe he would do a little digging himself in that department.

*

A blanket of silence connected them as they headed towards The Lane. Ruby felt a need to explain. She could imagine the turmoil he was going through. She wondered if he now hated her, even though what had happened had not been initiated by herself. Her voice was quiet, barely audible. 'I know what you must be thinking but I never led him on, Ray. Honest.'

He cleared his throat. 'Don't presume to know what's going on in my head, young lady. What's done is done, chewing it over won't help anyone and it certainly won't change anything.'

His manner confused her. She had seen a different side to him back at the house. She hadn't imagined the kindness he'd shown her yet now it seemed as though he was laying the blame at her feet.

No one was more pleased than Sal to see Ruby propping up the counter. 'Don't tell me he wants feeding again for heaven's sake? I swear that man must have hollow legs.' She sighed.

'No, he didn't mention food, just told me to help you out today.'

Sal eyebrows rose in disbelief. 'Hope he's not taken a queer turn. I'll be run off my feet otherwise. And you needn't look so glum either, duck.' she jested. 'I mean, there are worse places to work: take the laundry for starters down Manor Pl...' Her voice petered out.

'I didn't mean, I was just ...'

'Away with the fairies. Yeah, I can see that, but you do know that if the wind changes your face'll be stuck that way forever?' Sal was surprised to see Ruby lower lip tremble. 'Whatever's the matter?' she asked, drawing closer.

'Me mum used to say that a lot, about me face.'

'And I dare say she'll be saying it again when she sees you. You soppy date.' Tucking Ruby's hair back behind her shoulders, Sal gasped at the obvious bruising developing on the girl's neck. 'Who on earth's done this?' She glanced towards the window and blanched. 'Not my Ray. No, surely not?'

Ruby shook her head, encouraging her hair forward. 'No, it was Mickey.'

'Who? Ray's Mickey? Attacking a girl. Goodness gracious.' She pulled Ruby into her arms. 'What's the world coming to, lovey? Now don't you worry, I'll soon put a stop to his lark.' Her voice deepened as her anger grew. She stepped back. 'You watch that door while I call the police.'

'Ruby panicked, grabbed the woman's hands, and quickly explained. 'There's no need. It's all sorted Sal. Ray stepped in. He saved me.'

Sal puffed out a noisy breath. 'Good for him. Well, I don't mind saying duck, that's spared us a heap of grief and an evening down the station. The Old Bill, bless 'em, don't like families sorting things themselves, but between you and me, I reckon they turn a blind eye. Saves them a job, doesn't it?'

To avoid further fussing and questions, Ruby moved swiftly into the alcove and began stacking the drained crockery. Sal followed and worked alongside. 'I'll never understand folk. You think you know someone, and then this,' Sal rambled on. 'Whatever could have possessed him?'

'Who knows? The man's a proper maniac.'

'I think you could be right,' said Sal, walking back through the empty seating area. 'You're safe now, that's all that matters. And if he shows up here, I'll soon deal with him.' She crossed to the door, and stilled her shaking hand by twisting the catch to secure the lock.

Chapter 21

Within a few days, life had slipped back into its usual routine. Mickey had kept his distance and Ruby no longer jumped like an Olympic hopeful, whenever customers approached from behind.

Ray's jaw jutted back and forth as he ground his teeth in anger. His face reddened and beads of perspiration glistened on his creased, freckled brow. He mopped the dampness up towards his hairline with the back of his wrist before manoeuvring his barrow into position. Being late in setting up meant he had missed the early birds and takings would be down. 'That lazy git of a boy is costing me a bloody fortune,' he grumbled to himself. 'I'll give him take the piss.' Inhaling long drags from his Woodbine cigarette helped to take the edge off.

'I take it Joe's overslept?' called old Hawkeye, from his vegetable stall opposite. 'I dunno,' he rambled on. 'Kids today, so bloody unreliable.' Holding the corners of a paper bag he spun it over to secure the ends, trapping the tomatoes inside. Handing the bag to his customer, he continued, 'Now in my day ...'

'Yeah, yeah, rein it in granddad. I've heard it all before,' countered Ray, clicking his tongue.

'Well, pardon me for breathing. There's no need for that attitude.'

Ray let out a sigh. He had been out of order and knew it. The guy meant well and he should not have cut him off like that. Everyone knew the old codger prattled on like an old woman, but he was harmless enough, a good sort. 'Look mate, don't mind me, I'm having a git of a morning. I get what you're saying. I really do. Listen, do us a favour, keep an eye out while I nip and grab a bite to eat. Me stomach's about to start noshing itself.'

'Right you are, son,' he nodded. 'Trust me, no one will have it away with your gear while I'm about.'

Ray gave the thumbs up and plastered a grin on his face that would have rocketed toothpaste sales had it been displayed on a billboard. Satisfied that he had curbed his anger before any real harm was done, Ray walked the short distance to the Cafe. He watched thoughtfully as Ruby sliced through bread pudding ready to place in the display cabinet, while Sal fetched him a cheese roll before pouring the tea. Sensing his gaze upon her, Ruby turned and met his stare.

'I want you over on the stall when you've finished there,' he said.

'Hold up a minute, Ray. I need the girl to help prepare for lunchtime.' Sal raised her hands, palm side up in despair. 'You might have mentioned something sooner.'

'I would have if I'd known that drip of a boy would leave me in the lurch.'

Ruby's ears pricked up. She guessed that Joe had clocked-on at the cheese factory, but it wasn't her place to say.

'I won't be messed about, not where business is concerned,' Ray fumed. 'I've warned him no end of times.'

Ruby sidled up to Sal. 'Would you like me to run round to his house? It's only up the road. Wouldn't take me long.'

'No, we bleeding don't, little miss fix-it,' snapped Ray, lifting the tea mug from the counter. 'Now make yourself useful and get the door for me.' He flicked his head. 'You'll have to work the stall with me till I get someone else, and that's all there is to it.'

Come late afternoon, Ray started packing up and motioned for Ruby to push off. She wandered along towards the main Road, thinking that she might stop off at the library before closing. With its huge plate glass window facing the main road she could keep a look out for her family. A woman, striding yards ahead of her, oozed a confidence rarely seen locally. A group of builders, taking a break on the new housing development, steadied themselves on idle spades. Low, drawn-out whistles caused Ruby's cheeks to rise when she saw them ogling the woman.

She increased her pace to close the distance between herself and Lady Muck, as her sister Ellen often called her. Ruby had only met with Cecelia a handful of times, and although the woman spoke in a lah-di-dah fashion, she never found reason to badmouth her in the way Ellen did. A smile split her face. Ellen had once warned, *Be sure to duck the minute Cecelia opens her mouth, cos she'll be firing plums for sure.* How they came to believe that posh people developed their upper crust accents, by talking with plums in their mouth was anyone's guess.

Ruby followed the willowy figure decked out in a smart belted suit, head high like a tailor's dummy as her black stilettos tapped out a purposeful, timely beat.

'Cecelia!' Ruby shouted breathlessly.

The woman flushed at having her name bandied about to all and sundry. Her features softened into an embarrassed grin as she noticed the builders checking her out. Her hand smoothed the back of her French pleat hairstyle.

Ruby, who was at her side in a trice, gave an exaggerated huff. 'Flaming Nora. You don't half move fast.'

Cecelia kept her voice low; leaning into the girl so as not to be overheard, she gave her a gentle ticking off. 'You really shouldn't yell in the street like that. It's not very lady-like and now everyone is staring. And just so as you know, I don't use my full name anymore. I much prefer...'

The ear-splitting wolf whistle cut all conversations dead and turned every head in the street. The cheeky builder was jokingly chastised and pushed by his fellow workers, before they continued their work with great smirks on otherwise weathered faces.

Placing a hand on Ruby's arm, Cecelia steered her towards the entrance of the nearby block of flats. 'I've been frantic these past months, wondering what had happened to you and your sister. Why on earth didn't you drop a note through my door saying you were settled elsewhere? It would have saved me a whole lot of grief.'

Ruby nodded glumly, realising that the thought never once occurred to her. 'We never meant for you to worry. We were in such a state, couldn't even think straight, and anyway,' she continued, with a more confident lilt, 'we knew the block was called Speedwell, but forgot the number,' she fibbed, not wanting to lay the blame on Ellen. Noting the way Cecelia's tangerine-coloured lips tightened into a thin line, Ruby knew that the woman hadn't believed a word of it.

'You have a voice, as you've just demonstrated. You could have asked any of my neighbours.'

Considering herself told off, Ruby stepped back and clamped her mouth shut. White lies, as far as she knew, were meant to be OK. In future she would try and stick with the truth and save herself a rollicking.

'Look, forgive me for snapping pet. It's no excuse, but I've so much to deal with right now,' she explained. 'I'm organising an exhibition at the War Museum tonight and I'm behind with everything.' She placed an arm around Ruby's shoulders, drew her in, and gave the girl an apologetic hug.

134

Cecelia and Ruby's mother, Kate, had been friends and neighbours since 1945 when both their Air Force husbands had died in Germany at the end of the war. Cecelia, unlike Kate, had never remarried. Although their lives went in different directions, their friendship remained. With only herself to consider, Cecelia had the means to afford the lifestyle Kate had lost all those years before. The woman's smooth, powdered complexion was testament to that, regularly lathered with expensive potions, while Ruby's mother put her faith in a dab of Pond's Vanishing Cream to perform the same miracle.

'She doesn't need it, but she won't be told,' Ruby's grandmother once said. Ruby recalled a particular visit, and the time spent cuddled with her grandmother in the large faded armchair on a winter evening, with only the flames from the open fire to light the room. How her grandmother loved to talk about days gone by. Her words painted pictures of a younger Kate. A Kate Ruby didn't recognise. *Your mother,* she'd once told her, *had the poise and grace of a lady.* Such memories were like fairytales to an insatiable Ruby. Her grandmother's eyes would twinkle, *your mother loved her hats, delicate things with feathers and netting. We all teased her about it. It never fazed her though. Such a proud lady, your mum.* Ruby wondered about those beautiful hats and where they had disappeared to. The floral headscarves her mother replaced them with, although pretty, didn't conjure so grand an image.

So, what stopped mum wearing hats? Ruby had asked, nuzzling closer.

Five beautiful kids and a ruddy great hole in her purse, her grandmother had said, laughing and poking her ribs, until a bout of hiccups saw Ruby dash to the scullery for water.

Ruby never understood her grandmother's words back then, but she did now, and the laughter she recalled became overshadowed with sadness. She made a vow that one day, she would buy her mum a hat; the prettiest hat she could find.

Snapping out of her reverie, Ruby realised she had missed most of what Cecelia had said.

'She's worried sick.'

'Who is?' asked Ruby

'Why, your mother, dear. She came looking for you sometime last week. I had no idea of your whereabouts so I couldn't help I'm afraid' She checked her watch. 'Ruby, I really must be getting along.

'But where's me mum now? Where's she living?'

'I really have no idea. It's unforgivable I know, but I completely forgot to ask.'

Ruby couldn't believe her ears. Didn't think to ask! What kind of a woman was she? Some friend she turned out to be. Had the boot been on the other foot, it would have been her mother's first question.

Stuff it, she thought. If she wanted to yell out in the street then she damn well would. 'Did she say she'd call back?'

Cecelia had gone but a few yards when she glanced back, lifted her shoulders and shook her head.

Leaning against the iron railings surrounding the low-level block of flats, Ruby stared across at the new dwellings taking shape in front of her. Enormous ugly grey slabs of concrete swaying precariously from a crane, waiting to be slotted into place. The vast new estate had completely changed the borough she had grown up in. She'd never really given it much thought before, and even now she was little more than an observer. Her thoughts were locked into the fleeting conversation she'd had with Cecelia. The short exchange between them had initially left Ruby feeling down in the dumps. Before long, a sudden brightness crept up on her as though a secret had just unfolded. She realised the news had a positive side and was just what she needed to lift her spirit. To know that her mother remained in the area, actively conducting her own search could mean only one thing: that a new home had been found. One where her father waited anxiously at the door to welcome his children home.

Ruby's pulse quickened, prompting a slight woozy feeling, similar to the time she had guzzled a half glass of beer that her father failed to keep a watch over. Then, as now, she couldn't wipe the silly grin from her face. Her emotions were topsy-turvy. She didn't know whether to laugh or cry, as the feeling of happiness continued to build. Walking alongside the small parade of shops, the elderly newsagent, on sentry duty as usual in the open doorway, mirrored her grin.

'Now there's a rare sight,' he winked. 'A smile to warm the cockles. Well, whoever said, you don't get anything for nothing in this world, clearly didn't come from these parts.'

Ruby's mouth stretched wider. The man never passed up a chance to engage in friendly banter with the locals. He was as much a part of their lives as saveloy and chips.

'I'll give you a penny for them?' he called, as she sailed past.

Ruby laughed. Feeling braver than she had felt in a long time, she answered, 'That's rich, coming from a skinflint,' remembering how he'd refused to sell her an orange flavoured jubbly when she was a penny short.

'Now then Missy, don't get lippy. Some things are worth forking out for. I'll give you a tanner. Final offer.'

Without looking back, Ruby brushed him off with a high-handed wave. She couldn't risk diluting the joy she felt by sharing it around. Even a sniff of the bank notes recovered from that Great Train Robbery wouldn't tempt her, let alone a measly tanner.

Chapter 22

Ray had a swagger in his step and a smug expression on his face. To take on an experienced worker like Luca had been a wise move. Not only could the Italian be trusted to run the stall single-handedly, he came with additional benefits. His charisma knew no bounds, especially where the ladies were concerned. Who better to flog handbags? Business was booming, profits well up, and Ray's mood was closer to cloud nine than it had been in years.

Ruby could work her days in the Cafe. Not that he wanted rid of her; after-all, she was a spirited so-and-so, no longer afraid to stand her ground and piss him off when she felt the need. He admired her for that if nothing else. The fact remained; the girl needed a woman's guiding hand, and who better than Sal to pour the oil when needed? Everyone's a winner. He gave himself a surreptitious pat on the back and continued on his way, leaving Luca to deal with his growing entourage.

Catching Ruby nosing in the pawn shop window, he crept up behind. 'This you skiving again, girl?'

She jumped, dropping the fruit Spangle she'd found in her overall pocket, and cursed under her breath. 'If you must know, it's me break. Sal told me to take my time, since Tuesdays are slower than a limpet on Librium.'

'She said what?'

'Yeah. I haven't a clue either. You off to the bookies to chuck away your fortune, again?'

Ray's usual scowl had disappeared, softening his trademark frown. 'Cheeky little mare,' he waggled her chin. 'Not that it's any of your business, but I'm off to add to my nest egg.' He patted the canvas money bag that filled his deep inside pocket. 'Building nicely for my retirement in the sun. Aussie-land seems a safe bet, and at ten pounds a ticket, what's not to love?' he said, walking off.

She called after him. 'Why go all that way? Leysdown's cheaper and the sun shines there too, you know.' Ruby's focus returned to the window. She stared open-mouthed into the empty corner, as a scream bubbled up and exploded inside her head. Her mother's ring had gone!

*

The first blow landed in his stomach. Winded, Ray bent forward gasping for air. A double handed fist crashed down on the back of his head, forcing him to his knees, while a kick from behind caught him between the legs. His eyes flickered, barely open; he clocked their outline, bright as streaks of lightning, transparent figures, merging, drifting. With his strength ebbing away, he still managed to latch onto the hand riffling his jacket. The underside of a boot connected with his shoulder and sent him sprawling to the ground. The moment his head hit the concrete the lights dimmed.

'Leave it for fuck's sake,' the youth behind Ray ordered, giving the collar of his accomplice a firm tug. Unable to part Ray from his cash, the lads bolted.

By the time the traders realised what had gone down, it was over. The muggers scrammed, running full pelt in Ruby's direction. Too stunned to move, she held her breath as they hurtled towards her. Racing past, they knocked her off balance. Luca stepped forward to catch the tumbling girl, when an inquisitive bystander suddenly blocked his way. Before he could react, Ruby had also hit the ground.

Dusting herself off, she dashed the one hundred yards to Ray's side. Her heart plummeted on seeing the blood spilling from his head wound. She knelt beside him, placing a hand on his shoulder. Her gentle calming voice appeared to rouse him. Although his eyes remained closed, his weak groans and faint mumblings dispelled her worse fears. His head, turning slowly towards her, prompted a spurt of warm sticky blood to catch the back of her hand.

'Best lie still Ray, helps on the way.' Ray's struggle to communicate, saw Ruby place her ear to his mouth.

'Bastards. Busted me nuts.'

The men folk surrounding them encouraged her to move back. At the same time an engine started up a few feet away.

'Shouldn't we wait for an ambulance?' Ruby quizzed.

Four burly men took Ray's weight between them and laid him carefully into the back of a van. 'It'll take a month of Sundays for an ambulance to get through this lot,' one said. 'By which time we could be at the hospital.'

Ruby stared into the van, watching Ray's chest slowly rise and fall. He'd been so upbeat just minutes before, that to see his battered body lying there, cushioned on a mound of gaudy dresses, seemed unreal. She wanted to kick herself for all the petty thoughts she'd harboured about him over the past weeks. If she had known something so awful was lying in wait, she'd have been more forgiving of his so-called hot-headed guise, as Sal called it; because that's exactly what it was.

Ruby, first hand, had witnessed a different side to Ray. A gentle, more patient character had slipped through the hard exterior, and handed Ruby the confidence to be herself. She owed him for that. In future she would handle things differently. She would not allow his sarcastic arrows to puncture her skin and in turn she'd pull back on winding him up. She just hoped it wasn't too late to put her plan into action.

'Tell Sal we'll be taking him to Guy's hospital,' the older man announced. 'It's a bit closer than St Thomas's. Now we've really got to step on it, love, so move away please.'

About to close the van door, Ruby remembered the nest egg. If nothing else, she would make sure the money arrived safely at the bank. Climbing in the back, she retrieved the canvas bag, kissed the tip of her finger and placed it softly against his cheek. Ruby tucked the folded bag inside her overall pocket for safekeeping. As the van pulled away a breathless Jimmy turned up.

'What's happened? There're all sorts of stories flying around.'

'I'm so glad you're here. It's Ray, he's been beaten up. They practically knocked him out,' said Ruby, close to tears. 'I really need to speak to Sal. Would you come with me?' She had no right to ask anything of Jimmy. Hadn't she purposely avoided him these past weeks after his Billy Beaufoy rant. A rant she believed to be jealousy inspired, causing too much hurt in too short a time. Her mistake, glaringly obvious by all who knew Jimmy, was soon realised. Admittedly, she had got it wrong. But to put things right, she first had to ditch the embarrassment that dragged her down like a sack of washing.

'Blimey Rube. Course I will. Hard to imagine that anyone would get the better of Ray, what with his boxing history. He's the last person I'd expect to take a pasting.'

'It happened so quickly. They caught him by surprise,' she said, before explaining about the money.

In her haste to reach the Cafe, Ruby's ankle snagged on a wooden slatted box, propelling her forward. Jimmy made a grab for her elbow. 'Steady on. You'll be kissing the floor yourself in a minute.' The blood seeping through her torn sleeve had coated his palm with its sticky residue. 'Hell Rube. What's happened here then?'

'A graze,' she murmured, 'Nothing that a plaster won't sort.' Ruby made no attempt to move forward. She couldn't shake the eerie feeling of being watched. It troubled her, like ants creeping over her flesh. She shuddered.

'You sure you're, OK?' asked Jimmy.

'Yeah, it's just...' She spotted the figure in the shaded recess of a shop doorway, his chin angled towards his chest. That menacing twisted grin hastened her pulse. Taking Jimmy's hand, she stormed ahead, skirted round the remaining stragglers and stopped outside the Cafe. 'I'm just worried sick, that's all.' Her thoughts ran riot. What was Mickey doing there in the first place? Had he played a part in Ray's attack? The man scared her. There was something very wrong about him. She had seen the evil for herself, his cold, steel grey eyes boring into her: first along the main street and again at the house. She could still feel the pressure of his hand at her throat.

Struggling to get him out of her head, a brief window appeared and her mind skipped momentarily to the young men who set about Ray. Thugs, to her way of thinking, no matter how cocksure, rarely demonstrated their handiwork in front of an audience, unless they were two sheets to the wind, plain mental or paid-up front! Their botched so-called daylight robbery had something to do with Mickey. Of that she was convinced.

'Ease up mate,' Jimmy begged. 'You'll yank me arm off in a minute. What's the panic anyway? Sal's bound to have heard it a hundred times over already.'

142

Ruby stopped short of pushing open the door. She looked over Jimmy's shoulder, expecting to come face to face with Mickey. *He wouldn't have dared*, she thought, feeling braver, on seeing the shop recess empty. Her tension slowly ebbed away, as each muscle in turn began to thaw. 'What if they come back though?' She leaned closer. 'I've still got the money. Remember?'

Jimmy matched her gentle pitch. 'Yeah, but they don't know that, do they? Look, nothing else will happen. Trust me. I'll go with you to the bank if you like; once you've spoken to Sal, I mean.' He gave her a hug, and Ruby allowed herself to respond. feeling his arms tight around her made her feel more secure.

'What about George? Won't he throw a fit, with you not being there to help out?'

'He'll be fine. We'll fill him in on the way. Now let's get inside and see how Sal's doing.'

'OK, but can I just say, I owe you an apolo...'

'Jimmy touched his fingers to her mouth. 'Let's not do this now.'

Jimmy was right. Fragments of information had reached Sal beforehand. Most of it guesswork, Ruby decided, but plenty enough to get her into a state. Sal brightened instantly on seeing Ruby. The paper towel Sal used to blot her face disappeared up her sleeve. 'Thank the Lord,' she cried out, rushing from behind the counter. 'I can't make head nor tail of what's gone on – is my Ray all right – and what about you? I've heard all manner of snippets, believe me.' Her breath gushed in fits and spurts.

Ruby gestured to Jimmy to fetch a tea. With only a handful of customers remaining, she flipped the door sign over. The customers left soon after and Ruby turned the key in the lock.

Sal's anguish was etched into every line of her face. 'For pity's sake, you're bleeding duck. Here let me take a look.'

'It's nothing,' Ruby insisted. 'Come and sit-down Sal, and I'll explain everything.' Presently, Ruby booked a mini cab to take Sal to the hospital. 'I wish you'd change your mind and let me come with you?'

'I'll be fine. I promise. Let's close up early. One of yous pop a note on the door.' She patted Ruby's hand. 'I'd prefer you here with Pam. She'll need help getting cleaned up, ready for the morning. Sod's law, me letting Mandy shoot off early.'

Jimmy piped up. 'We'll all muck in. Won't take long with the three of us.'

Sal and Ruby waited at the back gate for the cab to arrive. 'I hate leaving you like this, but I must go to Ray. Make sure he's all right.'

'Don't give it a second thought.' Ruby squeezed Sal's hand. 'I'll tell Luca what you said, about him running the stall till Ray gets back. He practically runs it anyway and there's plenty of stock in the lock-up.'

For a short time, the roles had reversed and Ruby was the one doing the reassuring. Sal was a strong woman in many respects. She was also a loving, caring soul and in need of a little guidance herself. She climbed into the passenger seat, slammed the door shut, and wound down the window. 'I'll back as soon as I can.'

'He's in the best place, you know. They'll get him sorted out. If me dad was here, he'd tell you the same. They gave him a new lease of life once, sent him home feeling ten years younger.' Ruby smiled. 'Imagine that.'

Sal's eye's tapered and wrinkled in the corners. 'Best not lovey. Long as no real harm's done, I'll be satisfied with that.'

Ruby waved as the car drove off, while battling with her hair that continually whipped across her face. She scooped the tangled mess into a ponytail, looped it through the elastic hair-tie from her wrist and made her way back along the path. Later, with the Cafe cleaned and ready for the morning, she handed the key to Pam, before setting off with Jimmy down The Lane.

'We'll make the bank before closing, won't we?' she asked.

'Yeah, we've got half hour to play with. Don't worry.'

She felt a good deal safer with him by her side. Stopping briefly at George's stall, Ruby allowed Jimmy to explain the situation before escorting her to the bank, then home to wait for news.

Chapter 23

The remains of Tom's dinner coated the kitchen-diner wall like abstract art. Trails of thick gravy cut a winding path down through the faded leafy pattern. A jigsaw of razor-edged crockery pierced Grace's fingers as she gathered the pieces into a neat pile. 'For fuck's sake woman, leave it be I tell you,' Tom snapped, thumping the table.

Heaving himself out of the chair he hobbled across the room. Stooping behind her, he grabbed a handful of hairand yanked her backwards onto the tiled floor. She lay there, trembling, arms waving frantically to ward off expected blows.

He watched her flapping, every second hating her more than the last. Her near silence angered him. Not once did she cry out when he laid into her, except for the slightest child-like whimper. The blows came harder. Her lack of response made him feel inadequate, weak.

He'd heard about women who screamed blue murder for less. He nudged her with a slippered foot, and as expected, she made a grab for his leg. Slapping her hands away, Tom launched his foot into the folds of her hip. She rolled over, clutching her side. Her body curled, every muscle tensed, prepared. He stood over her awhile, watching, waiting for her to do something, say something. Anything! The blinding rage that coloured his face and left his whole-body glistening with sweat, slowly began to simmer.

One solitary word floated out on a sigh, 'Tom.'

'Yeah, well, you bring it on yourself, every fucking time. I'm off out, so get this mess cleaned up before I'm back. Oh, and keep the bloody door locked too. I've told you before I don't want that nosy prat next door in this house.' He walked through the sitting room to the cupboard under the stairs, pushed his feet into black slip-ons, buttoned his coat and stormed out.

*

The moment the street door slammed and windows rattled from the force, Grace knew to expect her neighbour, Jean. She pulled herself up and into a chair moments before Jean arrived at the side door leading to the kitchen. Her heady Tabu fragrance wafted in ahead of her. 'So, you've finally come to your senses and turfed him out?'

Grace expected nothing less from her friend. Jean's no nonsense, straight for the jugular approach had taken some getting used to, but Grace soon came to realise that the woman's 24 carat heart would help guide her through her darkest periods. From that very first 'Coo-eee' over the back fence, when Jean presented Grace with a rhubarb pie, their friendship had grown stronger by the day. Knowing they had both left London for a new start in Bromley, was the glue that bound them together.

'You shouldn't be so hard on him, Jean. The damage to his leg from that car incident has devastated him, plus he's had a lot to put up with over the years.'

Jean rolled her eyes. 'Too right he has, the poor man. Home cooked meals and a full-time skivvy at his beck and call.' She soaked a tea towel under a running tap, before wringing out the excess. 'I can see how that would get him down,' she added, placing the wet cloth on Grace's bruised cheek. 'He's a sly, two-faced son-of-a-

147

bitch, and I wouldn't trust him to hang the washing out. How long you lived here, fifteen, twenty years?'

Knowing where the question was leading, Grace remained silent.

'You know this place inside out, every nook and cranny. So how come you haven't worked out where the bloody doors are?'

It was a lame excuse, Grace knew that, but how else could she pass off the facial bruises?

'So, what set him off this time?'

Grace knew full well that Jean had loathed Tom with a passion, even before she'd got wind of his violent streak. Grace never delved too deeply as to the cause - never wanted to be caught in the middle. She could so easily lay the blame for every mishap on Tom, and Jean would accept it as gospel, but she refused to do so. He was a good man at heart. A good man who'd been dealt a dud hand. She was his wife, for better or worse.

'It's me. It's always me, Jean. I should choose my words more carefully. He mentioned doing someone a favour, watching their youngster for the evening. I expect it's one of the mums that he helps out?' Grace, unaware of Jean's shaking head, continued. 'I'd cooked a special meal for our anniversary. Thought we could spend a nice evening together, but he wouldn't budge.' Grace's voice dropped. 'I hinted, jokingly of course, that he must be having an affair. I'd really upset him, Jean. He hit the roof, went ballistic. I've only myself to blame. I shouldn't have said such a thing.'

Jean guffawed. 'Listen lady, you're definitely barking up the wrong tree. He might have fancied himself as a looker once upon a time, but I'm telling you straight, he is not a pretty sight now!'

'He sees me as a burden, I know he does.'

'Burden my arse. He lives the life of Riley. You more than compensate for not looking at his ugly mug all day long. You take my Willy,' she paused for effect. 'Turned into a right lazy git. The man thinks he's a frigging ornament.'

Grace's downcast countenance lifted slightly, giving Jean the reaction she had hoped for.

'Whenever he catches me looking his way for longer than usual, the silly sod gets a bit edgy. He says, what're you looking at me like that for, woman? Poor man thinks I'm after his noodle. Truth is, I often think he would have made a smashing dad. Anyway, I swivel me hips, nice and slow, while mentioning the Kama Sutra book I picked up cheap. Have I got a surprise for you tonight my little honey bun, I tell him. I'll just nip up and run us a bath.'

'You don't, surely?'

'Too right I do. Then suddenly he's got a list of jobs that need doing. He's out of that bloody armchair in a heartbeat, tearing round like a blue-arsed fly, polishing, dusting, you name it, he's on it. I now got the cleanest windows in the whole damn street!' She laughed.

Grace's rheumy eyes brightened. Her friend's tactics, obvious as they were, never failed to lift her spirits. The woman was truly a gift.

They had both suffered losses. Grace thought back to her own stillborn daughter. Like Jean, she too had wondered what sort of dad her Tom would have been. She forgave him his initial accusations of being trapped into marriage, when he warmed to the possibility of a daughter. However, his damning words six months later, laying the blame firmly at her door, would remain engraved on her soul forever. She couldn't bring herself to share the vile names he'd called her, when their beautiful tiny girl, delivered blue, slipped away. She knew that their daughter's passing was not a result of anything she had done, but the blame Tom foisted on her would haunt her days, forever.

Jean filled the kettle and placed it onto the glowing cooker ring. She prised the broom from its hiding place and set about clearing the floor. 'Kettle's on, Grace. Nothing like a good cuppa to sort things out.'

Acknowledging her friend's optimism, Grace's cheeks rounded into a half smile. The heightened pain made her flinch and wish she hadn't bothered. *I have a feeling it will take more than tea to put things right this time*, she thought.

*

Tom's mangled leg had healed faster than expected. The unrelenting nerve pain and pronounced limp were a different matter altogether. His ladder climbing days were over. With his job no longer viable, his time dragged by between the house and potting shed. The bastards who mowed him down were lodged in his thoughts. He knew, deep down, it hadn't been a random attack. They had set him up, lured him to that spot for one purpose only. To take him out. Someone must have cottoned on to his little game. It didn't matter how many times he turned it over, he'd no way of knowing for sure but didn't intend hanging around to find out.

The late TV news had come to a close when he looked across at Grace, seated on the sofa. The relentless clicking of her knitting needles drove him to distraction. He focussed on the mole above her lip. A beauty spot she'd called it, back in the day when she blackened it with pencil. It made little difference then and a sight less now, with a single coarse hair sprouting from its centre.

She wasn't exactly ugly, and boy, he'd seen some ropey women in his time. She just wasn't his type, never had been. Thinking back, she'd been nothing more than a convenient bunk-up. If only he'd had the balls to stand up to her old man with his self-righteous moral code. He could have left her at the registry office to irritate some other bugger's life. Well, he'd had enough. He would wipe that sickly fucking smile from her face once and for all. Shame he wouldn't be around to see it though.

He manoeuvred his gammy leg up the stairs and into the bedroom. Taking the holdall from the bottom of the Ottoman, he packed enough clothes to see him through. His spinster sister in Rotherhithe would take him in until he got settled in his new life. He set the alarm clock for six, giving him an early start. He wasn't lacking in the skills department, and prided himself on his handiwork. Always had. Someone would spot his potential in the coming weeks. It was just a matter of playing a waiting game. A game he excelled at, and more often than not, came out on top.

Chapter 24

Sal's eyes drooped. Sitting for hours at Ray's bedside somehow zapped her energy. The kindly matron in her starched navy uniform, noticing Sal's head lolling and jerking, sidled up to her. 'Why not get yourself home, dear? He'll probably sleep through until the morning. We'll call immediately if the situation changes.'

A reluctant Sal gathered her bits together and made her way to the exit. Crossing the road, she joined the lengthy queue at the bus stop. 'Looks like the earlier ones didn't turn up?' she said to the well-dressed woman in front. 'It'll be all push and shove for a seat. You mark my words!'

'I think you could be right,' came the reply.

The women eased into idle chit-chat. 'Don't see many like him round here, especially at this time of night,' nudged Sal, discreetly nodding towards the city gent standing ahead of them. 'Looks well dapper with his briefcase and bowler.'

'I agree. He does seem a little out of place.'

Sal's eyes fixed on the brown leather case. 'I've often wondered what they carry in those things. What's your best guess?'

'Important files I imagine.'

'More like lunch.' Sal chuckled.

A loud bang from a car backfiring had the queue jumping and cursing. A startled pidgeon swooped across the gathering and pooped directly onto the gentleman's bowler. Sal and her companion drew breath simultaneously before turning away to hide their amusement. Sal dabbed at her eyes. 'Sad to say, but that's tickled me. Cheered me up no end, and believe me, I needed something to smile about.'

'I've heard say that it brings good luck.'

'I doubt he'll see it that way,' said Sal.

'Shall we let him know? It seems wrong not to.'

'Nah, let's not ruin his evening. He'll find out soon enough.'

*

The mantel clock in its cumbersome wooden casing chimed the hour. Nine p.m. and still no word from Sal. Ruby paced up and down the kitchen. What was taking so long? She should have been back ages ago. Ruby checked the back door a second time. Satisfied that all was secure she popped the kettle on a low gas and returned once more to the sitting room.

The instant heat from the gas fire drew her closer. Kneeling down, she offered up her hands, capturing the warmth from the glowing flames. The constant low hiss from the gas jets filled her ears with its calming magic.

The painting of the old greyhound, high on the chimney breast, evoked a much happier time period. Memories of skipping through woodland, arms heavy with bluebells, touched by shards of sunlight piercing the dense green canopy; of hopscotch and daisy chains, and golden summers tempting butterflies into achingly steady palms.

She traced a finger along the smile that touched her lips. She remembered the fun shared with her giggling sisters, Ellen, Daisy and Mary: their streaming eyes and aching faces. There had been a time when her shadow stood for something other than fear.

Exactly when things began to change, she couldn't fathom and neither did she want to. She'd become her own worst enemy, tormenting herself with all manner of morbid possibilities. Her thoughts mocked her. You're sixteen years old for Christ's sake. Try acting your age for once in your miserable life.

There were occasions when she truly detested herself for being so lame, so bloody needy. But she despised Mickey a whole lot more. The backbone she'd always promised herself was almost fully formed. Allowing him to chip away at it would undermine everything. She couldn't let that happen, not having come this far. She might well be just a kid in the eyes of many, but her shoulders were ancient in comparison. In future, she would keep a tighter rein on her thoughts. What could be simpler?

She recalled the night that Sal had taken her in. How excited she'd been, barely able to stop herself jumping with joy. Luck was finally on her side. The cosy sitting room seemed to welcome her with its old-world charm, not dissimilar to her grandmother's flat in Suffolk, with similar chunky, near black wood furniture taking up most of the wall space. Sal's favoured armchair stood angled by the green tiled hearth, its cushion sagging from two generations of backsides. Close by and stuck precariously in the middle of the floor sat the coffee table, leaving little room for manoeuvre.

Rising to her feet, Ruby zigzagged across the room, making her way to the front parlour. The heavy floral curtains acted as draught and natural light excluders blocking the grim view of the shortcut alleyway that Sal often used. Ruby pressed her forehead against the cold glass, half expecting Mickey to leap out of the shadows and barge his way into the house as he had done previously. She could still feel him choking the life from

154

her. She returned to the kitchen to check that the kettle hadn't boiled dry.

Hearing the front door open and Sal cursing the rising fog, Ruby raced along the hall. Sal removed her coat, hung it on the hook to the side of the mirror and shivered. 'My toes are that bleeding numb it wouldn't surprise me if they've dropped off.' She stamped her feet on the doormat. 'I hope you've got the fire on, duck? I'm that cold, I'd swear I've got ice clunking through me veins.'

Ruby nodded. 'I've had the kettle on low for ages too. Expect you're dying for a cuppa?' she gushed, overjoyed at finally having someone to talk to.

'What on earth would I do without you?' Sal encouraged Ruby back to the sitting room. 'Quick smart, there's a girl, before we catch our death.'

Ruby fetched the teacups from the kitchen and placed them on the coffee table in front of the settee. She perched herself on the edge of the nearest cushion. With her palms pressed together and held tight between her knees, she waited, itching to hear the news. It seemed an age before Sal unbuckled her shoes and settled back into the armchair.

'Well, he's got that gash on his head as you know, but there's a bit of concussion too. They're going to keep an eye on him for a couple of days. He should be right as rain in no time. I'm that relieved, I don't mind telling you.'

Ruby's lungs emptied with an exaggerated sigh. Finally, her muscles lost their rigidity. She slumped backwards, as though every bone in her body had been sucked out. 'Did you tell him they didn't swipe the money? That I paid it in for him?'

'I certainly did. He's well chuffed. Said what a good kid you are. Kept rambling on about Leysdown and

155

suntans of all things. I couldn't understand a word of it. Must be something to do with the bang on the head?'

'No, he did mention retiring to Australia, on one of them cheap tickets.'

The furrows in Sal's forehead deepened as she blew and sipped her tea in equal measure. 'So, what's that got to do with Leysdown of all places?'

'I suggested he go there instead. It's got a beach and a penny arcade. Me Dad got sunburnt there once, straight through his string vest. Dripping in diamonds for months he was, so Mum said.'

'Now that makes sense, but our Ray, well, he talks a lot of rot.' Sal shook her head knowingly. 'So don't you believe a word of it. He went on one of them fancy holidays once, to Spain with his mates. They had to ply him with booze just to get him on that aeroplane. Cried like a babe. Or so I heard,' she winked.

Ruby realised that her mother and Sal were not that different. They both said stuff just to cheer other people up.

Sal continued. 'He reckoned he'd never get on a plane again. Scared of heights see! He insisted that the next time he flew it'd be with his own wings. You know love, dead and buried. I told Ray in no uncertain terms, that him upstairs only takes in the guddens. There'll be a pitch fork and furnace waiting for him.'

Ruby gulped her tea. 'Yeah, but he's not that bad really, is he?'

Sal's heart swelled. 'Hark at you changing your tune,' she chuckled. 'To be honest, he's had it tough one way and another. It's turned him into such a bloody misery, as well you know. Doubt he'll ever change his ways, not now.'

Ruby took the empty cups through to the kitchen. Grown-ups were a weird bunch at times, digging at each other like playground bullies, always striving for the last word. Despite their differing opinions, she knew that Sal loved her brother deeply and would see no harm come to him. As individual as they were, they were family; tied by that special bond which would sustain a higher degree of friction than they were willing to chance. There were of course other ways to sever a tie. Ruby scolded herself for welling up. She hadn't really understood the word poverty until it stormed unexpectedly into her life, scattering her family like windblown seed heads from decaying dandelions.

'I'm sorry to hear about your mum's ring,' called Sal. 'Must have been a blow to see it gone? I'd have mentioned it sooner, but with Ray and all.'

Ruby returned to the room. 'It's OK. Should have known someone'd buy it. It was that nice. Feel sad for Mum though.'

'Oh, Lovey, try looking on the bright side. What's to say she didn't buy it back herself?'

Ruby toyed with the notion, and nodded. 'She could have. I s'pose?'

'Anything's possible. Listen, I think I'll crack on with some paperwork. I won't be late going to bed. It'll be an early start as usual in the morning.' Sal had already worked out how the shift pattern would work until Ray's discharge. Pam, together with the part-timers, was more than capable of running the show if necessary, giving Sal a much-needed break. She would visit Ray on Thursday morning, her day off, allowing her to miss the evening rush. 'I don't mind telling you, the idea of crawling into bed at a decent hour gets me that excited, I doubt I'll catch a wink.'

Ruby kissed Sal's cheek. 'Might go up myself then, if you don't mind?'

'Course not. You scoot. I won't be far behind.'

Unable to sleep, Ruby concentrated on the house sounds. The creaking of the landing floorboards would tell her that Sal had turned in. She waited, and waited some more.

*

A ray of morning sunlight settled on Ruby's face. She stirred, checked the time and bolted from the bed. Sal's bedroom door remained open; her bed empty. Ruby's feet skimmed the floor as she flew down to the sitting room. Sal lay slumped in the armchair, her paperwork, a heap on the floor. Close to hysterical, Ruby tip-toed across and placed a trembling hand close to Sal's mouth. The moment she felt the warm air touch her skin, she fell to her knees and laid her head on the sleeping woman's lap.

Chapter 25

Seated in the Wimpy bar at the Elephant, Ruby strung out her Pepsi for a good half hour while waiting for Ellen to show. A few weeks had passed since the sisters had last met, and with much catching up to do. Ruby arrived early, hopeful that Ellen would do the same.

As the young woman strolled towards her, slipping off her coat in one smooth action, Ruby gawped like an imbecile. The shapely figure, clad in a suede mini skirt and flouncy top, flashed a band of midriff for good measure. Her usual chestnut coloured hair, ousted for a dramatic eye-catching ebony, was styled in a fashionable pixie cut, made trendy by the model Twiggy. She looked the bee's knees and Ruby could not have been prouder. As the girls hugged, Ruby was struck by the immediate change in the male staff. Their sudden ramrod backs and sucked in bellies had her laughing on the inside. 'You'd better sit down, Ellen, before you cause a riot. They've got steam coming out their lug-holes.'

'And it's nice to see you too, Rube!'

Things changed for Ellen the moment she took possession of her first wage packet, and spied those crisp notes though the brown perforated envelope. Ellen kept the fashion trade in business. She wore what she wanted, for no one but herself. Looking good kept her sane, bolstered her self-worth, and stopped her from popping the Valium that clueless doctors tried forcing down her neck. Demure as she looked, she would not be messed with. Her angelic features lulled many persistent Romeos into thinking otherwise. Few survived her acid tongue.

'Let's grab a burger here, then nip over to Kennington Park before the sun disappears altogether, Ellen said, glancing casually at the other diners. 'To be honest, you never know who's listening in these places.'

'Oh come on, they're too busy getting an eyeful if you ask me,' Ruby ribbed.

'Don't you be so sure.'

Her sister's response had Ruby curious. It was unlike Ellen to be so cautious. 'Has something happened?'

'No, but we don't want every Tom, Dick and Leroy knowing our business, do we?'

Ruby sat back in the chair. Her sister being cagey had Ruby doubtful that the news would be good. It was completely at odds with Ellen's trademark tell-it-as-it-is attitude. This, in Ruby's eyes meant only one thing. Trouble. And she was in no hurry to learn what that might be.

A while later, still chatting like a couple of gasbags, the girls left the Wimpy bar and headed towards Kennington, where they made a dive for the lone bench in a semi secluded section of the park. Ellen elaborated on her new life in Chatham as a married woman. 'You can still change your mind you know. You'd love it, I know you would. We've got a right nice place close to the docks. Our own back garden too! 'Ere, you'll never guess, but my Steve got a deal on some tiny plant bulbs. I only cooked the bleeders; didn't I. Thought they were those little onions Mum used to bung in the stew. 'Fruit cake or what?'

No amount of persuading would tempt Ruby from London. She had landed on her feet with Sal, and made mention of her own plans. 'You can be a right stubborn mare at times,' said Ellen. 'But I do get what you're saying so I'll get off your case, long as you know where I am if you get stuck? So, any idea where Daisy might be? I've been worried sick.'

'What're you on about? She's with Mum. We know she is.'

'Not anymore. Mum struggled to find somewhere, so thought it best if Daisy went to Grace's for a while.'

'Does Aunt Grace know where Mum is then?'

'As far as she's concerned, we're still at the flat. And before you ask, I've no idea where Mum is either. To be fair, you've more chance of finding her than me.'

'How come Daisy's not with Aunt Grace now then? It doesn't make sense.'

'I figured you already knew, Rube. Daisy left there late August.'

Ruby paled. 'I'd no idea she was even there!'

'It's just as well if you ask me, as he'd be leading her a dog's life now that he's laid up.'

Ruby sprang to her feet. 'I don't understand any of it. What's going on, and how'd you know all this?'

Ellen filled her lungs. 'Because I phoned Grace. You could have phoned too, any time you wanted so don't get on your high horse.'

Shame-faced, Ruby bowed her head. 'I did ring. Several times. But he always answered so I hung up. He's so weird. I hate talking to him.'

Ellen nodded in understanding of her sister's actions. 'Well, he won't be jumping up so fast from now on, that's for sure. The old sods had an accident. Real messed up by all accounts.' Her voice quietened. 'More's the bloody pity.'

'What's that supposed to mean? And what about Daisy? Where the hell can she be?'

'If I knew that I'd tell you, wouldn't I? Keep your hair on. We're on the same side, remember? Just sit your backside down and we'll try and work it out.' All Ellen knew was that Daisy had supposedly come back for the new term in secondary school, according to Aunt Grace. And with Ruby being closer in age, she'd be the one most likely to know who Daisy's friends were. 'The best chance we've got of finding her is through her mates.'

'Well, there's no point ringing round schools, as they're the last place she'd turn up,' Ruby decided. 'She's a worse truant than I ever was. And now, with a genuine excuse.'

A light suddenly illuminated Ruby's brain as the penny finally dropped. Julie Brinton! How many times had Ruby walked past those flats, imagining Daisy and Julie swinging from the monkey bars in the park area, without fear or dignity? Ruby doubted that Mrs Brinton could afford to take Daisy in, knowing as she did that the woman's purse held mainly dog-ends for emergencies. Everyone knew the Brintons were barely surviving, practically skin on bone the pair of them. Many there abouts were struggling in silence. She'd seen it herself. Hadn't her own mother, Kate, taken in others when they'd nothing to share but a joke and an armchair. 'I've got an idea where she could be,' beamed Ruby. 'It's our best hope.'

Thrashing out a plan, the girls were oblivious to the Laurel and Hardy duo sizing them up. The slimmer of the two with more pluck than sense, decided to try his luck. Ruby cringed and looked elsewhere as he sauntered over, an unlit cigarette hanging from the corner of his mouth.

'All right girls?' Directing his question to Ellen, he tapped his cigarette. 'Was just wondering like...' he said, full of bluster. 'Don't suppose you've got a match?'

Ruby blanched as Ellen sprang from the bench and was in his face faster than a slap. 'Yeah, I do as it goes.

Your face my arse. How's that suit you? Now piss off before I really lose my rag.'

The lad backed away, losing face in front of his mate who was creased up a safe distance behind. He jabbed a finger at Ruby. 'You should keep that bitch on a lead,' he called, before sprinting towards the nearest exit. Ellen turned and grabbed the wooden armrest. Lowering herself to the bench, her head slumped against Ruby's shoulder. Her rapid breaths slowly evened out.

Ruby knew she should at least say something, but not so much as a muscle twitched. To blame the turmoil of recent months as the trigger for Ellen's mouthing off would be a cop out. Her sister's anger was far more deeply rooted. That much was obvious, even to her. She'd received her fair share of tongue-lashings down the years. The last thing she needed was to wade into another.

Ruby had never seen Ellen cry, not even in temper. The sinking feeling in her stomach would not let up. Somehow, she had to find the right words. 'You're really scaring me, mate. I've not seen you this bad before. I'm worried you might be ill or something.' Scared that her concerns would create more tears, she tried a lighter tack. 'Getting wound up like that can't be good, can it? I mean, look what you did to that bloke. Poor sod nearly messed himself. All he wanted was a light; not a bloody blow-torch!'

'You think I'm round the twist?'

'No, don't be silly. But I am worried about you.'

Easing herself upright, Ellen's gaze followed the group of squealing kids playing catch around the defunct water fountain. 'I was just six years old. Not much younger than them,' she said, ignoring the clear mucus tricking from her nose. 'He reckoned it was me own fault, that I was a bad egg. I've always convinced myself that he must have been right. But you know

163

Rube, realising all these years later that I'd got it wrong, doesn't alter a thing. I'm still that same gasket ready to blow. It's not like I'll suddenly change into that folk singer, Mary, prim-and-proper Hopkins, is it? To be honest, I'm sick of the constant battle.' Her fingertips brushed the tears outwards across her cheekbones, leaving a smudged trail of black eye-liner.

Ruby was stunned into silence, shocked by her sister's cryptic outpouring. With no idea as to who or what her sister was referring to, she waited for Ellen to continue.

'Mum bought me a party frock, from Old Jack's. All puffed up with poncey pink frills and lace, can you imagine? But I loved it so much: even slept with the damn thing by me bed. To anyone else it was another ragged cast-off, but to me, Rube, it was everything.' The floodgates fully opened as memories played out in her face. 'He shredded it, right there in front of me. I didn't deserve it,' he told me. Every punishing rip left a scar. I sat with fingers rammed in my ears to dampen the sound. I'm sure I cried more over that poxy frock than the things he put me through.'

Ruby's heart thumped, threatening to burst through her chest any minute. She grabbed Ellen's hand. A thousand and one questions competed for space in her head. Comforting words were called for and yet not a single one sprang to mind that would do an ounce of good. She felt completely useless, just sitting there, squeezing her sister's hand tighter still and wondering who had brought this about and brought down the one person that Ruby herself had always strived to emulate. All the while Ellen wanted to talk; Ruby stopped short from butting in. She knew from her own experience that the smallest of worries could grow at a monstrous rate if kept under wraps.

By dredging up the past, Ellen had unknowingly rocked both their worlds. With a tissue taken from her tote bag, Ellen began to tidy her face. A snotty-nosed girl skipped away from the fountain and stopped in front of their bench.

'You all right lady?' she asked. 'Did yer cat die or something? You can share me gob-stopper if yer want.' She pulled the smooth yellow ball from her mouth and offered it up. 'Ain't sucked it much.'

'Nah, you're all right, but thanks anyway.' Ruby smiled. 'Me sister's OK, just poked herself in the eye, that's all.'

'Suit yerself.' The girl skipped off back to her mates.

'Guess I look a bit of a state then?' said Ellen.

'I've seen worse,' Ruby teased. 'Best stick your face back on before your hubby turns up. We don't want Steve doing a runner now.'

'I could try and get a message to him, at his mum's. Maybe put him off till later. That way I can go to the Brintons with you.'

'And where will we find a phone box round here?'

'I didn't think of that.'

'Let's leave things as planned, and I'll walk you back to the Elephant. I'm guessing Steve's already on his way. I've got your neighbour's phone number, so I'll let you know as soon as I get word of Daisy.'

Ellen's lingering stare, with bare lips locked in a half smile, caused Ruby to feel self-conscious. 'What?'

'I often wondered if mum brought the wrong baby home from hospital. You're nothing like the rest of us, apart from looks of course. But that's not what I'm on about. You're much smarter than you think. You always find your way, no matter how much crap gets dumped in your path.'

'Oh yeah, takes a real brain-box to dodge a bully's fist, then hide out in the toilet block waiting for the home bell.'

'Precisely, that's exactly what I mean,' Ellen added. 'Hear me out. I'm not bullshitting. See what I mean though? You had the sense to dodge and scarper rather than stand there like a moron and take a battering. And believe me many do. Sorting things out with your fists is not always the best option. I should know. I've never said it before, but I'm really proud of you. You and Daisy. Sticking together, is what kept you safe. That and your ages of course. Little dots like myself I guess, were easier prey. He'd have to be mental to chance his luck with older kids.'

Feeling as though someone had pulled the plug on her blood supply, Ruby fought to hold herself together. 'Holy cow! You're talking about Tom. Uncle Tom?'

'Oh Rube, I never meant for this to come out. I wouldn't upset you for the world, you know that. Can't think what came over me. I've never breathed a word of it before. Not to anyone. Everyone thinks the sun shines out his arse, but it's all a con. I wouldn't make it up. And I'd never forgive myself if I thought for one minute that by keeping quiet, I'd put you both in danger.'

'I didn't even know you'd stayed there!' Ruby gasped.

'Why would you? You were just a toddler.' Ellen's feather light voice preceded a brief, agonising silence between them. 'You're right as usual though, little miss know-all. I'll get myself sorted as soon as, so don't go worrying. Promise? I wasn't called best girl fighter for nothing you know.' She forced a smile. 'In the meantime, I need you to be honest with me, so we can bury this crap in the past where it belongs. OK?'

Ruby swallowed, already knowing the question on the tip of her sister's tongue.

'Did he ever? I mean, when yous were there together? You know what I'm saying, don't you?'

Under different circumstances Ruby might have opened up, but the timing was all wrong. It would only create further heartache. Ellen had clearly suffered enough. They all had. Shaking her head, Ruby mouthed a silent 'No,' all the while silently praying that he hadn't got his dirty mitts on Daisy.

She kissed her sister's cheek and quickly changed the subject. 'What you were saying, about Tom and the accident. Did aunt Grace say what had happened?'

'Yeah, some car ploughed into him. Hit and run they reckon. He's still alive though. Pity it didn't take him out altogether, if you ask me.'

A shiver ran down Ruby's back. She shuddered. 'So, he's finally got what he deserved then. It's all about karma and stuff. I've heard them say as much.'

'Who we talking about?'

'The hippies. I met some down The Lane. They were going on about Karma, so I looked it up at the library. It said, if you treat someone bad it'll come right back at yer.'

'Sounds about right. Shame Tom didn't read the same book.'

'I'm glad he got his comeuppance. D'you reckon he was scared, like you, when you were a kid? I know it's wicked to say, but I wish I'd been there, seen his rotten face.'

Ellen reached for her sister and hugged her tight. 'Well let me tell you Rube. His face was a picture! The man was fucking petrified. And I should know, because I was the one behind the wheel.'

Chapter 26

The street door snapped shut, leaving Ruby staring blankly at the eye-level section of glass. Glued to the spot, she heard the rattle of the security chain slot into position and the woman's footsteps fade out along the hallway. Ruby willed that the letterbox cover would lift from the inside and Daisy's giggly, girlie voice would sing out, *made you look, made you stare, made the barber cut your hair.*

Daisy never missed an opportunity to catch her sister out. Ruby's breath stilled in her chest as the seconds ticked by. Her hopes were dashed by the unbroken silence. Dragging her feet back along the landing, she sat dejectedly on the grey stone steps of the council flats. Her head rested heavy on her knees. The flickering of the light-bulb appeared to echo in the stillness. Green tiled walls, defaced with chalked slogans, cast a gloomy shadow over the stairwell, sending a rash of goosebumps down the length of her arms. Daisy had been within hugging distance and now she was gone.

Shifting the blame onto Mrs Brinton might have lessened her guilt, her stupidity, but there was no mistaking the pain in the woman's face or the quiver in her voice. She had done her best by Daisy, and like the woman had said, *I just couldn't give her what I haven't got.*

Ruby had heard of Sidcup, everyone had, although knowing it was somewhere on the Kent border didn't help one iota. The very idea of her sister in a Childrens' home, lost amongst strangers, brought Ruby lower than a worm's belly. If only she had turned up sooner. Presently, making her way back to Freemantle Street, moving swiftly through the darkness, she found comfort in knowing that Daisy was not cowering in some doorway. She was safe. She'd have a warm bed and food in her belly.

The heat in the back sitting room engulfed Ruby like a blast from a dryer at the launderette. Sal, struggling to keep her eyes open, shifted position in the fireside chair and rubbed at the red, mottled pattern forming on her calf.

'Didn't mean to be late Sal. Hope I didn't ruin dinner? Only once me and Ellen got talking, we'd lost track of time.'

Sal rubbed the girl's frozen face with her warm hands. 'Don't need to apologise, silly. I saved you some shepherd's pie, it's warming on top of the saucepan. How'd you go with Ellen then? I'll just grab your plate then you can tell me all the news.' Sal moved off to the kitchen. 'Oh, and Jimmy turned up to let you know that the 'do' at the youth place in Brixton has been cancelled. Went rabbiting on about calypso and that Reggie stuff you both like. It's all double Dutch to me I'm afraid.' Sal mopped up the moisture from the rim of the plate with a corner of a tea towel.

'It's Reggae, Sal, and to be honest, I'd forgotten all about it.' Tickets for the visiting calypso band sold fast, with Jimmy snaring the last two. Ruby's heart hung heavy with regret. They'd been counting down the days to the one-off event. Without doubt, Jimmy's disappointment would match her own, but with Daisy gone and Ellen's revelations, Ruby had no room in her head for calypso.

Sal sat the warm plate down on Ruby's lap. 'He looked a bit upset if you don't mind my saying? I'm to tell you he'll be at home if you want to pop round.'

'I can't face him. Not tonight, Sal. I wouldn't be good company. I'll see him tomorrow though.' By the time Ruby had explained about Daisy, her half-eaten meal had gone cold. 'I don't mean to waste it, but my appetites just...'

'Don't give it a second thought. Next door's cat will soon polish it off. Look here,' Sal lifted her bag from beside the fireplace. Taking out a magazine, she handed it to Ruby. 'I picked this up on the way home. *Fabulous 208*,' said Sal, reading the title like a telephone number. 'Figured you might like it?'

Ruby flicked through the pages. 'Thanks so much. It'll help take me mind off things. Might take myself upstairs, if you don't mind?'

'Do what you have to, duck. I'm here if you need me.'

Ruby sat on the bed, knees up and back resting against the headboard. Quietening her mind proved an impossibility. The day's events played out, rewound and re-played. Halting the bombardment of the nagging 'if only' fast became a lost cause. Had she knocked the Brinton's door sooner, Daisy might well have been with her, right now, asleep beside her. Rooting for the small transistor radio beneath her pillow, she turned the dial. The Bee Gees, *Don't forget to remember,* was part way through. She knew the words by heart. Singing along in her head, eyes closed, she glimpsed Daisy's smiling face, clear as a bell in her mind's eye.

A build-up of tears seeped through her thick lashes and into her hairline. She let them fall. The lyrics demanded nothing less. With the curtains pulled back along the wire, she caught glimpses of the night sky. The remains of the drifting fog formed little more than a fine mist slinking off into the distance. Wrapped in her

170

misery, she drifted into that welcome place, that woozy weightless haven, somewhere between consciousness and sleep.

*

The freckle-faced ginger haired girl, fragrant as a wrestler's armpits, blocked the entrance to the common room. 'You ain't coming in, shrimp. Not without the password,' she hissed through bucked teeth. 'So, buzz off before I clump you one.'

Reliving the slapped face from the previous week, Daisy backed away from her tormentor. She wandered along the corridor and into the kitchen. The resident female cook welcomed a break from the monotony of stocktaking. Hearing the door thud against the stopper, she emerged from the walk-in larder, quietly cussing her varicose legs. The split sack of flour, trying her patience and clogging her lungs with its plumes of white dust, would have to wait. With a film of the flour covering half her face, muting her usual high colouring, she appeared to Daisy as someone closely related to the Pilsbury Doughboy.

The youngster's infectious giggle filled the room. The cook grabbed a hand towel from the central work station, and snapped it back and forth, as though swatting flies. 'I'll give you make fun of me, young lady. Get out of my kitchen this instant. The very cheek of it. And don't go giving me that butter-wouldn't-melt look either. I've got the measure of you.'

Daisy stood at the opposite side of the counter, ready to dart if the cook so much as blinked. She loved the game, the pretence of it all, knowing full well there would be no loser. The heavy-set woman with more rolls than a bakery gave cuddles to die for, and Daisy felt the need for one more than ever. The past week had dragged like a lame dog, and she missed her family dreadfully.

The cook knew her behaviour was a sackable offence. Favouritism would not be condoned. Period. It topped the list of rules. Never, in all her years of bolstering a timid youngster's appetite, or curbing a ravenous one for that matter, had she broken it, until now. The petite, golden-haired scrap had reduced her to putty. Keeping her at arm's length was one battle already lost. There was something about her: her eyes, those large vivid blue pools, knowing and deep, that pulled you in with their unmistakeable sadness. An old soul if there was, disguised in knee high socks and a corduroy tunic, sent to inflate a lonely heart. Smitten didn't even come close.

'I've never known such a hungry bunch of kids,' said cook, plating up a triangle of cake and sliding it in Daisy's direction. 'Good job I keep a lock on these food cupboards, else between yous the shelves would be stripped bare in a jiffy and I, little miss, would be out on my ear.'

Daisy, picking out the sultanas from her wedge of fruit cake, spoke without thinking. 'I'll be gone soon anyway,' Her tummy tightened and she clammed up instantly. Words had a habit of tripping off her tongue willy-nilly. She wasn't wholly responsible.

The woman's eyebrows shot up. 'Gone! What's this? Tired of us already?'

Holding fast to the side plate with its home-made treat, Daisy stood before the woman, now crouched down to the youngster's level. 'Me Mum must have a new flat by now. It's been ages.' she huffed, loudly. 'She'll be here any day to take me home. I know she will.'

Cook's bruised heart skipped a beat. As much as she loved her job, and love it she did, there were times as now that she could don her coat and walk away. Or so she told herself. There were easier ways to earn a crust, surely, without the emotional ties that pulled tighter as each year passed. Her love for the waifs and strays that crossed the threshold, and there had been so many, held her, a willing prisoner dishing out portions of hope where needed, and always with a ready smile. She was a great big softie, too damn old to change either her ways or direction. Not wanting to dampen the girl's spirit, she kept the conversation light. 'Well, maybe you'll come back for a visit?' She brushed crumbs from the girl's chin. 'Or what about sending me a letter? That's a splendid idea. I'd really look forward to that,' she brimmed, encouragingly.

Daisy hung her head. 'I'm not very good at that stuff,' she admitted. 'But I can come back and visit you. Might bring Ruby too!'

Daisy liked Rowan House, named after the tree planted close to its main door. The house, as big as a mansion and almost identical to the others scattered about the vast grounds, was filled with similar aged kids, but with no real friend amongst them, she felt lonelier than ever.

Daisy strayed up into the bedroom she shared with three others. With her roommate's downstairs, goggle-eyed in front of the television, she leant through the open window and stared out across the garden. Huge mounds of red crispy leaves, painstakingly raked up by the gardener, cried out to be trampled through. If Ruby were here, they would have dived in head-first and loved every minute. Opening the cupboard, she pulled her coat from the hanger and slipped it on. With the remains of her pocket money clutched tight in her hand, she crept down the stairs.

'Off out are we?' called Cook, catching the youngster sneaking past her door.

'Just going for some sweets,' she said, opening her hand, revealing the pennies.

Cook pulled a sixpence from her pocket and placed it in the girl's palm. 'Get yourself something nice, and be quick about it. It'll be dark before long.'

Daisy draped her arms around the woman's waist, her head pressing into the warmth of the ample bosom. Sniffing back a dewdrop, she pulled herself together. She wouldn't cry, not now. It would give the game away. Besides, she was hardly a baby, despite her smallness. She had stuff in her head that didn't ought to be there. Some things she knew could never be changed, but there were other's that could. Her mother had trouble finding money for the gas meter. She hadn't a chance in hell of finding her here, stuck in the middle of a dirty great field, Daisy decided.

'And what's this in aid of?' asked Cook, not that she needed an excuse for a cuddle. 'You are a funny one and no mistake. Off with you now before the shop shuts.'

Daisy's feet crunched along the gravel path leading to the road. Fighting the temptation to look back and arouse suspicion, she continued on to the bus stop. Sticking out her hand she hopped aboard the bus that would take her back to the place she knew as home.

Chapter 27

It had been less than a week, but the strain of visiting Ray was beginning to tell on Sal. The cold bus journeys and the route march through the ever-expanding hospital was playing havoc with her corns. Ruby saw through the brave face Sal maintained for the customers. The fake smile and the half-hearted retorts went unnoticed by the barrow boys, but not so Ruby. She saw the despair, the daubing of dull eyes in a quiet corner and the constant wringing of tea towels. She had tried to help by offering to visit Ray herself. 'Bless your heart, but I can manage. It shouldn't be for much longer. Maybe in a day or two I'll take you along, how's that sound?'

Come Saturday evening things had taken a turn for the worse. Ruby had a bowl of water already in place for Sal to dunk her feet. She coaxed her into the armchair and sat opposite. Ruby had a childlike notion. If she broached her question quietly enough then maybe the answer would be less painful. 'So, is everything OK?' She guessed from the look on Sal's face that things were anything but. The ticking of the clock appeared louder than ever as the seconds dragged out.

'He's been acting up a bit, throwing his weight around,' Sal started. 'I told them, he's never been one to curb his tongue under any circumstances.' As she plunged her feet into the water her drooping eyelids closed, albeit briefly. 'There're other things too, which aren't suitable for young ears. Gist of it is they've had to operate. Didn't look like my brother lying there.' She sniffed. 'His head all bandaged like one of them foreign Johnnies with the turbans.'

'I don't understand. I thought he just needed rest?'

'So did they duck, till he went all peculiar. The doctors tried to explain, but you know what it's like. They talk in that medical jargon; all those highfaluting words that no one can understand. I told them straight, give it to me in plain English. It turns out he'd got a blood clot, from when his head hit the pavement. I'll give them their due, soon as they'd worked out the problem they didn't hang about. They mentioned something about a procedure called a Burr hole to drain it through. I was tempted to say, don't suck the brain out with it. It's only small but it's in there somewhere.' Sal tittered. Ruby understood that whenever Sal became nervous or worried, she laughed. It was a coping mechanism that Ruby knew well. She and her sisters had the same affliction which their mother labelled as a wicked sense of humour. Sal continued. 'I'm not one to poke fun at others misfortunes, especially my own brothers, but sometimes you've got to see the funny side else you'd end up in the loony bin.'

When George turned up a short while later, Ruby left them to it. If Sal opened up to anyone it would be him. Ruby hadn't planned on listening in but couldn't prise herself off the bottom stair. Hearing the chink of glasses, she knew the advocaat, gathering dust in the larder, had been opened, together with the bottle of light ale Ray had tucked away the week previous.

Sal explained about the blood clot and its worrying symptoms. 'He's been leading them a merry dance, George, let me tell you. Wouldn't have believed it if I hadn't seen it for myself. Only yesterday, right there he was, in the middle of the ward.' Her voice changed to an exaggerated whisper. 'He fished out his old John

Thomas and peed all over the bleeding floor. Nurses flapped like bed sheets in a blizzard, trying to sort him out. His dingle-dangle on show to the world. I was mortified. Didn't know where to put my face.'

'Never!'

'I swear on my life I'm telling the truth. Then later, he grabbed this nurse's thingamajigs, squeezing the life out of them like some oversexed teenager. Nice young thing she was too. An Irish girl, took it all in her stride, bless her. I tell you; those nurses deserve a medal for what they put up with. Wouldn't do for me, I'd have clouted him one, good and proper.'

'Have a heart, Sal. The poor sods not himself. You know as well as I do that Ray wouldn't behave like that. He'd be mortified to know you'd witnessed it.'

'Never, in all my life have I seen such a palaver. Me own flesh and blood too.'

'Could be the jollop they're giving him triggered something?'

'Painkillers,' Sal broke in. 'That's all he'd had. Hardly a reason to go flashing his, his bits. Mind you, the doctors were on the ball. Soon as Ray started his lewd behaviour lark, they knew exactly what was going on, and had him on that operating table faster than a toupee in a hurricane.'

George choked on his beer. His hacking cough brought a halt to the conversation as he struggled to retrieve the amber fluid from his lungs. Ruby could hear the thuds as Sal pummelled the man's back, ignoring his weak, mumbling protests. Ruby tensed in anticipation of the door opening and being caught red-handed by a flustered Sal. She darted swiftly into the parlour, and waited for things to settle down before returning to the stairs.

'I'm not comfortable discussing my old pal's todger, Sal.' His final cough was little more than a forced puff of

177

air between his tonsils. His rasping voice remained difficult for Ruby to decipher. With her ear pushed firmly between the banister spindles, she concentrated for all her worth.

'As I was about to say,' he cleared his throat. 'He'll be back to normal before you know it, and be none the worse for his ordeal.'

'I hope you're right. I really do. I don't think I could cope with that sort of carry-on.'

Ruby sensed that Sal was close to tears. Her words had lost their confident, no-nonsense edge. She stood up, ready to intrude and give the woman a much-needed cuddle.

'I don't mean to go on, George, but me head's all over the shop. I'm that worried about him. He's the only family I've got left. And as for them ruffians knocking him about like that, what was that in aid of?' George had barely opened his mouth to answer when Sal continued. 'I'm no gossip, you know that, but I've heard mention that they'd probably taken drugs.' In fear that the walls had suddenly sprouted ears, she lowered her voice again. 'Things called purple tarts.'

George patted her hand. 'Hearts, Sal.'

'You what?'

'Purple hearts. It's what they're called. I get what you're saying but I reckon they were chancers, out to rob him. Probably got wind of his trip to the bank.'

'Everything is such a mess, George. It's a living nightmare, it really is.'

'Come on girl, I'll support you all I can. How long before he's home?'

'They hinted at a couple of weeks. All being well.' She stifled a yawn.

'Listen, I'll make tracks so you can get your head down.'

'I am whacked, I'll give you that,' she hesitated. 'Tell you what, give us a top up first.' She offered up her empty glass. 'I'll sleep all the better for it.'

Ruby chose that moment to pop her head round the door. 'All right to grab some water?' she asked.

'Course, lovey. I thought you'd already turned in?'

'Just on me way. I did have a nose in your front room though. It's amazing, Sal, like a museum. And all those books about tanks, enough to start a library! Were they your dad's? Oh, I hope you didn't mind?' she hastened to add, looking from one to the other. 'I should have asked first. Just thought I'd keep out the way, give you time to chat.'

Sal gave a nod of understanding. 'She's a real treasure, George. Always thinking of others.'

He smiled in Ruby's direction, causing the girl to colour up.

'About time someone disturbed the air in there. Them books are Ray's, duck. He's always been fascinated with tanks. Can't see the appeal myself, but there you go, wouldn't do for us all to be the same. It used to be mum's pride and joy, that room. All her best furniture and trinkets in one place and no one to get the pleasure of it. We're a daft bunch us females.'

'Don't get me started on that one,' said George, before supping the remains of his beer and heading towards the door.

Taking a tumbler of water to her room, Ruby set it down on the patterned runner alongside her bed and slid beneath the covers. On hearing the street door close and the bolts slotted into place, Ruby relaxed back into the feathered pillow the minute the creaks from the floorboard faded out, letting her know that Sal had also called it a night. Ruby glanced at the small travel clock on the mantel; its illuminated face showed close to midnight and sleep had no plans to visit her anytime soon.

She had come to love her room. It felt like home. Even more-so with the little touches Sal provided. The framed print of a Chinese lady, resplendent in her gold-collared robe and green painted face, watched over her from the far wall. Similarly, the selection of ornaments lined up along the shelf atop the boarded-up fireplace added a rainbow of colours. She didn't want to think about leaving, but the conversation between George and Sal troubled her. What if Ray didn't return to normal? There's no way she could stay, not with him like that. Selfish as it was, she shuddered to think of where she might end up.

Wrapped in her thoughts, she hadn't heard Sal's footsteps along the landing. The sudden click of the door opening jolted Ruby upright. Snatching up the pillow, she held it close to her chest.

'You awake, lovey?' asked Sal, staring into the gloom.

'Gawd, Sal. You scared me half to death. What's wrong?'

Sal remained ghost-like in the doorway. Her white flowing nightdress and chiffon headscarf, keeping her curlers in check, had the makings of a late-night horror.

'I guessed you'd be awake. I just wanted to say, don't go worrying yourself about Ray, that's all. I know things are a bit up in the air at the minute but it'll all come good, believe me. I can feel it in my bones.'

Ruby slipped back between the sheets, feeling partly relieved and partly embarrassed. Sal must know she'd ear-wigged the conversation; why else would she try to reassure her? Truth was, she had thought about Ray more than she cared to admit. Strangely enough she missed him sounding off, demanding the whereabouts of some inanimate object, obviously tidied away by interfering females, only to show up later in the exact place he'd left it.

She would never figure him out if she lived to be a hundred. There were days when his manner had been so pleasant that she truly believed he liked her. And others when, if she'd have been a man, she would have knocked him through to the following week. If his personality had become permanently altered, then she was the one being out of order, and for that she felt a pang of guilt. But she couldn't budge her sneaking suspicion, that his grumpy git mode had become a habit too hard to break. And that some people, as her mother once told her, weren't happy unless they were downright miserable.

Chapter 28

Mickey Loughty was a coward of the first order. His precious, pretty-boy features, often twisted into a threatening grimace, fooled no one but himself and unsuspecting females. They alone felt the brunt of his grievances. His sadistic streak shone through during those early school years, when he consistently tormented others, before hiding out in the cloakroom, leaving his older brother, Luke, to take the flak and calm the mayhem that Mickey had created: was always creating.

Mickey justified his actions, or lack of them, by convincing himself that he was doing the wimp a favour. Luke, the golden boy, the sensitive one who could do no wrong, especially in the eyes of their parents, needed toughening up. His namby-pamby ways, the butt of many a joke, heightened the maternal urges in the so-called weaker sex, regardless of age. The boy lapped it up, a runt if ever there was.

Mickey was a lot of things but blind he wasn't. In his eyes his brother was a weakling, a mummy's boy, and he hated him for it. Little things plagued him the most. The irritating way his head rolled backwards when he laughed. His nose, forever stuck in some poxy book, not forgetting those gut-churning impeccable manners, that left old ladies swooning like toothless teenagers. Everyone's little darling, that was Luke.

Mickey became a law unto himself. As a young man he had no time for niceties and all that rubbish. People liked him or they didn't. Their choice. He had his mates, fall-out guys he called them, clearing up after him as Luke had done before.

They made him feel good, pandered to his expanding ego. The day Luke packed his bags was cause for celebration. It had been a long time coming and Mickey couldn't wait to see the back of him. The fact that Luke had landed himself a job in a university library in some far off place that Mickey had no idea even existed, was of no great importance. He for one, would be glad to be shot of him. However, their mother, Jane, as expected, made a spectacle of herself, clinging to him like a wet blanket. It had taken their father, John, an age to prise her arms, thin as they were, free from the hold she had on her boy. Her first born, no matter what age, would always be her baby. Her little Lukey.

Mickey silenced the alarm clock before it rattled the other tenants in the dingy, overpriced bedsits. He couldn't shake the remnants of his dreaming mind, the unwelcome memories that infested his quieter moments. He saw the three of them, his father John, mother Jane, and himself at the dinner table, going through the motions of everyday life. Life after Luke.

Why didn't you go with your brother to the train? Jane had asked him.

Because I had better things to do. OK? If he can't make it to the station on his tod, how will the daft git find his way across the bloody country?

The less time Mickey spent with his brother the better. The idea that Luke's dubious character traits might rub off on him scared him witless. He was afraid at times to breathe the same air, let alone share a bedroom. You didn't have to be Einstein to spot a pansy in the making. It was glaringly obvious to some.

His mother's voice piped up. *He might meet a nice girl and settle down.*

He'd hardly entertain a battle-axe, now would he?
John replied.

Trust you to split hairs, Jonathan Loughty.

John slapped a hand against his forehead in mock surprise. *Well blow me down, I no sooner open my mouth and I'm back in the dog house.* He'd looked to Mickey for backup, only to be greeted with a blank, I-don't-give-a-toss stare.

We might get a grandchild after all? Oh, John, wouldn't that be lovely?

Let's give the boy a chance, love. He hasn't even settled yet, and already you've got him married off and pacing outside the maternity unit.

I know. I know I'm being silly, but I have such dreams, and time passes so quickly.

Mickey had lost count of the times that scene rolled about in his head. They had been totally oblivious to what was staring them in the face. Although, give the old girl her due, she had been right on one count. Time waits for no man, or woman. Within eighteen short months there were two more residents interred in Brenchly Gardens, and not a grandchild in sight to mourn the loss.

Ray had it coming to him. Mickey would sting him where it hurt the most: his wallet. Checking his hair in the mirror, he buttoned his favoured Crombie, smiled his crooked smile and locked the bedsit door behind him.

Glengall Road stretched before him, empty and silent. The high back gates to the R. Whites Lemonade depot remained locked and patrolled by an unseen watchman wearing metal heel taps. The dense early morning frost, glistening beneath the haze of street-lamps, had Mickey pulling the rucksack closer to his chest for both warmth and safekeeping. He hadn't bargained on pavements like skating rinks. The last thing he needed was a tumble. Going down and spilling his cache was not an option. He would tread more carefully. Adding extra minutes to his time plan was not an issue. With a good couple of hours before the traders stirred, he'd have the job sorted and be back between the sheets before anyone was any the wiser.

Turning into Alvey Street, he paused outside the house he once called home. Different curtains hung in the windows of the terraced house. Two up two down, Jane, his mother had called it. Her pride and joy. He imagined her seated on the upper window ledge, leaning out, over stretching as usual with her worn square of chamois leather. One phrase lodged in his brain. She keeps a clean house. Geez, how many times had he heard those words?

The neighbours were saps. All taken in by the little woman with the big heart and possible shares in the Ajax factory. They envied her perfect English. Tits, they were, the lot of them. Spewing out their misplaced aitches in a bid to impress Lady fucking Jane. It appealed to his sense of humour, given some of the women there about, the ones forever on his case, were like navvies in lipstick and heels. Christ, in comparison his mother was a ringer for Little Bo Peep, albeit a sullied one.

She'd been a rarity, a human tornado sucking up every ounce of shit from their lives. In hindsight, it made perfect sense. Scrubber by name and nature. He was her dirty little secret, a daily reminder of the time she had dropped both her standards and her drawers; and try as she might, no amount of cleaning paraphernalia would obliterate her shame. He fought the urge to slam his fist through the window, shatter the lie that had shaped his life. There were times he had loved her, must have done, even during his angst-ridden teenage years when she'd hacked him right off. But that was before, before he

185

found out the truth, heard it from her own mouth. Those same thin lips that had caused and kissed away a trillion hurts, had, as a final act, completely floored him without so much as a single apology.

Had he not set foot in that hospital he'd have been none the wiser. It was his old man's doing, jawing his head off like some old nag. The conversation played out in his head. *Have a heart, son, for heaven's sake. She's your mother after all. Don't let her go without saying goodbye.*

How many more times? I just said I'd go, didn't I? You want it in blood, or what?

Well, there's no need to be like that. I was only saying…

Yeah, and you made your point so can we just drop it now?

You do know that I'd swap places with her if I could?

Geez, here we go again. I can't be doing with all this morbid claptrap. I'm out of here.

I'll be there a bit later, give you two sometime alone. His words were punctuated by the door crashing against the frame.

Mickey's feet had dragged along the hospital corridor. Why he'd allowed himself to be badgered into visiting was anyone's guess. He hated hospitals and the damn stench that permeated his clothes. His head was near bursting with half-baked excuses to turn-tail and slink off. Chances are she wouldn't know him from Adam anyway.

For ten agonising minutes he waited on the outside of the drawn curtains while the chaplain spoke with the dying woman. Jane's laboured breaths carried her voice on a whisper. Mickey edged closer. His crooked smirk fell away as he deciphered her strung-out words.

John doted on him. We both did. Couldn't tell Mickey the truth. It would have destroyed him.

186

And Mickey has no knowledge of this?
None.

Arriving back home in a blur of red mist, Mickey paced his room until a plan had evolved. How could he have failed to make the connection? Ray's presence at the house had been as regular as the need to piss, and yet it took a dying confession to spell out the obvious; Ray was his biological father. A confrontation, if met with denial, could well jeopardise his future prospects. He'd decided to play it safe and take the man for all he could get. After-all, his need for another father figure was on level pegging with a dose of the clap. Ray's humiliation of him gnawed away in his gut like a suppurating abscess. To be tossed like garbage in the gutter over some slut of a girl needed to be addressed, personally.

Mickey's stride lengthened. The Lane stood empty, weirdly silent and bathed in shadows just as he'd expected. He slipped quietly into a side turning. Ray's lock-up, the first on the corner of a short row was ideally situated. If rumbled, he had three escape routes. Piece of cake. kneeling down, Mickey emptied the bag onto the pavement. Knowing that Carter Street Old Bill were holed up within throwing distance made the task that much sweeter. He felt the adrenaline flood his system and swallowed back the laughter bubbling up in his throat. The faster his hands moved, the more they shook. Mumbling, like some deranged biddy having a heart-to-heart with a long-dead parrot, he put everyone in their place. All the crap stored in his head, all the slights and put downs came tumbling out. The constant pressure finally began to ease.

Uncapping the nozzles, he squirted half the petrol through the gap below the door; the remainder, aimed through the top, promised a longer reach. Shaking with nervous energy, Mickey cursed his numbed fingers as

187

match by unspent match fell away. He couldn't fuck up, not now. Word would get out. He'd be labelled a prat, made a laughing stock. Panic crept up on him. Gripped him, python tight. His breathing quickened. Short, regular explosions of white breath, draining his strength, messing with his head. His thoughts mocked. *You'll be collared, red-handed any poxy minute, and for what? Move your sodding arse or get the fuck out of there.* With seconds to spare before his heart burst through his chest, a tiny delicate flame, protected by a trembling hand saved the moment.

The initial flare rocked him, forcing him further back to admire his handiwork. An orange glow rapidly framed the door. The first plumes of black smoke curled up into an already dark sky. He could barely contain himself. He'd done it. He'd fucking gone and done it. Finally taught the big man a lesson. 'Up yours, Dad,' he said smugly, before heading back to the bedsit.

The outline of a man emerged from a darkened doorway, clocking the unmistakable swagger of the figure passing by. Close to choking on his Rothmans, he backed up, stepped inside and quietly closed the door.

Chapter 29

The torching of the lock-up quickly became old news, much to Sal and Ruby's relief. They'd welcomed the added trade in the previous fortnight, but not so the relentless questions.

Ruby passed the time by refilling the condiments. 'Bit slow today, Sal.'

'I'm not surprised. Look at that poor man,' said Sal, watching an elderly gent rush past the window in pursuit of his trilby storming ahead of him. 'I'd hoped the sausage toad special would draw them in. If things don't liven up I might just shut up shop. Look, you and Pam may as well take the rest of the day off lovey. Can't see a stampede happening any time soon.'

'Wouldn't mind if that's OK?' Fancy a bit of a walk to be honest.'

'Like you don't get enough of that here,' Sal quipped. 'Off you trot, but slip a coat on first. I'll give Pam a shout.'

Ruby wandered through the deserted Lane, heading nowhere in particular. The overcast sky had rumbled throughout the morning. Cold as it was, and with the wind biting like a feral dog, it nevertheless allowed a brief respite from the Cafe's stifling atmosphere. Ten minutes into her stroll a thunderclap split the slate grey heavens and a downpour ensued. Ruby dashed into the nearest sanctuary, Arments, the pie 'n' mash shop.

The warmth, as she pushed open the door, gathered her in like a lost friend. Combing her fingers through tangled hair, Ruby placed her order and waited at the counter. The place was buzzing as usual. She glanced from table to table, and smiled back at grinning kids with bloated faces, but quickly looked away when an overly-stuffed boy in a sleeveless pullover began to retch. The boy's pullover reminded her of Gary, her brother, and how when younger, he'd lived in those V necked patterned tops. She smiled at the memory; those tops and snake belts had been his favourite items by far.

'Here you go, love.' The assistant, handed Ruby her meal. Ruby settled at an empty marble-topped table tucked away at the rear. She doused the food with vinegar and popped the first delicious forkful into her mouth.

Working between the stall and the Cafe had been good for Ruby in many ways: it kept her busy, allowed less thinking time, less time to stew about her loved ones. Daisy had always been her main concern. The rest of the family would find their way, she didn't doubt that for a minute, but Daisy, being a nipper, was vulnerable. But she was a savvy little so-and-so, and streetwise too! Weren't they all. Young heads on old shoulders, their grandmother had called them; grown up too fast for their own good. Ruby, at times, wished she was privy to the goings on in her siblings' heads.

They rarely spoke in detail about their futures, the possibilities, or more importantly the lack of them. As siblings go, they shared only the joy and their day-to-day triumphs. Everything else was secreted away, to protect themselves and each other. They mastered their own, nothing-can-touch-me front, and hoped for all their worth that the guise would be strong enough to carry them through.

Ruby fought the urge to look up as two mountainous men shifted their bulk into the seats opposite her. An overpowering waft of stale sweat brought her close to gagging. She considered moving, searching out another table, but with her embarrassment levels already spiralling, could she chance looking a complete idiot if forced to return to her seat?

'Some people got no manners,' she said quietly into her plate. Even she knew it was impolite to plonk down at another's table without asking. Neither of them had ordered, making their arrival doubly suspicious. She could feel their eyes boring into her, second by excruciating second as they sat, fixed in position, like a pair of defective manikins. Their bulbous heads posed in her direction caused the heat that had reached her chest to storm quickly upwards, and cover her face in crimson blotches.

'What's that you're saying?' asked one.

Without looking up, Ruby answered. 'Wasn't talking to you.'

Her appetite flew out of the door on the heels of the green-faced boy heading for the nearest drain.

'A little bird tells me you work with Ray.' said the one directly opposite.

Ruby mumbled, 'None of your business.'

'That's not very nice, is it? I'm only trying to be sociable.'

Holy moly, she thought, *they're after Ray! Were they involved in his attack? Have they shown up to finish him off? One wrong word could spell disaster for Ray, for all of them.* She wanted to blast Pinky and Perky, tell them to shove off and be done with it, but instead, she pushed her food idly around the plate.

They would get nothing from her. Nothing. With her back arched and tension creeping into muscles that she never knew existed, she kept her mouth shut. Although being watched at such close proximity was unnerving, she had been in worse situations and survived. Ruby also knew they wouldn't dare take liberties with her in front of so many people. The other diners would be on them like a ton of coal. That's what she loved about Walworth: people looked out for each other.

'I'm looking for an acquaintance of me son. I hear he hangs about with your boss. Bit of a flash geezer, name of Mickey. It's my guess that you know him. I've a message see, and thought I'd deliver it meself while I'm in the area like.'

Ruby spluttered on a sip of warm tea. The coughing fit that followed showed no sign of abating. Red-faced and gasping, she wanted nothing more than to slip beneath the table and hide herself away.

The man opposite stood up, moved to her side and landed a blow to her back. 'Gone down the wrong hole, girl? Cough it up, might be a gold watch.'

Exasperated, she knocked his arm away and wiped tears from her face. The man's sidekick hadn't moved a muscle. He remained transfixed by her minced beef pie. She half expected it to levitate, whizz across and slosh him in his greedy chops.

'All right now girl? Like I was saying,' said the man returning to his seat, 'this Mickey bloke, any idea where I'll find him?'

Using Ray's choice of words, Ruby thought they looked like a couple of old bruisers. However, their prey would have to be tied to a lamppost or legless because they hadn't a hope of catching anyone moving faster than a crawl. She breathed easier knowing that Ray did not appear to be in danger, and with Mickey already on remand in Brixton, their so-called message would simply have to wait. One day Mickey would get his due; a taste of his own medicine would be a hard swallow, and hopefully wipe that cockeyed grin from his face once and for all. Until then, Ruby would put her trust in what the hippies swore by, what goes around comes around. Under normal circumstances Ruby had no idea where

Mickey hung out. He just popped up, appeared from nowhere, similar to a bad smell in a packed lift.

'Haven't a clue who you're on about.' Ruby pushed her chair backwards and got up to leave.

'Right you are, darling,' the main man smiled. 'We'll take it up with Ray.'

His sidekick snatched the remains of Ruby's pie from her plate. With his mouth full from one enormous bite, his words tumbled over mounds of mush. 'Can't waste good grub.'

Ruby grimaced as the coating of green parsley liquor dripped through his dirty fat fingers. 'So disgusting,' she mouthed before spinning on her heels and marching out.

*

The smell of frying bacon greeted Ruby the moment she stepped inside the house. She could hear the frenetic sizzle from the hallway as the smoky haze from burning fat filtered through the rooms. Sal would have a canary fit. Yet another pan ruined. How many times had the woman reminded him to turn the gas down? Ruby shook her head in disbelief. Patience and Ray had never walked side by side. He wanted everything yesterday.

No surprises that he had ditched the turban, pronto. Ruby hung her jacket on the door knob, and surveyed the landscape of his shorn head, which had more lumps and bumps than rice pudding. His so-called miraculous recovery was driven solely by his work ethic, which Sal had referred to as a blessing in disguise. Whatever the reason, Ruby could not be happier. The man was back and life had returned to normal.

Ray turned to face her. 'What's up? I like it crispy. You want some?' Ruby scoffed at his offer as he forked the charred strips onto the large wedge of bread.

193

'Your loss,' he grinned. Ruby had warmed to him of late. His mood was good and he was fun to be around, more often than not. She hated to be the one to change that. She dismissed Sal's idea that the bang on the head had forced his grumpy nature into hibernation and it was just a matter of time before it was business as usual. Nevertheless, Mickey was a touchy subject now where Ray was concerned. She knew that more than anyone. He wouldn't thank her for keeping quiet about something that could bring trouble to his door. She brewed him a treacle-thick tea in his British bulldog mug and took it through to the sitting room.

Ray eyed her suspiciously. 'What's this then?' He nodded towards the mug placed on the coffee table. 'If you're about to tap me for money you can save your breath.'

'Why do you always think I'm after something?'

'You're a teenager. It's par for the course.' He watched her face drop. 'I'm winding you up you silly mare. What's going on? Out with it.'

Seated on one of the armchairs, Ruby twiddled nervously with the gilt button at the neck of her pink paisley top. 'Two men followed me into Arments today, asking after Mickey. They've got a message to pass on.' She held her breath and waited for the explosion. It never happened. Ray placed the empty plate down on the hearth and reached over for his tea.

'So, these men, local you think?'

Ruby shrugged her shoulders. 'Doubt it. I would have remembered.'

Ray frowned. 'How come?'

'They were built like dump trucks for starters. Brothers I'd say. Getting on a bit too, at least forty.' The gilt button plopped into her lap.

The moment she saw Ray smile, followed by Sal's home-made cushion hurtling towards her head, she knew he wasn't overly concerned.

'You taking the piss or what?'

Her face splitting with the widest grin was answer enough. 'Oh, and they mentioned you by name, told me they'd look you up.'

'Yeah, cheers for that.'

'D' you reckon Mickey's in trouble?' she asked.

'Wouldn't be the first time. I'm sure those blokes will let us know soon enough.'

The street door snapped shut. Sal had barely kicked off her shoes when Ray grabbed his keys and wallet and headed out to the Bedford Arms for a quiet pint before afternoon closing. Listening to his sister's inevitable belly-aching about burnt pans, elbow grease and the amazing properties of the Brillo pad was not his idea of a relaxing afternoon. He had more important things to worry about.

*

Mickey Loughty had one main habit: he pissed people off, left, right and centre. He could cause ructions in a mortuary that one; Ray would take bets on it. Hadn't he warned the dozy prick time and again to get his act together. And did he listen? Of course he bloody didn't. Ray rubbed his temples. He had the beginnings of a headache, all thanks to Mickey. A promise is a promise, Ray reminded himself. Didn't he say he'd look out for the lad? Lord knows he'd tried. At this rate he'd still be wading through the toerag's shit when he's in his dotage. He always knew that someone would come looking. It was just a matter of when. Well, they would get short shrift from him. Mickey was a pain in the arse, granted,

195

and a liability to boot. After the kind of day he'd had, he could seriously take the little shite out himself.

The Bedford Arms had a few locals propping up the bar, so Ray settled at a table out of earshot. Last thing he needed was to get roped into discussing the bleeding weather.

Clutching a small parcel, the landlady squeezed through the bar opening and stood by Ray's table.

'Good to see you on the mend, Ray,' she said, eyeing up the short tufts of hair sprouting through the top of his head. 'Bet you're feeling it now though without your turban?'

'I am as it goes. Might have to get me one of them hair pieces till it grows back proper.'

'Well, if they're good enough for Sinatra, then why not?'

Ray liked the woman. Her humour, often close to the mark, had got a few backs up over the years, but not his. She gave as good as she got, a natural piss-taker. He envied her style.

She placed the parcel next to his pint. 'Got a treat for you. Thought it might do you a turn?'

Opening the paper bag, Ray burst out laughing. 'A frigging woolly hat! You're kidding me?'

'A little something to keep your bonce warm. It's actually a tea-cosy, but I won't tell if you don't. And Millwall colours too. Right up your street.'

'Woman, you're a diamond. Best laugh I've had in ages. Have a drink on me. Sod it, have two. You deserve it.'

'Carry on like that, and I'd swear that crack on your head did more good than harm.'

Ray stared absently into his pint, slowly digesting the landlady's parting words.

Chapter 30

Cutting through the Georgian elegance of Surrey Square, Daisy's feet danced up and down the steps at the pavements edge. The four storey houses shaded the girl slipping by in the semi darkness. With no place to hurry to she stopped at the school gate. Her fingers followed the lines of rust-coloured names scratched into the grey metal panels. The crudely shaped hearts surrounding initials and finished off with an X was to Daisy, incomplete. Her name wasn't there, as though she had never existed. Yet her childhood remained beyond that gate. She could feel its closeness, wanted to grasp it with her frozen, blue-tipped fingers: snatch it back and run with it, forever. She imagined herself, arms outstretched, spinning, faster and faster. Her face upturned and bathed in glorious sunshine, with her golden hair flying free and the sound of laughter filling the space around her. An unbroken circle.

The metal gate was cold to her face. A stinging, penetrating cold that gradually warmed her reddening cheek. She pushed her face harder into the hinged gap, glimpsing a section of the freshly painted hopscotch. She felt the weight of a stone, tight in her hand, leaving small dents as she jumped those squares back to victory. For a brief moment she caught herself smiling. A flash, beacon bright. *Ha ha, cracked your face. I win*, Ruby would have shrieked, and together they'd have cracked the faces of all within earshot of their infectious giggling. Unexpected sobs bobbed in her belly as warm salty tears flowed unchecked. Silent tears; for without the noise, the wailing, it wasn't proper crying. It wouldn't count. Besides, crying served no purpose except to make her more miserable.

The footsteps of the lumbering temporary caretaker went unheard. He clapped a heavy hand down on the girl's shoulder. 'What you hanging about 'ere for? Up to no good by the looks of it.'

Jumping back from the perimeter and free from his grasp, Daisy stared up at him. The pending scream dissolved in her throat. 'Jeepers,' she uttered between quick breaths. Why'd you sneak up on me like that? I nearly peed meself,' She stared up at him, watching for the moment he recognised her. The seconds dragged by. He couldn't have forgotten her already, surely? 'I was just thinking...'

He cut her off. 'Well, do your thinking elsewhere. Now clear off out of it.'

Her shoulders slumped. 'But I've done nothing wrong. I was only looking. It's me, Daisy. I used to be the litter monitor, remember? The girl with the smile,' she beamed, cocking her head.

The man's scowl relaxed. She was obviously one of the multitudes to cross his path. But names and faces rarely matched, if remembered at all. 'Of course,' he nodded, totally bemused. 'Best get yourself off home. Your mum'll be sending out a search party.'

'Me mum's not...' she stopped. 'But thanks anyway.'

'For what?'

'For remembering who I was, silly.'

With a skip in her step, Daisy turned the corner and made her way towards the small parade of shops, tugging rose-hips from spent bushes along the way and flicking them into the air. The display boxes outside the grocers were too tempting to ignore. Swiping the closest apple to hand, she rushed away and sunk her teeth into its juicy redness.

'You must be mental coming back here,' Julie Brinton groaned on answering the knock at the door. 'What if me mum cottons on, spots yer? She'll kill me stone dead, that's what.' Watching Daisy's backside disappear into the gap beneath the metal bed-frame didn't make her feel any easier. Down on all fours, with her face touching the lino and hair trailing the floor, Julie peered through the gloom and haze of dust particles. 'You do know this is the first place they'll come looking?'

'Not on your Nelly,' said Daisy. 'No one's ever been under here, 'cept me.' She sneezed, sending balls of fluff skittering off on a merry dance. She pressed her palm to her nose, forcing it round in a continual motion to ease the fiery itching. Thoughts of stolen pinches from her granny's snuffbox came back to haunt her. 'Achoo!' sounded Daisy, purposely stretching out the 'oo'.

'Glad you think it's funny. And I don't mean the bed either. Julie jumped up and went across to the window. She moved the curtain just enough to see the area below. Catching sight of her mother threw her into a panic. 'She's sodding well coming. What'll I do?' She paced the room. 'I'm in for it now, I know I am. If you so much as fart I'm never talking to you again. I'll get myself a new best friend. I'm not kidding!'

'Oh stop being such a scaredy-cat. Nothing's gonna happen to you.'

Daisy had it all planned out; she would stay in the flat while Mrs Brinton cleaned at the pub and the funeral parlour. When the woman was home and on the warpath, Daisy would re-visit the parks that she'd missed the most, except at night-times. Night-times were trickiest of all. But Julie had promised to sneak her back in, somehow.

'I might even bump into me dad.'

'Well, if you do don't fetch him back here, cos there's no way *he* will fit under me bed!'

Daisy tensed with excitement and held her breath, waiting for the moment that key turned in the lock. Once upon a time she would have been petrified, but today, with her friend close by, it became a game, an adventure. After all, being caught was not the worst that could happen. She would simply run away again.

Chapter 31

Thursday, Sal's official day off, found her at the kitchen sink, rinsing newly washed hair with jugs of tepid water. Ruby, snug in her layers against the cold, poked her head around the door. 'I'm just off out for a walk, Sal.' She eased her fingers into her woollen gloves. 'You're missing the Archers, you know. It's all kicking off in the other room. The racket from that radio's got the neighbours banging a hole through the wall. Surprised you can't hear it.'

Sal sprang up quickly. Streams of soapy water drenched the upper half of her blue, button through shirt dress. 'Oh, for goodness sake, you little madam,' she grumbled, snatching up a towel and wrapping it round her head. 'Look at me now. I'm blimming well drenched. You and your pranks. One of these days my girl...'

Ruby stifled a giggle. 'Couldn't resist it. Sorry. Let me grab you a clean frock before I go.'

'I'll sort it. You get going, else you'll be late for your date. And we don't want to keep Jimmy waiting. Do we?' She planted a kiss on Ruby's head.

Ruby's heart swelled. She had come to love this woman, who, in spite of being pranked, still spoke and acted with a motherly tenderness.

'I'm a bit early for that. Thought I'd wander round the flats first.'

'Is that wise?'

Ruby shrugged her shoulders. 'I miss the place, Sal. Won't hang about too long.' Ruby's light-hearted, playful mood had Jimmy written all over it. Sal had been right to call her a wally. It forced her to look at her actions. Only then did she realise she had created her own misery. And likely Jimmy's too.

The wire mesh fencing surrounding the waste ground had been cut through and the beginnings of a bonfire was taking shape beyond. Victorian houses, flattened and cleared in readiness for a modern estate, had once provided magical play areas for Ruby and her friends. Her fingers hooked over the metal diamonds. She breathed in the familiar scent of brick dust and the remains of wood fires. Endless fun-filled games with dented saucepans and rusty tin cans sprang to mind.

Her focus drifted as scenes from last year's celebrations crowded in. She fancied she could hear the roar of the bonfire, as the wood, piled high, spat bursts of red rain which fizzled out in the dirt underfoot. She imagined the explosions of colour shooting towards the heavens and the squeals of... Ruby screamed the instant she felt the tap on her shoulder.

'Goodness me. Nearly had kittens myself,' the woman apologised. 'Didn't mean to frighten you, dear. I just said to my neighbour, that looks like Kate's girl down there. Thought I'd nip down and have a word. Expect you're missing the old place?'

Ruby had been so immersed in her thoughts; she'd been totally unaware of the woman creeping up on her.

'We've been wondering where you disappeared to? I mean, so sudden wasn't it, and without a word! What a shock we got. I couldn't sleep with the worry of it.'

'Really?'

'Yes, dear. Really. And your mum's furniture, every stick of it left behind too!'

It had been a bad move to come back. Ruby knew there would be questions. Some people genuinely cared and were naturally concerned. She understood that. But there were others she needed to avoid, the ones who thrived on keeping the gossip wheels turning.

'Oh, it wasn't sudden at all. We managed to get ourselves somewhere nicer. A terraced house actually, with a garden too!' she emphasised smugly. 'As for the furniture,' she continued, keeping her tone friendly but lightly peppered with sarcasm. 'it's like Mum said, a new start calls for new belongings. Makes sense, don't you think?' Those pesky little white lies had a habit of creeping in when least expected.

'Very nice too, dear,' the woman answered, every inch deflated. 'Do remember me to your mum. Oh, and tell her the kettle's always on if she fancies a chin-wag.'

'Will do. I'm sure she would love that.'

Ruby walked off with a bounce in her step. She licked the tip of her index finger and made a downward stroke in the air, indicating one imaginary point gained. She was still grinning to herself when she saw the newspaper stuffed Guy with the painted cardboard face slumped against the wall surrounding the flats. The trouser hems and shirt cuffs were all neatly tied off with string. She had finished her Guys in the same way a few years before.

A small boy standing by rattled his money tin. 'Penny for the Guy, Miss?'

Ruby had been called many things, but Miss had a special ring to it. She liked it. A lot. She added a sixpenny piece to his collection, knowing the joy it would bring later when he counted out his bounty.

*

Jimmy and Ruby stopped for a bite to eat in the 'Quickie,' a popular cafe along the main road. They placed their order at the counter and waited, ready to grab the next available seats. Romantic notions had attached themselves to every cell in Jimmy's brain. He wanted Ruby to be his girl more than he'd wanted anything in life. He'd rehearsed his lines time and again in the privacy of his bedroom. It all came down to timing, he decided. With odds stacked against him, given his interference with the Beaufoy situation, he came close to backing out.

From the moment he saw the billboard advertising the funfair, he had visions of himself with Ruby on the Waltzer. She'd scream above the records playing back-to-back, as they're thrown together with each breakneck spin of the carriage. He would hold her tight, as a rainbow of lights would blur into streams of colour around them. With her eyes tightly closed, she'd be unaware of the contented grin stretched across his face.

Girls had hardly figured large in his life. Oh, he liked them, no mistake, and there were plenty hanging round when he got together with his mates. His jokey nature set him apart though. He likened it to a safety net. The girls never took him seriously, which was just as he wanted. He'd watched his mates pulling the birds, all that tosh they came out with. All those empty promises just to get their way. He didn't want to be the odd one out, but he couldn't be like that. Being with Ruby was different. He never had to pretend to be anything other than himself. She was a good friend, but he couldn't deny his feelings had changed.

Ruby had also seen the poster. 'I used to go there with me sisters,' she cooed.

'It's the last weekend before they pack up. Don't s'pose you'd fancy going?'

'Thought you'd never ask. I love the fair!'

'Saturday it is then,' said Jimmy, mentally punching the air as they rushed to claim the newly vacated seats. He watched her in silence, how the tiny flecks of gold in her hazel eyes appeared to sparkle. And her smile, soft at the edges, causing her cheeks to dimple and colour under his gaze.

'What?' she smiled coyly.

'Nothing. Just looking,' he said, hoping that the news he needed to share, wouldn't cast a shadow on what had the makings of a perfect afternoon.

'Rube, I know where Gary is.' Keeping his voice upbeat to hopefully stall any sign of tears, had the desired effect.

Ruby swiftly closed the distance between them. Her words rolling like a thrown dice. 'Never! I mean where? Is he round here? - Is he OK? I don't understand. I'm his sister and I hadn't a clue.'

'Slow down, let me get a word in will yer,' he teased. 'It was purely by chance. My mate, down the Dun Cow last night, told me Gary was in Hollesley Bay.' Jimmy reached for her hand. 'But now he's at...'

Ruby butted in. 'Well, good for him; starting over somewhere else. I had a feeling he'd taken himself off. I've been to his mate's place a few times, where he's s'posed to be lodging. No one's ever there. Even knocked the neighbours. They'd never even heard of me brother.'

A waitress emerged from the kitchen. 'Sausage sandwiches,' she yelled, watching for a hand to shoot up.

'Over here,' Jimmy answered, half out of his chair.

Lifting a triangle of bread, Ruby squirted a wavy line of tomato sauce from the squeezy bottle, careful not to dislodge the dark blob caked around the nozzle.

'So, what's this Bay place then? Some posh hotel I guess. Or even one of them Butlins camps. Yeah, that'd be right. He's a jammy sod, my brother.'

205

Jimmy stopped mid-bite and popped his sandwich back on the plate. 'It's a borstal Rube! He was there a day or two, some administration cock-up, so they moved him to Stamford House. He's on remand. For a couple of months, I think?'

'Remand,' she repeated, incredulously. 'What the hell did he do?'

'Shh, keep your voice down. He nicked a scooter. One of them flash jobs loaded with chrome mirrors and headlamps. Guess the feller really fancied himself, eh?'

Ruby couldn't face the remains of her sandwich. She pushed the plate aside.

'That doesn't make sense. I didn't even know he could ride one.'

'That's exactly it. He can't. I'm told he fell off the bloody thing. Zoomed off like a pro, took a corner too fast and tipped the thing over. Right in front of a copper too! Talk about bad luck.'

'You sure he's alright? I mean, his cheeky manner's got him through dodgy situations before.' Her face suddenly dropped. 'Blimey. You don't think he'll get sent back to borstal, do you?'

Jimmy's swift, and positive come-back helped relieve the building tension.

'Nah, course he won't. He's had scrapes before, who hasn't? But it's only ever been petty kid stuff. It's hardly gangster league, is it?'

'You're right. He'll be out soon enough. Sooner still if he starts with those lousy jokes of his. And as horrible,' she faltered, 'as it sounds, at least we know where he is.'

Chapter 32

With two hours spare, Ray joined the queue outside the prison. Waiting to be escorted in, whilst inmates dreamed of breaking out, appealed to his kind of humour. Brixton remand wing, as a place to visit, had never been on Ray's priority list. It's all thanks to Hawkeye, a slave to his Rothman cigarettes that Mickey got nabbed in the first place. Looking out for the lad, as Ray promised to do, had been no easy task, and brushing off his snide remarks that seriously warranted a pasting had proved even more difficult.

He'd lost count of the times he'd come close to wringing the bleeder's neck. Yet here he was, having passed through security, seated at one of the few empty tables, soaking up the sob stories that had mothers and girlfriends drowning in snot and tears, and himself on the verge of puking up his ham roll. The stench of unwashed bodies and stale cigarette smoke hung heavy in the air, clinging to the fibres of his newly cleaned jacket. Ignoring the huge wall clock to his left, Ray checked and re-checked his wristwatch.

Finally, Mickey ambled into the visiting area. His triumphant smirk, big enough to park a bus in, was a dead ringer for an old comic Ray had seen on the telly: a bloke with an obscene elastic mouth.

'Make it quick,' said Ray. 'I've better things to do with my time than stare at your ugly mug.'

Mickey slumped back in his chair and laced his fingers behind his head. 'Didn't think you'd show.' He paused. 'Guilty conscience disturbing your kip?'

'Don't push it sunshine. Just say your piece and I'm out of here.'

Mickey swung forward. Folding his hands on the table, he cleared his throat. 'You think you're so clever, don't yer? But I've got you well and truly sussed. I used to think you were a top geezer till I found out the truth.'

The white lump of gum being mashed in Mickey's open mouth had Ray shifting in his seat. It grated his nerves. He'd been within a hair's breadth of yanking it out and plugging it forcibly up the bloke's nose, when a woman's ear-splitting cackle broke his thoughts. He'd had it with these stupid guessing games. Standing up from his chair he went to walk away.

'Wait up pop, or should I say Dad?' Mickey braced himself for the fall-out.

'What the fuck are you on about?' Ray dragged his chair back across the wooden boards and sat back down.

'Thought that might get your attention.' His eyes bored into Ray's. 'You doing the business with my tart of a mother is what I'm on about. Heard her telling that vicar bloke, dying confession and all that. Didn't take long to work it out, what with you always sniffing round. Uncle fucking Ray. Nice one. Who came up with that? You? John was your pal and you did the dirty on him. Shagged his missis behind his back.'

Ray quelled the need to laugh. 'You've no idea what you're talking about, and if you think I've nothing better to do than sit here and listen to you preach about morals,' he shook his head. 'I'll tell you this much: you're right, John, Jane and myself had been close friends since school, and sure, back then I fancied Jane. I'd have been some kind of numbskull not to. The girl was a looker and I'm not ashamed to admit, that when she did that pouting thing with those candy pink lips, us boys dive-bombed into the bogs to sort ourselves out. At the end of the day, she chose John and broke a lot of hearts. Disappointed? Of course I was, but I'd never do the dirty on a mate. Now, you're seriously on the wrong track, so best you drop this bullshit before we both say things we regret.'

'The truth will out. Ain't that what they say?' Mickey sniggered. 'Guess your old lady didn't rate you as a dad either, her carting your kid off to America like she did.' Mickey's upper body pushed forward as his fingertips chiselled into the table edge. 'So, what now, Dad? You turning your back on me too? Me being blood and all.'

Ray slapped his palms forcibly on the table, becoming the focus of the room. His hands were up in a flash, signalling an apology to the officers moving fast in his direction. 'You are one deluded fuck. Where you get these crazy ideas from is anyone's guess. You're not right in the head, pal. Not right at all.' His stomach muscles clenched as the burn of acid swirled in his gut and pushed up into his chest.

'A chip off the old block then,' Mickey laughed, mockingly.

Ray took a breath before his words ripped into Mickey's pretty boy features. 'Get it in to your thick skull once and for all. You are not my son. Not now. Not ever. Your old man took off before you were born, doing himself the biggest fucking favour in my opinion.' Ray hadn't meant to blurt it out like that. He had wanted to be upfront with Mickey long before now but the right time never presented itself. Until recently it was not his truth to tell. Now, with both John and Jane gone, the cock-sure pillock staring back at him needed putting straight, if he was to stand a chance of sorting out his head and his life.

'Lying through your teeth comes easy, don't it? Wouldn't do your reputation much cop if people knew the real you,' spouted Mickey.

'I don't give a monkey's arse about what people think of me. All these years you've swanned around sticking two fingers up at the world. Anyone who's tried to help you has had it thrown back in their face. Without John and Jane stepping in, bringing you up as their own, you'd have been stuck in Barnardo's or some such place. You've been spoon fed all your miserable fucking life. Others have gone without for you. You ungrateful little git.'

Mickey's bravado dissolved faster than pissed on snow. He shook his head in disbelief, trying to dislodge Ray's words, stop them taking root. 'You're a lying sod. Just trying to get me back cos I torched your sodding lock-up. And as for Jane, your lovely fucking Jane, psycho doesn't come close! The devious bitch hated me, laid into me on the sly. A waste of space she called me; a snivelling piece of shit basking in the shadow of her golden boy, Luke. Any idea what that does to a kid? Have you? Have you?'

Ray's shoulder's sagged, as a sensation of icy fingers ripped into his chest wall and tightened around his lungs.

'What? Think I'm making it up?' Mickey shouted. 'Got the scars to prove it, pal.' Springing up from his chair, he began to remove his top, when a guard quickly intervened, putting an end to the free show.

'You either calm it down now, Loughty, or you're out of here.'

Mickey parked his backside and gained control of his emotions. 'Oh, I was grateful Ray, for every fucking minute she was out of the house.'

Ray's thoughts moved faster than a whippet round the track. *Surely if something untoward was happening with the kid, I'd have known, seen the signs?*

Presently Ray spoke. 'Whatever's gone on in the past, I hope for your sake you can bury it and make something of your life. I'm not pressing charges and the witness has backed out, changed his statement. There's nothing to implicate you. I must be the biggest mug going, but the lost gear is replaceable. Had someone been hurt, it would have been a different matter altogether.'

Mickey's sheepish demeanour showed him up for what he was; a boy desperate to fill man-size boots. 'How come I'm still tucked up here then?'

'You'll be out soon enough.'

Mickey reached out a hand. 'No, hang on a minute. Wait up. You can't leave it like this...'

The kid was struggling, Ray could see that, but rushed explanations were never a good fix. He'd already said far more than he intended. Pulling the wallet from his inside pocket, he eased out a dog-eared black and white photo and slid it across. He'd carried it with him for twenty odd years. 'I was given this to pass on when the time was right. I think that time is now. I hope it'll give you the strength to get yourself sorted. Get in touch when you're out. This lovely lady was your mother, Lily.'

The photo lay face down on the table, covered by Mickey's shaking hand. His heart flickered, similar to the time he smoked his first joint and promptly threw up. He was afraid to look. Ray's words rang loud in his ears time and again. His whole life had been a series of lies. He turned his palm side-on. His vision blurring as he struggled to read the message scrawled on the back. *For Mickey, my world. Now and forever. Mummy xx.*

He flipped the photo over, prompting quick-fire sobs to bounce quietly off his stomach wall. A beautiful young woman stared up at him, with a tiny bundle cradled in her arms. 'Lily.' The word drifted from his mouth on a gentle breath. 'My Mum.' He marvelled at the mass of fine corkscrew curls tumbling down her back, before his gaze came to rest on her eyes. For the first time in his life, he could see himself in someone else. There had been a time when he belonged after all.

'But how come?' He looked up. His eyes darting every which way. The room had partially cleared. Ray had left, slipped out, while Mickey was otherwise engaged.

Chapter 33

Ruby peered time and again at the young girl standing by the wall of the East Street Mission Hall. From their regular pitch she could just about see the building a few hundred yards away. She fancied she saw a resemblance to Daisy in most fair-haired girls of a similar age. Heaven knows how often she'd called out, only to have her hopes dashed. Fears for her sister's safety gnawed away at her. Snatches of conversation she'd had with Sal in the Cafe that very morning jumped in and out of her thoughts. *It's not that I've given up on finding my mum, Sal,* she'd said. *But Daisy's just a kid, and she's out there on her own. Anything could happen. She must be scared stiff, poor little thing.*

But you don't know that for sure, lovey, about her being on her own I mean. So no use getting in a stew about it. Look, I know it's hard, but something will turn up.

Ruby knew instantly from Sal's expression that the woman struggled to hide her true feelings. Her concern was obvious from the moment Ruby had hinted at the sordid palaver with their so-called uncle.

What's to say that Daisy isn't with your mother this very minute? Did you think of that?

Maybe Sal was right? If she could hold onto that thought it might block all the other stuff worming its way through.

The girl remained in the same position, every inch, a dishevelled doll left behind by a careless shopper. Her dark, unbuttoned cardigan, stretched and doubled across her chest, was held fast by folded arms. For the most part she stared at the ground, showing no interest in those passing by. She stood alone, unquestioned, a little dot in a frantic world eager to lighten its purses. She was waiting, Ruby surmised, for nightfall, when she would slink away into the shadows.

Moving constantly back and forth within the short space allotted, Ruby could not settle the edginess consuming her. She bagged up customer purchases and took their money without the usual small talk. What was taking him so long? It seemed an age before Ray finally showed his face. How long does it take to down a couple of rolls for heaven's sake? With her takings belt already untied, she handed it to over before yanking her skinny-rib jumper back down to hip level.

'In a hurry are we?'

'You could say that.'

'Shoot off and get yourself something then and don't take all day about it.'

Ruby didn't rise to the bait. She refused to waste precious minutes arguing the toss over agreed breaks, knowing full well that whatever she said would likely antagonise him. Although he had softened towards her in past weeks, showed a humane side which surprised her, he was still the boss and writing a new rule book every day was his prerogative. As much as it irked her, she decided to play along. Better that than endure the prolonged silences that reigned after a petty squabble.

By the time Ruby reached the hall, the girl had gone; simply vanished, as though swallowed up by the thickening fog. Had she imagined her there? Turning to leave, she noticed the blue painted door, left slightly ajar. She eased it back further, a fraction at a time. Its creaking hinges reverberated through the hall. She peered in, praying there'd be no ministering angel waiting to nab her. The girl she'd seen earlier sat at the far end in front of the makeshift altar. Her shoulders rounded, as though the weight of silence was too much to bear. Creeping inside, Ruby pushed the door to and stood on the welcome mat, deciding how best to approach her. The last thing she wanted was to frighten the poor thing.

Presently, realising that she was no longer alone, the girl's head lifted. In slow motion, she stood up and moved into the aisle, fiddling nervously with the edges of her cardigan. Her grubby socks had concertinaed around her ankles.

Ruby clapped a hand to her mouth. Her heart soared. She threw out her arms and the sisters raced towards each other, neither fully believing the evidence of their own eyes. With arms tight around each other, their faces touched, cheek to cheek, as their tears merged. They stood alone in the eerie stillness of the mission. A place that had been their Sunday school; back when days were graded in measures of fun, and the only cloud to dampen their spirits came in a bottle labelled 'Nit Lotion.' There was no immediate exchange of words, or whooping with joy. They stood as one. Whole again. Cocooned in love.

Their favourite hymn, *All things Bright and Beautiful*, played out in Ruby's head. The happy tune tingled on her lips as a soft, broken hum pushed its way through. They would sing that song at Sunday meetings as though their lives depended on it. Louder and louder, their voices would rise in unison with smiles so big, so infectious, that the whole ensemble had no choice but to mirror their happiness.

Ruby stroked away the dampness from her sister's face. 'Everything will be OK from now on. I promise.'

'I thought you were them coming in to take me away again.' She sniffled.

Ruby's voice rose with concern. 'Who?'

'The welfare people. They stuck me in a home, miles from anywhere. But I didn't like it so I left.' Feeling safe at last with her big sister to cling to, she wanted to share her moment of daring. Her words rushed out like gobstoppers from a torn bag. 'The girls in me room were fast asleep, so I climbed out the window and hid behind the trees. The garden was bigger than a park!' Her eyes, saucer wide, as she waited for her sister's reaction.

'How did you find your way here then?'

'On the buses, silly.'

'But where'd the money come from? You didn't pinch it did you?'

'Nope. I wouldn't do that. I had some already.' Her cheeks lifted, presenting that happy cherubic face that Ruby had missed so much. 'Oh, and I've got a secret too,' she remembered, standing proud as a peacock.

Fear walked its clammy fingers down Ruby's back.

'I put rose thorns in Uncle Tom's bed.'

Ruby's mouth gaped in disbelief. 'You never did?'

With a smile that reached from ear to ear, Daisy's head rocked slowly up and down. 'Yep. I picked a whole load of 'em one day after he'd left for work.'

Ruby's hand gripped a chair back. There could only be one question, which now hung precariously on the tip of her tongue. Dare she even ask, throw it out there and hope for the best. Finally, the word crept out of its own volition. 'Why?'

'Huh. Like you don't already know!' Daisy tut-tutted. 'Cos he's the worst ever old moaner in the world, that's why. So, I gave him something proper to moan about.' She grinned. 'Did I do good or not then?'

Her words kick-started Ruby's breathing. 'That's the best and funniest news I've heard in ages. Remind me not to mess with you anytime soon.' The girls' laughter rebounded off the walls, and the lucky stars that people gave thanks to, touched Ruby's world for the first time.

216

Closing the door behind them, she took Daisy by the hand and led her through the market to the Cafe. 'Let's get you something to eat. I guess you're starving as usual.'

'I had cakes for breakfast.'

Ruby, about to ask how she'd paid for them, quickly decided against it.

'D'you know where Mum is?' Daisy asked.

'Not yet, but she's around here somewhere, so don't go getting upset. You'll have to put up with me for the time being, as I'm never letting you out of my sight again.' Ruby's hand tightened around Daisy's. She had made promises that she knew she'd struggle to keep, but keep them she would, whatever the cost. She would run it by Sal. The woman had answers for most things. She would know what to do.

The mid-day rush hour had petered out by the time the sisters arrived at the Cafe. Sal was not in her usual place behind the counter. Ruby checked the alcove area before calling across to Pam, busily stacking crockery on the vacated tables. Pam flicked her head in the direction of the yard and continued with her task.

Chapter 34

Hearing the door open behind her, Sal shifted her bottom and slunk back further into the chair she'd dragged from the dining area. Without turning a hair, she said, 'Whatever it is you'll just have to deal with it. I'm whacked.' She sighed with such ferocity that her lips puckered and trembled like a worn-out beach donkey. The girls burst out laughing. 'What the hell?' Sal's feet dropped down from the upturned bucket that she'd used as a footrest, and she levered herself up. She rested a hand on Ruby's shoulder. 'It's all right yous laughing, but my poor feet feel like they've been scalded. Think I'm getting too old for this lark.'

'Give over, Sal.' Ruby chuckled. 'Women your age are like matured brandy: full bodied and something else along those lines, according to me dad.'

'Sensible man, your dad.' Sal straightened up. 'Maybe there's hope for me yet? Anyhow, what're you two doing here? And who's this young lady?' Daisy was too busy starring at the big toes poking through Sal's stockings to pay much attention.

'It's Daisy, me sister. You'll never guess, but I found her in the mission up the road.' Her eyes sparkled as she spoke. 'Nearly died of shock when I saw her. Thing is,' she paused. 'I should be back on the stall by now, but I'm scared to leave her on her own in case she disappears again.' She linked her fingers with Daisy's and pulled her closer. 'Thought you might be able to suggest something?'

Sal's mind emptied of all but one thought: Ray, and the ructions that would undoubtedly kick off. She was overjoyed that the sisters had found each other, but what to do about the situation was another matter entirely. Sal had always been a firm believer in things happening for a reason. The girls had landed on her doorstep, no one else's. It would be up to her to sort the mess out; and for that she would need time.

She looked at the two of them standing there, willing her to come up with a solution. How could she tell them that she didn't have one? Looking away, she slipped her feet back into her shoes. Although the little girl had put on a brave face, it didn't hide the fear emanating from her eyes. Knowing what the poor mite might have been through had been bad enough, but to see her there, in all her smallness, made it all the more painful somehow. She would see them right. Meanwhile, she'd don her thinking cap and try to scratch a plan together.

'Well, there's not much left in the way of dinners but I reckon I could rustle up some bangers and chips, girls. Sound good or what?' She locked eyes with Ruby; silently imploring her to jump at the idea, to give herself the time to work things through.

'Thanks, Sal. I'm starved. D'you need a hand?'

'No, you go through and grab a seat. I'll see to it.'

Daisy gave Sal's elbow a gentle tap. 'There were currant buns on the side when we came in. Could we have one for afters?'

Ruby gave her sister a discreet nudge.

'Please,' she added, remembering her manners.

Sal stooped down to Daisy's level. 'Afters indeed. Well, there's no flies on you that's for sure.' She tweaked the girl's nose. 'You can take your pick, but only when you've finished up the chips. Deal?'

'I love chips,' smiled Daisy, who went and sat with Ruby by the drooping triffid along the back wall.

*

Sal kept her distance while the girls caught up with past events. It warmed her to see Ruby step into a motherly role, as naturally as taking breath. She hadn't realised before now, but Ruby had roused in her those same protective feelings. They'd crept in, silent as the night and filled a void in her life which, up until that point, she was blissfully unaware of. She had fooled herself into thinking that Ruby had been the one in need. Suddenly, it all became clear. How had she not seen it before? The girl had given her purpose amid the daily commotion that she had mistakenly considered to be a full life. The boot was truly on the other foot, and she had been nothing short of a dimwit not to have cottoned on sooner.

Sal screamed out as the sausage skins burst and showered her in hot fat. Ruby rushed to the kitchen. 'You OK?'

'Yes, duck. It's me own fault for not concentrating. Now look, I've cremated your poor bangers.' Sal wiped the spots of grease from her arms onto a nearby towel as Ruby made a move back towards her sister.

'Here, just a minute,' Sal gestured.

As Ruby stepped closer, Sal planted a kiss on the girl's forehead. 'What's that for?' she asked.

'Because,' smiled Sal. 'Just because.'

*

Presently, with bellies filled to groaning, the girls pushed their empty plates to the tables edge. Bubbles from Daisy's Fanta erupted in a loud burp. Ruby suppressed a giggle. Avoiding eye contact with the old dears who stared disapprovingly from their corner seats,

220

she flicked Daisy's thigh beneath the table. 'What's that for? Burping? Me teacher says that in some countries it means I'm being polite.' she added, chuffed with the opportunity to air her knowledge.

Ruby kept her voice low. 'Well, it doesn't here. It means uncouth.' Her voice was breaking up. She eased her chair back ready to dash out to the yard before she made a spectacle of herself.

'That you being posh?' asked Daisy.

Ruby raised her eyebrows at the very idea but remained tight-lipped.

'What's uncouth then?'

'You,' she relented. 'You sound like an old drunk from the bomb-site.'

Daisy pulled back. 'I sodding well don't. 'Sides, everyone knows that drunks are men. Smarty pants.'

'There's always a first!' blurted Ruby before fleeing the room with Daisy chasing behind.

The girls huddled together outside the back door; tears of laughter dried on the heat from their faces. 'I've missed you so much,' said Ruby.

The door opened and Sal joined them. 'Listen up my lovelies. I've squared it with Ray. Told him you're not feeling too good, Ruby, and that I've sent you home. So, don't be doing a highland fling when we get back and drop me in it. You got your key?' Ruby checked the side pocket of her trousers and nodded. 'Best you keep out the way this evening while I sort things with his nibs. You'll have to top and tail for the time being.' Sal unlocked the back gate. 'Better if you go this way and cut through.'

'Thanks, Sal. Hope we didn't get you in any bother?'

'You worry too much for a young 'un. Just like your mother. Be off with you.'

Daisy laughed with excitement, part skipping and part dragging Ruby along the street. 'We're staying together, sharing a bed again just like before. I love Sal,' she sang out, her voice bouncing between the neat rows of terraced houses.

With her sister back where she belonged, Ruby could not have been happier. Sal was right though. She did worry and with good reason. In a few hours' time everything could change. Ray's reaction would decide their fate. There was no point in upsetting Daisy with a fistful of maybes. She would keep schtum and deal with the consequences later, whatever they might be.

*

It was close on eight when Ray eventually arrived home. His dinner, left warming in the oven, had dried out and cemented itself to the plate. With the plate now balanced on his lap, he chiselled away at the slab of liver with his knife, popping a bite-size piece into his mouth.

'Blimey, girl, it's like a slab of cement.'

'Ah, and I wonder why that is?' Sal interrupted jocularly, not wishing to antagonise him before sharing her news about Daisy. 'Oh, give it here, and I'll run it under the tap,' she joked. 'That'll soften it up.'

'You taking the biscuit?'

Before Sal could reply, a bout of giggling from upstairs had Ray glaring at her for answers.

'Ruby's got her little mate up there. The girl has never laughed so much, Ray. You should've heard them earlier, they had me in stitches.'

'What mate? Didn't know she had one?'

'Well, no, actually, it's her little sister. Now, before you blow a fuse, I've already said she can share Ruby's bed for the time being.'

'You did what?' Ray's plate crashed down on the coffee table.

The door opened unexpectedly, catching them both unawares. Daisy appeared in the opening, her chin down and imploring blue eyes fixed on Ray. Several seconds passed. No one moved. No one spoke. His head, just minutes before, close to bursting with fiery objections, emptied. Something deep inside him physically tugged. He felt it, like a stopper released, and his pent-up anger swiftly melted away. 'What the f...' Rather than seeing a nipper in a grubby frock as an irritant, sent by God's knows who to drive him barmy, he saw instead, someone's daughter. A child, misplaced. Lost. Stolen even, just as his had been.

The girl momentarily stood still as a portrait; a four foot nothing subject caught in an oversized frame. He watched her. Watched her mouth move, a flicker at a time, until her full-on beam lit up the whole damn room.

'Well move yourself if you're coming in. And shut the door. You're causing a draught.'

Daisy eyed up the discarded dinner. 'That liver?'

'It was, before it got turned into shoe leather,' Ray answered.

Sal dismissed his taunt. She tittered, knowing what to expect from Daisy. She'd already experienced the girl's ravenous appetite.

'Don't you want it?' asked Daisy. 'Me dad says liver's good for yer. It turns your blood to iron. Did you know that?'

Ray shook his head, while snatching up the newspaper from the armrest. 'Can't say I did.'

'Ha ha, well now you do. So, cos I've learned you about blood, I think it's a fair swap if I get to finish the liver. Do we have a deal?' She poked her thumb in the air, waiting for Ray to do the same.

Totally mystified by this whirlwind of a girl, Ray copied her gesture and raised his thumb. 'I guess we do,' he said, hiding his grin behind the local headlines. 'So yeah, get on with it then. Fill your boots.'

Chapter 35

'For goodness sake,' grumbled Sal from the Cafe kitchen, when an overstocked shelf suddenly collapsed. 'As if I haven't enough to contend with.' The length of wood, now hanging precariously by one remaining screw, had her scared that it would fall down altogether and do someone a damage. She turned to Ruby. 'Get Ray for me, there's a love. Tell him it's urgent.'

Ruby settled Daisy on a stool in the alcove, out of view and harm's way. With a colouring book laid flat on a tea tray and balanced on Daisy's lap, Ruby handed her a glass jar half filled with an assortment of coloured pencil nubs left behind some weeks before.

'Don't go getting in Sal's way. I'll be back as soon as I can.'

'But I want to come too.'

'It'll be quicker if I go myself, but if you promise to stay put, I'll fetch you back a doughnut. How's that?'

'You best get going then, cos me belly's already gurgling.'

Sal called out as Ruby reached the door. 'And don't take no for an answer.'

Luca was in his element, poncing about like a prize bull, sweet talking the ladies. Ruby never tired of watching him. The speed at which purses, handbags, and the occasional phone number leapt off the stall held her spellbound. The man was a wizard. Ray had definitely struck gold when he hired Luca, and well he knew it.

You women are suckers for a winning smile and a dollop of charm-laced drivel, Ray had answered once, after Ruby commented on Luca's magnetic draw. Ruby's comeback had been instant: *Pity you missed the queue when those qualities were handed out?*

You cheeky little mare! I'll give you bloody qualities, he'd said, swiping her around the head with his newspaper.

The market was packed solid. Ruby tried and failed to manoeuvre herself around to the back of the stall. With no sign of Ray, she needed to get closer in order to speak with Luca. The female customers had other ideas and quickly closed ranks. Banding together, they erected an impenetrable wall. They weren't about to allow an interloper, especially some slip of a girl to get first dibs. Standing on tip-toes, Ruby retrieved the last fluff-covered cough candy from her pocket and threw it at Luca. With arms waving in an agitated fashion, she hollered. 'Over here!'

Finally, Luca looked up.

'Where's Ray?' she mouthed.

With his dazzling pearly whites permanently on show, Luca pointed towards The Masons pub and quickly returned to his near mutinous fan-club.

Moving with the crowds, Ruby was within yards of the pub when the door opened. Ray stepped out, deep in conversation with the person following behind. As both men stepped onto the pavement, Ruby stopped dead. People directly behind banged into her, tutting, shoving and cursing. She remained fixated on the shorter man. Her distant memory placed her in a hospital side room. A white room, like the heaven she'd seen portrayed on bookmarks at Sunday school. She was seven years old and clinging to her mother's hand. They'd stepped slowly towards a bed, centred in the room. Ruby drew back; their arms stretched like rope between them. Her small voice, barely trickled out. *Is Daddy an angel now?* She'd asked.

Her mother had ruffled her hair. *No darling. He's just sleeping. Come and see.*

Ruby edged closer, her grip tightening with each tiny, noiseless step. He didn't look like her dad. The chunky plastic mask hid most of his face, his smile. She tensed in readiness. Any minute now he would surprise her. He'd spring up, shout Boo, make her jump and scream and laugh till her belly hurt. He often played that joke while pretending to sleep in the fireside chair. Feeling braver, Ruby noticed the little clump of hair sticking out above his ear. She licked her fingers and smoothed the strands back into place. His eyelids flickered before slowly opening. She watched for the little crinkles to appear at the edges. And there they were! She had known then that he was smiling; that everything would be okay. She blinked away the memory.

Ruby threw herself into her father's arms with such force that Charlie's cap went sailing to the ground. Ray picked it up, bashed it against his leg to remove the dirt, and handed it back. 'Ease up, girl. You lost your mind or what? You'll have the poor man over in a minute.'

With their arms locked tight around each other, Charlie and Ruby laughed and cried at the same time.

'Let us in on it then,' said Ray. 'Or do I start charging the audience you've just drummed up?'

'This is Ruby, my girl. The one I was telling you about.'

'Well blow me down. I had no idea mate.' He flicked his head towards Ruby. 'You'll be telling me next you've more like this little madam tucked away?'

Ruby understood Ray's probing. He was testing the water: protecting his mate, her father. Two shocks in one day could prove one too many. Ruby liked him all the more for his concern.

Charlie's chest expanded. With his arm locked around Ruby, he spoke with pride. 'She's one of five.'

'Five! Strewth! No wonder I haven't seen you in years. I mean, I know you re-married, but Jesus, Chas, you'd have been wiser to stay aboard ship.'

Ruby laughed along with the men, but the questions were already piling up. She knew her father had been a merchant seaman. She had vague memories of her mum talking about the quayside at Deptford, but learning of her father's previous marriage had thrown her completely. She had no idea. It had never been mentioned. Not once. Unlike her mother's short marriage to a wartime Airforce pilot. It felt surreal to imagine her father also in another life: a life before Kate, a life before herself and siblings. Her questions would have to wait. Her father was here, with her. She refused to allow any child-like imaginings to spoil what was turning into the best day ever.

Charlie spoke about Daisy. 'We've searched everywhere: followed her footsteps from the Brinton flat to a kid's home in Sidcup. She's like a mini-Houdini that one. Trouble is, the girl's got many friends it's hard to keep track, but the police have been diamonds and reckon they'll have her home soon.'

'We?' said Ruby.

'Me and your mum, girl. We finally managed to get ourselves a flat off Tabard Street, down at the Borough. All we need now is our family back to fill the beds.' He gave her hand a squeeze.

Ray forced a cough and glanced over at the Cafe; his cue instantly picked up by Ruby.

'Listen mate, come and grab a bite to eat. I'll drag a couple of chairs out back. It's a damn sight quieter there. You've clearly got a lot of catching up to do.' Ruby mouthed a thank you and stuck close to her father as they weaved through the crowds, while Ray followed closely behind.

Ruby peered over her shoulder. 'I didn't know you were mates with me dad,' she said, her eyes narrowing.

'Give us a break. Do I look like some overfed biddy, flogging fortunes and heather?' He chuckled heartily. 'I can turn a hand to most things, right enough, but mind reading?' He scoffed. 'A load of old rubbish.'

Her face dropped. 'No need to make fun of me.'

Upsetting the girl had never been his intention. 'Oh, come on, lighten up. Any other time you'd have laughed loudest at my wisecrack.' Ray nudged Charlie. 'Teenagers eh. What a bloody minefield. One wrong move and the whole thing blows. Kaboom!' Ray attempted to smooth the ripple before it powered up and drowned the lot of them. He never considered himself an authority on women, but he did know that they analysed the shit out of everything: good, bad or indifferent, it made no odds. The girl would feed off his comment for days if he didn't make things right.

'We go back a long way, me and your dad. Bit of sparring down The Becket, rubbing shoulders with the best of 'em. Your old dad was a bit nifty on the pitch too. We both were. Had our pipe dream of playing for Millwall scuppered. Missed the try-outs. Remember that, Chas?'

'Bloody hell, Ray, you're going back some.'

'Got drunk as lords instead and woke up in a stinking railway carriage other end of the country.'

Charlie nodded. 'Them were the days alright. Couldn't do it now. It'll just about finish me off.'

Ruby hadn't meant to be so tetchy, but the whole situation seemed unreal. Details about her father's past, that might otherwise have never come to light, were having a huge impact on her. How a friendship had even developed between her father and Ray was

229

unimaginable. The pair were as different as night and day.

'Anyway, Chas, I'd do a runner while you can. She's a right bossy mare this one,' he joked. 'I should know; she works for me.'

'You having a laugh?'

'No mate. Straight up. Thinks she runs the show, don't you, sweetheart? I could tell you stories that would that would turn your hair...'

Ruby landed a playful slap to his upper arm. 'Give over. You're really not funny.'

'See what I have to put up with, Chas? The sooner she's off me hands, the faster I can ditch the aspirin.'

Ruby noticed that Ray's features had definitely softened. The way he laughed and acted the goat came across as surprisingly natural, unlike past efforts, which were mostly forced and overblown. When Sal had spoken all those weeks ago about a different side to Ray, Ruby dismissed it as wishful thinking. She now realised, perhaps for the first time, that hidden behind that grumpy shell, a humorous soul was chipping away, desperately trying to break through. A person with a heart who actually cared and whom she would miss very much if she decided to return to her family.

Chapter 36

As they approached the Cafe door, Ray and Ruby stood back, allowing Charlie to take the lead. Once inside, the men dragged chairs out to the yard, while Ruby spoke with Sal at the counter. 'That's my Dad with Ray,' she gushed. 'They know each other. Can you believe it? You wait till he sees Daisy. I bet he'll wet himself.'

Sal's complexion suddenly paled. 'Good Lord, I hope he doesn't.'

On finding the alcove empty, Ruby returned to the counter. 'So where's my sister hiding out?'

'She got bored, bless her, so she's skipping in the yard. Pam found a length of old washing line in the outbuilding.'

'Oh no,' cried Ruby, deflated. She wanted to be there for the reunion. She dashed out only to rush back in again. 'She's not there, Sal!'

'She was a while ago when I nipped to the lav,' a customer butted in. 'Could be she's gone off with that chap she was talking to.'

Ruby panicked. 'What chap? What did he look like?'

'Snazzy dresser. Young. Friendly sort, you know? I wouldn't worry though. The girl seemed happy enough.' Ruby gasped. 'I'm sure he mentioned the park?' the customer added, gesticulating towards The Masons.

Ruby shot to the back door, called for Ray, and as quickly as her breath allowed, explained the situation.

'We're just stepping out a minute, pal,' said Ray, leaving Charlie blissfully unaware and tucking hungrily into a cheese roll that Pam had prepared. They raced to the park area.

The small grassed area, surrounded by flats and rows of houses, was blanketed with kids. With no mistaking Daisy's infectious giggling, Ruby and Ray found the missing duo, partly hidden by the only tree in the vicinity. Both were crouched down, enjoying the antics of the black and tan puppy darting from one to the other. Ruby took in the innocent display and in particular, Mickey's buoyant mood; something she had never witnessed before. Mickey sprang to his feet the moment he saw Ray striding over.

Ray's hands quickly balled into fists. 'I don't know what you're up to, sunshine, but it stops now. Right here.' He lashed out. Mickey ducked, managing to miss the punch that whizzed past his ear. He shuffled backwards.

'Hold your horses. What am I supposed to have done?' he asked. 'I brought the kid to the park to help out. She was stuck on her own, with you all caught up elsewhere. Nothing sinister, if that's what you're thinking. Listen mate, I'm trying to make amends here. Give us a break.'

'I'll give you more than a break, if I find you're playing me. How come you didn't tell Sal before sneaking off?'

'Now you hold on a minute. I did call out to Sal as it goes, but with wall-to-wall customers, there's every chance she didn't hear. What? You think I kidnapped the kid?' He gave a nervous laugh. 'You really think I'd do that?' A look of devastation crossed Mickey's face.

'What are we supposed to think? You've never cared about anyone except yourself. Why now?'

'People change. It's not unheard of." Mickey hung his head.

Ray snorted. 'Sure they do. Listen up, pal. Do us all a favour and clear off out of it.'

Tired of the shouting and with everyone ignoring her, Daisy cut in. 'Look what Mickey bought me off the man in The Lane.' With the puppy now in her arms and its head nestled beneath her chin she pleaded. 'Can I keep him, please. I promise I'll look after him.'

Not wishing to upset her sister, Ruby would leave the decision to her father, after-all, he would undoubtedly be taking Daisy home. 'We'll need to speak with Sal first,' she said, evading the question.

Ruby pulled on Ray's sleeve. 'Let's go, Ray, there's no harm done.' With Daisy still clutching the puppy and Ray reluctant to back down, Ruby turned to leave.

'Ruby promised me a doughnut, Daisy informed Ray. 'S'pect they'll all be gone by now?' She pushed out her bottom lip.

Ray steered the girl towards the gate. 'Come on sweetheart, we'll nip in the bakers.'

Mickey immediately reached for Ruby's arm. She shrugged him off.

Seeing the exchange, Ray shouted. 'Leave it be Rube. Let's go.'

'Just give me a sec.'

She never imagined she would see anything close to vulnerable in Mickey's face. Something about his manner caused her to waver. They were out in the open, she needn't feel threatened with people about. What's the worst that could happen? She asked herself. With no answer forthcoming, she faced him head on and allowed him to have his say.

'Look, you've really got the wrong idea. I honestly thought I was doing everyone a favour keeping the little one occupied. I'm trying to make up for all the - you know what I'm saying. I don't expect you to forgive me but I don't want you to be scared of me.'

His pitiful expression touched Ruby. The man looked genuinely upset.

'Give me a chance girl, my head is in a better place now, I've been a total bastard in the past. I know that and I'm not about to make excuses for the way I've treated you and everyone else, but please, believe me when I say I am truly trying to turn things around.'

Could she believe him? If nothing else, she fancied, that to walk the streets without fear as her companion, would feel similar to having wings on her feet. But could she trust his word, this man who tried to throttle her? Ray, and his gut reactions came to mind, how he'd acted on it, without fail. Ruby never understood how the gut thing worked. To her knowledge she'd never experienced it. Yet something deep inside prompted her to give him the chance he'd asked for. Some would call her a fool, and they may yet be proved right, but it was her choice to make. Her choice alone.

With Ray in close proximity, she summoned the courage to speak her thoughts. 'I really want to believe what you're saying, because I'm sick of living a life of two halves: half looking forward and half looking over my shoulder. Bet you've no idea how that feels?'

'You'd be wrong, Ruby. I know exactly, because you've just summed up my whole bloody life.'

'Sad then, that you'd put others through the same.'

Mickey shifted side-on as if to walk away. A sudden change of heart forced him back round to face Ruby. 'For what it's worth, I was in a bad way. Have been for years so the doc tells me; I just didn't realise. Funny thing is, the woman I called mum would often say, *there're more out than in*. I never knew what she meant back then. Maybe she sussed all along that I weren't right in the head?'

Mickey's whole demeanour softened. His once hardened jawline finally relaxed, as though any remnants of the anguish and misery that had dogged him, had simply melted away.

'I'm not that person anymore, Ruby. Things'll be different from now on in. I swear on my life.'

A moment's silence stretched between them. Ruby dithered as a barrage of responses crowded in. What did he expect of her? Why open up at all? 'It's good that you're being honest,' said Ruby, 'but what's going on? Why are you telling me all this? I don't understand.'

Ray's voice rolled like thunder across the park. 'Get a frigging move on, Rube. I got rigor bloody mortis setting in.'

'I best get going,' said Ruby, sprinting away. 'Hope it works out for you.'

Mickey's outstretched hand remained in position. 'Wait. Please. I need to tell you...' His words swallowed by squeals of overzealous, leapfrogging kids.

As Ruby neared the gate, she cast a quick look behind her. Her surprised look, on seeing that Mickey hadn't moved from the tree, did not go unnoticed by the man himself. His hesitant smile gave way to a mouthed, 'thanks girl.'

For what? thought Ruby. *For giving you the time of day?* Nothing made sense, not his change in attitude towards her or his completely altered character. Her mind ticked over. Ruby knew the dangers that a smile could hide. On closing the gate behind her, she walked ahead of Ray and Daisy.

'All OK?' he asked.

'Yep, everything's sorted.'

'Good. Now don't give him another thought. He won't bother you again. He's been given his marching orders.'

Daisy forced a cough. 'Does that mean we can eat now?' she asked, rocking the puppy in her arms. 'Only it could be that the doughnuts are getting stale?'

*

With the girls a few steps ahead, Ray reflected briefly on the past months. His thoughts concentrated solely on Ruby. *Any day now she'll swan off back to her family and rightly so, but damn, she'll be missed. No more back-chat! Christ, if I didn't know better, I'll think I've gone deaf!* He smiled to himself. *Get a grip.* He'd broken his one sacred rule: never become attached. He'd let the girl in, and chalked it up to the best mistake he'd ever made. She had unwittingly changed their lives, his and Sal's; added colour to their grey, regimented existence. It would be a wrench if she disappeared altogether, but with her love of the area, and a little gentle persuasion, his money was on her hanging around.

Chapter 37

Ruby had pressed her father for a description of their new home. She sensed his reluctance to share the details, so encouraged him with a playful prod.

'Well, it's far from new and it's definitely not the Ritz,' he answered, cryptically. 'But it is home, for now.' He adjusted his hold on the cardboard box housing the puppy.

As they turned into the entrance of Chaucer House, Ruby's steps faltered. She knew her father was watching her, trying to gauge her impression. The block was far more depressing than she could have imagined. Under no circumstances would she say as much. It would break him.

'There's room enough for Daisy to play out, that's for sure,' she smiled, holding tight to her sister's hand as they bypassed the remains of a burnt-out car. The sprawling ramshackle building appeared in imminent danger of collapse. Paint peeled doors offered a hint of colour behind the black iron railings fronting each landing area, where children's solemn faces peered through. It put Ruby in mind of a prison, with the addition of clothes on drooping washing lines strung along balconies, like faded misshapen bunting. The atmosphere was anything but celebratory.

'The whole caboodle is due for demolition, but in the meantime, it gives us a roof over our heads and for that we're grateful. We're all in the same boat here. I know it's not a patch on East Street, but for now it's better than nothing. We'll be re-housed soon enough. You'll see.'

Ruby opened her mouth to speak, when a brief conversation she'd had with Sal gave her reason to pause. Ruby once shared her dream of a rose covered cottage, after falling in love with an image on a chocolate box. *What would be the point?* Sal had replied. *You can't see the outside from inside!*

Ruby pulled herself up. Beyond that door they would be safe. They would be together, and something much nicer, as her father indicated, lay in wait for them just around the corner. Closing the street door behind them, Ruby's worries had all but faded.

'It's only me, Kate,' said Charlie, peering into the sitting room. 'You'll never guess what I found on my travels?'

Ruby handed Charlie her carrier bag.

Kate stood up from the sofa and smoothed out the creases in her green printed frock. She shook her head with amusement. 'Not more firewood! The coal cupboard's choc-a-block. We'll be storing it under the table at this rate.'

The door burst fully open and crashed against the wall. Fine white fragments of plaster floated down onto the lino. Ruby and Daisy's feet barely skimmed the floor as they rushed towards their mother. All three tumbled back onto the settee, a jumble of limbs amongst the laughter and tears. Little Mary, startled by the commotion, and the sound of her mother crying, abandoned her doll in the bedroom and flew to her father's side. She peered out from behind the safety of his legs.

'It's all right chicken,' he assured her. 'Those are happy tears. Nothing to fret about.'

Ruby rested her face against her mother's shoulder, inhaling the familiar scent of lavender and love. She sat bolt upright, remembering the carrier bag she'd handed to her father before bursting into the room. She quickly retrieved it and returned to her mother's side. She called for her father to join them. With trembling hands Ruby passed the small, unassuming package, that Ray had entrusted her with, to her father. Ray had kept his counsel on the contents, but given the size, Ruby's hopes had been lifted. The room seemed to hold its breath. Charlie unwrapped the wedding ring, the symbol of vows made decades ago.

As he slipped the gold band onto Kate's finger, time collapsed. Their wedding day, the laughter, the trials, all resurfaced, vivid and tangible, played out in their eyes. Delving again into the bag, Ruby, placed a larger, ribbon-tied package onto her mother's lap, and fidgeted excitedly. With the gift unwrapped, Kate stepped up to the mirror above the mantelshelf and eased the cloche hat over her fine waves. The pale blue fabric teamed with a lilac organza rose, needed little adjusting. The joy on Kate's face spoke volumes. Ruby had chosen well.

Remnants of a coal fire burned white-hot in the grate. The room had a cosy feel, provided by the soft glow from the standard lamp tucked in a corner. Ruby and her parents sat together on the brown fabric sofa, and talked long into the night while her sisters slept. The past months had been tough. The hardships, although rarely broached, showed in their eyes; their sparkle, clouded over. Ruby's heart bled. She forced herself to think of something else, anything to divert her sadness from spilling out. It would benefit no one if she broke down.

She pointed to the three flying ducks pinned high in the alcove, each positioned one behind the other. 'Blimey, Mum, those things don't half get about,' she laughed. 'I'd swear they turn up faster than buses. Didn't Nan have some too?'

Kate brightened. 'She did, and loved them every bit as much as we do. Isn't that right, Charlie?'

'Right you are, girl.' He turned to Ruby. 'They'll be worth a pretty penny down the line.'

'Yeah, if you say so. Just don't forget me when your horse comes in,' said Ruby, before kissing them goodnight. She climbed onto the top bunk, careful not to disturb Daisy and Mary sleeping below. The effects of the gift from Ray, that she'd been instructed to protect with her life, prompted a flood of emotion that she thought she'd never recover from. To watch her father, place the wedding ring back on her mother's finger, had been the most precious scene she had ever witnessed. It would remain in her memory forever, along with the knowledge that Ray, having bought the ring himself from the pawnbroker, displayed a flaw in his bolshie armour: the seams of which, Ruby decided, were held together with a sentimental thread.

The second gift, conjuring the touching image of her mother's face, reflected in the mirror, had melted Ruby's heart. The cloche hat had suited Kate perfectly, as Ruby knew it would the instant she saw it in the shop window.

Morning arrived with Daisy making grim noises in the tiny kitchen. The bottle of cow's milk, left standing in cold water overnight, had curdled. Hovering by the sink with her cereal bowl Daisy yelled, 'Mum, there's lumps on me cornflakes. Shall I see if the milkman's left some on the step?' she asked, re-filling the puppy's water dish.

Charlie waltzed into the kitchen with little Mary trailing behind. He emptied the cereal bowl into the bin. 'Be a miracle if he has. Not a problem though, as we're lucky enough to have a shop on the corner. Slip some shoes on yous two, and we'll go grab some. Your mum and Ruby will be gagging for their tea.'

Ruby and Kate sat at the drop-leaf table positioned beneath the back window. Kate left the end sections extended to help fill the otherwise empty space. The park area opposite appeared at first glance to be their own private garden. 'Blimey,' Ruby gushed. 'Not many people have a view like this.'

'Kate quietly agreed. 'Any news on our Gary?'

To save her mother's anguish, Ruby decided to hold back on news of Gary. She would come clean soon enough. 'Haven't caught up with him yet Mum, but I'm sure he's fine. I've been to his mate's place a few times, but there's been no one home. I expect they're all working, but I'll pop a note through the door with your new address.'

'I've been worried sick about you and Ellen too! When Cecelia told me you'd not been near or by, well - where've you been all this time?'

Ruby's altered version of events soon eased her mother's torment. 'Oh, and you'll never guess, Ellen's only got herself married! They've moved out to Chatham with his job, and she's doing great.'

Kate's colour faded. 'I missed my eldest daughter's wedding!'

'Oh Mum, come on, don't get upset again. It was a spur of the moment thing at the registry office. Hardly anyone knew till it was over. But she's happy, and that's the main thing. Right?'

The ruckus at the door put paid to their conversation, when the two squealing youngsters burst in, crunching their way through a handful of sherbet lemons.

Ruby placed her overnight things in her bag. 'I hate to leave so soon, but I'd promised Sal I'd help with lunches.'

'Not staying for a cuppa?' said Charlie.

'Not this time Dad. But I'll be back again before you know it.'

'Well don't disappear before I've shared my news.' He passed the milk to Ruby for safekeeping before lifting Kate clean off the ground and giving the baffled woman a quick twirl.

'Put me down, you daft bugger. Whatever's got into you?'

'I'm that excited girl. I Just bumped into a pal from my portering days. He reckons Claridge's are looking for staff; and since I know the ropes, he reckons I'm in with a chance. Hobnobbing with gentry again, Kate. Imagine that!'

'So, you'll be parting company with that threadbare waistcoat, finally?' she said.

'Ease up my love! Me and that waistcoat go way back. It'll be like ditching a mate.'

Content that things were looking up for her family, Ruby made her way to the bus stop. To have their loud, excitable plans for a brighter tomorrow, still ringing in her ears, went far beyond magical, far beyond anything she could have wished for.

Chapter 38

Ruby ignored the rattle from the letter box. She wanted to get the washing on the clothes horse before Sal got home. What kept her working beyond closing was anyone's guess. Sal was a stickler for order, everyone knew that. She'd find jobs where none existed. With the clothes draped over the narrow wooden spindles, Ruby dragged the horse into the recess by the fire. She nipped back to the kitchen and popped the kettle on the gas before heading down the passage.

The envelope on the mat had her name written in biro. She turned it over, looking for clues. She had never received a letter before. She opened the door and peered along the street. As her eyes grew accustomed to the darkness, she saw what seemed to be a small gathering crouched by the side of the fruit lorry, parked at the school gate. Presently, a cry for help sounded down the small turning. Tucking the letter into her waistband, Ruby dashed along the street: barely noticing the loose gravel biting into her bare feet.

'The wife 'ere, has already phoned for an ambulance and the police are on their way too,' said the old man as Ruby approached.

Ruby knelt beside the prone figure. The stranger's face, positioned downwards onto the road surface, remained hidden. With a slow, jerky movement he reached up for a hand and Ruby obliged; curling her fingers around his, she gave a gentle, reassuring squeeze.

'Help is on its way. They'll have you at the hospital in no time.' The elderly couple standing close by gave Ruby an encouraging nod.

The man's breathing remained shallow, laboured. Finding strength enough, he lifted his face from the road and angled it towards Ruby. His lips parted, offering the hint of a smile. Ruby held her breath. *Gappy teeth are lucky teeth*, she remembered. Blood now visibly pumped from a neck wound that Ruby had no notion of beforehand. Only now did she realise that a huge blood loss had seeped into the underside of his clothing.

Mickey's life was fast slipping away. Somehow, she managed to disguise her fear, knowing it would only escalate his. Likewise, the sobs, deep within her belly would remain trapped for as long as necessary. His narrowed eyes held her gaze. His mouth moved, yet no words carried on his faint breaths. With sirens and bells growing louder by the second, Ruby urged him to hang on. She leaned in. 'Be strong. They're just around the corner.'

Aware of his strength quickly diminishing and his struggle to speak, Ruby closed the space between them. She caught his final word, a breathy 'sorry' mere seconds before his eyes closed.

A torrent of sobs rushed out as one of the ambulance team unfurled Ruby's fingers from Mickey's hand and helped her to her feet. A police car screeched to a halt close-by.

'They came from behind the lorry,' the man informed the officer. 'There were two of 'em. Big buggers they were an' all. They dumped the knife over there,' he motioned towards a privet hedge.

After giving her personal details, Ruby stepped aside and turned towards home. The policeman questioned the couple on the victim's identity. 'Loughty,' said Ruby. 'His name was Mickey Loughty.'

A while later Sal returned home. Throwing off her coat, she dragged her aching body into the sitting room and flopped down in the armchair.

'Something's kicked off down the street, Ruby. It's crawling with coppers. Any idea what's going on?'

Ruby emerged from the kitchen with a cup of tea rattling in the saucer. Sal leapt up and grabbed the saucer before the girl scalded herself. She placed it on the coffee table. 'You're white as a snowdrop. Good grief, and there's blood all over you!'

'It's not mine,' said Ruby, bursting into tears.

Sal encouraged Ruby to sit down before she fell down. She lifted the teacup from the table and placed it to the girl's lips. 'Take sips. Don't gulp it. Sweet tea's the best thing for shock, and from the looks of it you need to down every little drop.'

Minutes later, Sal took the empty cup and placed it back on the table. She budged up closer to Ruby on the settee.

The girl was visibly calmer, her hands no longer shaking. 'He was just lying there Sal and I couldn't do anything to help him. I watched him die.'

Sal's sudden pallid complexion competed with Ruby's. She wrung her hands, almost afraid to ask the inevitable. 'Who's died, lovey?'

'Mickey. They stabbed him. He died just as the ambulance arrived.'

'They?'

'We don't know.'

'Lord above. Does Ray know? No of course he doesn't,' Sal answered herself. 'Poor man's not even home yet. I know Mickey was a law unto himself, but no one deserves to die like that, alone.'

'He didn't die alone, Sal. I was with him. He knew I was there.'

'Oh, duck, and you just a kid yourself. What an awful thing to have witnessed. Shall I ring Dr Clarkson, get something to help you sleep?'

'I'll be fine,' said Ruby, retrieving the crumpled letter from beneath her thigh. She passed the page to Sal, explaining how she'd read it several times, but, 'I just don't understand the part about my dad though.'

Ruby.

I'm not much cop at this letter writing lark, so I'm asking, please don't lob it in the bin before hearing me out. I've been seeing a shrink these past weeks. He's telling me that me wirings up the creek. No surprises there then. He's shovelling pills down my neck like no one's business, just to get me sorted. He's chuffed that they're working. Downside is I wake up every day knowing what a total dickhead I've been.

I've done some bad stuff. Fucked up big time, I know that. The way I've treated you and others, but especially you, don't bear thinking about, but I have been thinking about it, a lot. I wanna put things right, and I will, just as I'd said at the park. I'm sorry for what I put you through. I can't undo things, but I want you to know that I'd rather cut me own throat than hurt you again. I've decided to get out of Walworth, for good. Start again somewhere new. Good riddance to bad rubbish, I'm guessing that's what you're thinking, and I wouldn't blame you.

My head is full of 'what ifs' about your dad. He came to see me in Brixton. He's a good bloke. I really missed out there. Who knows, maybe in a different life me and you could have been mates! I didn't spell it out about our run-ins. I felt too ashamed, and as selfish as it is, I didn't want another person hating me. Word is that you're turning into a right gobby cow haha, joke. At least it shows you've got a backbone, more than I've ever had. That's it. That's me about done. Time to get on with your life now. Make it a good one.

Mickey

'My giddy aunt. What a sad state of affairs, and with him about to turn his life around too! Sounds like he's caused you more bother than you've let on?'

'We didn't like each other, that's all.' Ruby could see no point in dragging up what had gone before. It would change nothing and besides, something far more pressing had come to light.

'But it says right here,' she rattled the page, 'that he'd hurt you!'

'With words, Sal. Sometimes they hurt more than a slap.'

Although doubting the girl's explanation, Sal let it go. 'I'd no idea that Mickey and your father were even connected?'

Ruby shrugged. 'That's the thing, Sal, neither did I.'

Chapter 39

Ruby spent her first Sunday morning off work, turning rope for her younger sisters and their friends from the block. 'Nothing wears them out, Mum,' exclaimed Ruby, escaping into the kitchen and shaking life back into her arm.

'Tell me about it!' said Kate, her face bright with memories. 'You were worse still at their ages. I'd have had an easier time getting teeth pulled than getting you back indoors.'

Kate agitated the sink full of washing. Her thin, reddened hands created an overflow of soapsuds which saturated the front of her pinny.

'Shall I hang on a bit? Help you with this lot?'

'No need,' called Charlie from the other room. 'I'm an expert in the art of pegging out.'

'Best you get off, love, said Kate. 'I'm almost done here.'

Daisy and Mary charged into the kitchen, scooped up handfuls of foam and blew the bubbles up into the air. 'We're starving, mum,' bellowed Daisy, as though the whole world had suddenly gone deaf. 'Is it dinner time yet?'

Ruby hugged each of her family in turn before repeating the process. 'Can I borrow dad for a while?' she asked. 'Won't keep him long. Need some advice, that's all.'

'Course you can. You might want to nip to the park though. You'll get no peace here with these Minnie

Minxes. Oh, and make sure to give my thanks to Sal. I'm indebted to that woman, I really am.'

Charlie crouched in the open doorway to tie his shoe laces. A quizzical expression settled on his face.

It was close to lunchtime when Charlie and Ruby settled on a bench in Tabard Park. She had tossed and turned the previous night searching for the best way to broach the subject of his first wife. He may well say, albeit in a kindly manner, that it was none of her business. And that, she knew, would be the end of it. For the first time in sixteen years, she realised that her parents were individuals: people who started out quite separate from herself. People with their own past. It had never occurred to her during those younger years that they had been anything other than mum and dad.

There was much she didn't know, so many questions that seemed foolish now to even consider asking. Did her father have a favourite colour? Did her mother prefer a particular flower? She should have known these things already. Surely? The fact that she'd never taken time to find out bothered her greatly. But in her own defence she reminded herself that kids were a self-absorbed breed, whose main priorities were food and friends. She still had time to play catch-up. She would make amends: become a better daughter.

Ever since Ray had mentioned her father's first wife, Ruby was intrigued to know more. It was a sensitive subject, and although keen for details, she would never bring it up in her mother's presence.

'Come on then, out with it,' said Charlie. 'What's on your mind?'

Ruby fussed with her hair, winding it into a ringlet before releasing it and starting over. 'I wanted to ask about your first wife, if that's okay?' She paused, waiting for his reaction. 'Ray mentioned her, remember?' she added.

Charlie appeared suddenly fascinated by the clouds gathering overhead. Each second that passed had Ruby wishing she could withdraw her question in favour of one less painful.

'Many things get pushed so far back in the memory, that it takes your breath when they resurface.'

Ruby gripped his hand. 'Can we forget I asked?' Her eyes rolled in disbelief at her own child-like stupidity.

Charlie patted her knee. 'It's all right, love. Just took me by surprise, that's all.'

'Listen, Dad, we can talk about it another time. It doesn't have to be now.'

Charlie shifted position, and faced her. 'It was a different world back then, girl. Folk held back from sharing their grief; stiff upper lip and all that. The war had not long ended. Everyone suffered in one way or another. You coped best way you could; got on with it basically. What other choice did we have?' Ruby had no answer for him, so planted a kiss on his cheek instead.

'Lily was a Clapham girl, a petite thing with a mass of copper-coloured curls. On a good day her hair would make a judge jealous. Mostly though, the poor girl looked as if she'd passed through a wind tunnel.' He chuckled heartily at the memory. 'She'd be first to tell you what a nightmare it was. We were at Battersea Park, me and a few mates, when I spotted her sat under a tree with a nipper. The little lad, Michael, was out for the count, his head resting in her lap. I wandered over and we got chatting. An hour or so later me mates disappeared and left us to it.'

His shoulders dipped enough for Ruby to notice. She sat there in the silence, riddled with guilt and desperate to change the subject. But she knew, whatever she said now would not turn things around. She had taken her father back to a place steeped in sadness, and for that she would never forgive herself. She apologised, sheepishly.

'Don't be silly,' said Charlie. 'Not all memories have bells and whistles attached. but that doesn't mean we erase the ones we don't like: we just draw on them less often. All experiences, good, bad or otherwise make us the people we are today.' He suddenly perked up. 'And don't you go forgetting it neither.'

Ruby looped her arm through his and snuggled closer.

'Now, where was I? It turned out that Lily was a single mum. They were difficult times for girls in that situation. Not that it was her fault, mind! Her intended did a runner first chance he got. She had no family to support her. Anyway, I courted Lily and we married soon after. A year later we had a son. Sadly, Lily died from complications after the birth and our son, well, I lost him a couple of months later.'

Ruby's mouth dropped open. Not for a second did she expect such a tragic outcome. The one time she truly wanted to say something of value, something comforting, she found herself lost for words.

Charlie straightened up, opened his tobacco tin and took out a ready-made roll-up. The strong smell of sulphur from the lighted match caused Ruby to sneeze. 'Bless you,' he said. She watched the cigarette paper turn from white to brown as Charlie drew smoke into his already damaged lungs. 'And before you say anything, yes, the doctors have told me this isn't helping my chest. And yes, I'm trying me best to cut down.'

Ruby's eyebrows raised as he lapsed into a brief fit of coughing.

'I know. I know, so don't go giving me that look. You're as bad as your mother,' he teased. 'Now see what you've done. You've put the sodding mockers on it.

Damn things gone out.' He tucked the remains of the cigarette behind his ear.

They both laughed and bumped shoulders. She had missed him so much. His badge of kindness remained untarnished, in spite of the hardships that shadowed him. He jollied people along, softening life's blows with his turn of phrase, often at his own expense. A warm glow settled over her. He was the gentlest soul and she loved him all the more for it.

'So, I'm guessing you're wondering what happened to the boy?

'Well, the thing is,' Ruby started, easing the letter from her pocket. 'I got this a few days ago. It mentions you, but I don't know what to make of it? I figured you'd know what he's on about?'

The creased page shook in Charlie's hand. His ruddy complexion lightened. 'Good grief, girl. I should have been there for you.' Charlie clamped the letter between his knees, grabbed Ruby's hands and brought them to his mouth. 'I'm not a violent man, girl, but I'll swing for Mickey if he's hurt you in any way. Tell your old dad, love. I'm here now, and I'll get this sorted. I swear I will.'

'No, no, Dad, it's nothing like that.' Her words gushed in an attempt to calm him. His breaths came fast and shallow. She needed to reassure him and quickly. The man had been through enough. The truth would benefit no one, least of all her father. 'Mickey never laid a finger on me. Honest, Dad. I'd only met him through Ray. We got off on the wrong foot and to be truthful, we couldn't stand the sight of each other. I avoided him best I could. Tell you what though, his mouth would pass for a sewer.' she forced a smile. Her explanation appeared to work.

Charlie scratched behind his ear for the dog-end, re-lit it and took a long slow drag. 'As long as you're being straight with me?'

'Cross me heart and hope to ...' she replied, partly stealing her little sister's much used vow.

Although her father had bonded with Mickey, Ruby couldn't begin to understand how that bond became broken. One thing she did know: her father would undoubtedly have loved him, and there was no telling how he might react to learn of Mickey's death.

Daisy and Mary bounded across the grassed area and plonked themselves down on the bench. Kate called out. 'We thought you'd still be here. We've got Pease pudding and faggots on the table if you're interested?'

'Interested?' repeated Charlie, jumping to his feet. 'I swear on me life, love, if I wasn't already married, I'd be whisking you down the aisle.'

'You're a daft lummox, Charlie Denton, and don't I know it.' Kate laughed. 'Now shift yourself before it goes cold.'

'You sure we can't tempt you, Ruby? There'll be plenty to go round,' said Charlie.

'I'd love to stay longer, You know I would.'

'Let the girl get her bus,' said Kate. She'll be back soon enough. Meanwhile, the faggots are getting cold.'

Charlie slipped the sheet of notepaper discreetly to Ruby. 'We'll leave it there for now, Rube. I'll explain the rest another time. You have my word.'

Chapter 40

Saturday arrived and Ruby dressed warmly for the fair.

'Well don't you look a picture,' said Sal, as Ruby modelled her new coat.

'You're so kind to me Sal. I really appreciate it. Honest I do.'

'Only too pleased to help out, lovey. Now get your skates on. You don't want to keep your Jimmy waiting.'

'My Jimmy?'

'Well, he is, isn't he?'

'Might be,' Ruby answered cagily.

Sal pushed her out the door. 'Be off with you.'

Sal had made up the difference for the cost of the coat, a loose-fitting suede number edged with fake white fur. Ruby had hankered after one from the minute they appeared on the rails. Pleased as punch with her new look, she walked the short distance to the main road where Jimmy would be waiting. Sneaking peeks at herself in the shop windows, she was more than satisfied with her choice. Purple was definitely her colour. Jimmy's eye's popped when he saw her turn the corner.

'Blimey Rube, you're a sight for sore eyes! I'll need to keep a close watch; else you'll be snatched up from under me nose.'

It would take an ill wind to wipe the grin from her face.

Locking arms, they crossed the road to the bus stop. 'Let's nip in the garage first, get some change for the bus,' said Jimmy.

Waiting in the queue by the till, a customer barged through the door, red-faced and ready to go two rounds with the unsuspecting cashier. 'Ere guv, what's the idea of locking the carsey door? Frightened someone'll run off with the bog roll or what?'

The cashier handed over the key. 'It's a pain, I know, but some woman was caught kipping down in there. We've been told to lock it ever since. Fetch it back when you're done.'

Ruby loosened her hold on Jimmy's arm.

'What's up?' he asked. 'You look like you've seen a ghost.'

'I just need some air. I'll wait outside.' The coat had somehow lost its appeal. She felt uncomfortable swanning about in all her finery, while others out there were barely surviving.

They walked to the bus stop. The initial excitement abated. 'You sure you want to go? We could make it tomorrow instead?'

'No, let's stick to the plan. I'll be alright. Just felt a bit queasy, that's all.'

The travel clock showed ten thirty when Ruby arrived home. Slipping between freezing bedsheets, she curled into a ball. She could no more turn off her brain than she could sleep at the snap of her fingers.

Jimmy was lodged in her head. Every minute of the evening was now punctuated with an image of his bewildered face

His arm around her at the fair had been the defining moment when things changed. His closeness, as they laughed their way along the dried and cracked uneven walkways, conjured feelings so alien, so different from anything she had known; feelings that both excited and frightened her. The charged, hedonistic atmosphere had drawn her in. She lost herself in the music, and the intoxicating buzz of being with someone who made her feel alive.

The girls thereabouts, batting their stick-on lashes in Jimmy's direction, only served to confirm what Ruby already knew. He was a great catch. A catch who had chosen her. The moment he drew closer, the music faded as the sound of her racing pulse thundered in her ears. When his mouth covered hers, she feared her heart would stop and yet, being caught up in the sweetest sensation imaginable, she would not have cared a jot; until something stirred within her, something unfamiliar, as she savoured the feel of his tongue exploring her mouth. French kissing, she'd heard it called and had once considered it the most disgusting thing imaginable. Her knees weakened as the intensity grew. Her hands, gently tugging his hair, drew him closer still. Both were totally lost in the moment, and oblivious to small group now gathered. One on-looker jeered. 'Get stuck in you lucky git.'

Ruby pulled back, shame-faced and flustered. Her cheeks, a perfect match for the toffee apples on the stand directly behind Jimmy, were close to igniting. She had embarrassed herself. With her defences down, she'd allowed things to move along a route she'd promised herself to avoid. The hurt openly visible in Jimmy's face as she walked away, filled her with self-hatred. His stride lengthened until he was at her side. 'What did I do wrong?' he asked.

'Oh, Jimmy it's not you. Please don't think that.' She held his hands in hers. I'm just not ready for that kind of relationship yet. And before you ask, I do love you. I just need time.' She wanted to explain, but for Jimmy to understand she would need to relive the past; talk about the time spent in Bromley with Uncle Tom. In reality, she had more chance of beating Bannister's world record than forcing those barbed words from her throat.

'So, this isn't you giving me the elbow then? We can still go out and that?'

Ruby stalled. Those two little words, 'and that,' in another time and place had an entirely different meaning. One day, she would trust again. Until then, she had found a best friend in Jimmy. 'So where are you taking me next?' She smiled.

Chapter 41

Ruby made her way along Tower Bridge Road. She could hardly miss The Cat and Cucumber Cafe directly ahead. The large curve-fronted building sat pride of place on a bend. It had been her father's idea to meet there. He raved about the place. *Best fried egg sandwiches on the planet,* he'd said. Come late afternoon, with the main body of shoppers heading home, Ruby rightly assumed the cafe would be close to empty. She had no inkling what today's chat might reveal about Mickey's past. His connection to her dad remained uppermost in her thoughts. They had shared a home, her father and his stepson, something she found difficult to get her head around. Her thoughts galloped, all the while wondering what could have brought about their separation. Ruby adjusted the tie-belt on her black, wet-look mac and pushed open the door.

About to sup the remains of his tea, Charlie sprang up and held his arms open. 'Come and give your old man a hug.' Aware that the chap behind the counter had his eyes on Ruby, Charlie called across, 'Pop 'em back in their sockets, Bert. This little darling is my daughter,' he added proudly.

'Takes after her mother then,' came the reply.

Charlie chuckled, ordered teas and sat back down.

'Fancy a bite to eat?' he asked. 'Eggs are good.'

'I can see that!' Ruby tittered. 'Dried yolk on your chin is a dead giveaway.'

'Trust you to notice, he said jokingly, rubbing the area with a licked finger. 'I was saving that bit for later.'

Seeing her father in such good spirits had Ruby regretting that she'd started the whole sorry business. It would be a difficult conversation, since his memories of Mickey were a far cry from her own. Mickey's odd behaviour continued to haunt her. Had his obsession with her tipped the balance? Sal advised that she put it behind her: but in spite of the advice, Ruby couldn't let it go. That letter had changed things, showed a different, unexpected side. Something pushed her to know more, to understand what had made him tick.

'Come on, out with it,' said Charlie. 'I expect I know what's on your mind.'

'Would it upset you to talk about Mickey?'

With his hands wrapped around the mug, Charlie blew down into the rim to cool the freshly brewed tea. 'It's fine, girl. I've been turning it over since we last spoke. Still hard to believe he's gone you know.' He shifted in his seat.

'I guessed as much. That's why I stopped by the other day, didn't want to spring it on you here. I couldn't tell you at the park either, not after me sisters turned up.'

'You did right to wait. Now, let me tell you, best I can, before old Bert here charges us rent. It was a difficult time all round, back then, losing Lily and the baby, one after the other. Then not long after, I was due back on ship. I needed that wage, but with Mickey to care for I was at a complete loss. My parents weren't in a fit state and with Lily having no family, I'd no one to help out.'

Taking a roll-up from his tobacco tin, he reached for the Swan Vestas. His trembling hands scattered the pink tipped matches across the table.

'Here, let me.' Ruby scooped up the matches.

'It's a sad day when a man can't light his own fags,' his words drifting into the cloud of smoke whirling ghost-like above their heads.

'Where was I? Yes, it was Ray who stepped in. Said he had friends, a decent couple, desperate for a second baby. So, Ray arranged a meeting, Southwark Park as it goes. Hadn't a clue where these people lived. It was for the best; else I'd have been forever camped on their doorstep. They didn't want the little one growing up confused you see, with two dads and all. They brought Mickey up as their own. A private adoption. Wracked with guilt I was for giving up Lily's son, her pride and joy. He deserved a good start though and I couldn't give him that. Not then. I badgered Ray for the boy's whereabouts. He wouldn't budge on it: not an inch, didn't want to complicate matters. Best leave things be. So that's what I did, and hardly a day's gone by when I haven't wondered about that boy.'

A thin skin had formed on Ruby's cold tea. She pushed it aside, refusing the offer of a fresh one. It cut deep to see her father so choked up.

'You couldn't have known what would happen. It's hardly your fault.'

Charlie drew the baggy cuff of his shirt across his face. 'It's sad to think he'd turned out like that. It would have broken Lily's heart to see him in that place. It gets me, girl, right here,' he said, tapping his chest. 'Something must have happened, to turn him I mean?'

'It could have been anything, Dad. We've no way of knowing.'

'I've Ray to thank,' Charlie continued. 'He put me straight, told me about the damaged lock-up and Mickey being remanded. I needed to see the lad, explain stuff, about his mum and me.' The deep frown lines etched into Charlie's forehead began to smooth out. Ruby breathed easier, knowing the burden her father had carried for so long had finally begun to lift.

'I don't mind telling you, I was in a right stew beforehand, in case he changed his mind and blocked the visit. Got all churned up for nothing, No malice on his part, no blame card tossed about. We just chatted like old mates. I even got a slap on the back!' Charlie lifted his empty mug in the air. 'Gis a refill, Bert. I can't spit a bloody thruppence.'

Ruby got up from her chair and gave her father a hug.

'His letter makes more sense now, about us being friends. Who'd have thought it eh? We could have grown up together.' As much as the idea didn't sit particularly well with her, she refused to give it growing room. Collecting the fresh tea from the counter, she placed it in front of her dad.

With his vocals freshly lubricated, Charlie chatted on. 'We don't see much of you these days. Mum's always asking if you'll be moving back home any time soon? Oh, and Daisy's got herself a boyfriend. Billy says this and Billy says that, is all we ever hear. Drives us round the twist.' He laughed.

'Gawd,' mumbled Ruby to herself. 'Not another one!'

Ruby's plan had always been to get back with her family, but for the first time in ages she felt finally settled. Living within walking distance of work appealed far more than waiting for buses on cold winter mornings. She chose her words with care. After a little persuasion, Charlie agreed with her decision.

'On one condition,' he bargained. 'Don't become a stranger. It's all I ask.'

'As if!' exclaimed Ruby. 'Does Mum still cook those apple dumplings on a Wednesday?'

'There'd be a screaming match if she didn't my girl. I need some blubber back round my middle to help keep these sodding trousers up.'

'A belt might help,' she suggested.

Charlie lifted his waistcoat, showing off his belt and braces. 'Just to be on the safe side. Your mum worries that women will keel over if they catch sight of me long-johns.'

Ruby laughed heartily. Aside from everything else, it filled her with joy to know that his humour remained intact.

'Wednesdays it is then. And don't stint on the portions.'

Chapter 42

Ray had no issue with leaving Luca in charge. Tuesdays were a doddle, a warm-up for the weekend. The man could work the stall blindfolded and still be quid's in. The extra day meant Ray could dive off and check out new stock, content that his business was in safe hands. Today however, he had no such plans.

He woke later than usual. The tick-tocking of the clock irritated his brain. Under normal circumstances he'd barely hear the thing. Not so this morning. His stomach tightened as a sense of foreboding burrowed deep into his muscles. Every rhythmic tick hammered home its symbolic message. Reaching blindly into the semi-darkness, Ray sideswiped the clock to the far end of the room.

Last night's weatherman had promised grey skies and a northerly wind. With Ray's focus on the bedroom window rattling in its frame, there was no disputing that the man knew his stuff. Had the forecast been rain, the day ahead would be all the more dire. Rain and burials were never a good combination.

He wanted the day over with. It felt too close to home, like a personal dig, somehow; one of those so-called wake-up calls that get bandied about like dubious tissues whenever tragedy strikes. The old girls were the worse: couldn't wait to share their kick-up-the-arse mantras, *You never know what's around the corner*. No one did, for fucks sake. Getting into a lather about it would buy a one-way ticket to the funny farm. Popping his clogs was a subject he'd never entertained; just didn't have head space for it. Other people's demise, especially those closest to him, were a different matter altogether. Whichever way he looked at it, it made no sense. Tommy Gibbons had been fitter than most.

Boxing had been the life force that pulsed in the man's veins. Ray understood that more than most. When Tommy traded his gloves to manage the Thomas A Beckett pub instead, no one had been more surprised than Ray. The young man was clearly anchored to the place. Had his whole life in front of him. And now he was gone.

Before long, Ray was reflecting on his own life, something he promised himself he'd never do, since it contained more ups and downs than a slapper's drawers. Opening old wounds was a mugs game, yet here he was going over old ground. Lately, all things considered, he hadn't done too badly. He'd grafted, kept the bailiffs from the door and boosted the coffers in the betting shops. Job done. Thinking back to a time when he had swapped a chin full of bumfluff for a five o/clock shadow, and became a fixture at the Streatham Locarno dancehall, prompted the hint of a smile. He'd worn his life-and-soul label with pride. Things could not have been better. He took risks, fucked up on occasions, paid the price and moved on.

He blamed that sly mare for ruining his life. All these years later he still couldn't bring himself to say her name. Thoughts of her, although rare, still rankled, but she had given him a daughter. A beautiful daughter, who should have been celebrating her twenty second birthday this very day, the twenty eighth of October. The sound of her giggles was lost to him now. Ray took the framed portrait from the shelf and stroked a finger down her chubby, smiling face. He could almost feel the softness of her fine curls springing out in all directions.

She would always be his precious one, daddy's favourite girl. He replaced the photo next to the vase of silk daffodils that he bought in her memory.

A while later, and feeling restricted in his dark grey suit, Ray headed off towards English Martyrs Church. It didn't surprise him to see crowds already lining the streets. Tommy had touched a lot of lives. It was only fitting that his send-off reflected that.

Forced to jay-walk, Ray wondered how many would turn out for *him*. A handful at best, dragged screaming from their pints, to make up the numbers. Yesterday he wouldn't have given a toss, but today, with his conscience well and truly pricked, he toyed with the idea of change.

Two funerals in as many weeks were two too many. Mickey's send-off, a paltry affair, with only a handful of attendees resembling bookends on lengthy empty shelving, was reason enough to shed a tear.

The vicar's words, delivered in the usual sing-song fashion, pitched and dipped like a roller coaster ride. Ray tuned out, thinking instead of what might have been, had Mickey's life not been soured by circumstance.

Ray took stock. He summed up his own life these past years in two words, mundane and clockwork. Each day dragged its heels into the next. His 'grumpy git' attitude was more habit than design; something he slipped into along the way, like comfy loafers. He needed to sort himself out before it was too late.

Come the evening, Sal and Ruby cosied up on the settee, ready for a night in front of the television. Ray appeared from upstairs. 'Any chance of you grabbing fish and chips for tonight, Ray?' asked Sal. 'We're just about done in.'

Ray perked up. 'No need. I've booked us a table at that new Chinese place up the road. You've got half hour to get yourselves sorted.'

Sal and Ruby eyed each other suspiciously before staring blankly up at Ray.

'Must get these ears checked,' said Sal, tugging on a lobe. 'I could have sworn you said...'

'Yeah, all right, don't take the piss. I can always cancel.'

'Wouldn't hear of it, Ray,' said Sal, springing to her feet. She grabbed Ruby's hand and pulled her upright. 'We can be ready in a blink. Come on my lovely, snap to it. Let's not keep the man waiting,' she grinned.

With only a couple of tables occupied, the restaurant was as quiet as a nun's fart. Sal kept her voice low as she read from the menu, prompting Ruby to follow suit. Ray, ever vocal, tried deciphering the names of dishes. Only the prices were crystal, each one jumping out and stabbing his wallet.

'Don't think I can pronounce some of these, Sal,' said Ruby, scanning the list.

'There's no need duck. It's got the English in brackets. Think I'm going for the prawns.'

'I'll have the same as you then,' Ruby decided. 'But you can ask for them.' Her giggling brought the waiter to their table, and the girls placed their orders.

All eyes were on Ray as he dragged a finger up, down and across the page. 'Blimey,' he said, beneath his breath. Finally, he recognised words he understood. 'Chicken and chips. Bang on. I'll have me some of that guv'nor.'

The moment the waiter disappeared; Sal shook her head in disbelief.

'What's up with you woman?' asked Ray.

'You're paying over the odds here; you might at least try something different,' she suggested quietly.

'Listen up,' he said, imitating his sister's voice. 'I'm the one footing the bill. It's my treat, so it's my choice. And why the hell are we whispering?'

Sal looked over at the other diners and back again. 'Because dear brother, it's polite.'

With their meals placed in front of them, Ray was first to tuck in. 'Well go on then, get cracking. What'd they call them again?' he asked, his knife pointed towards Ruby's plate.

'Prawn balls,' said Sal, spearing one with her fork.

Ray came close to choking on a chip. 'Pity the bloody prawns dragging those monsters about. He dabbed his eyes with his serviette. 'Plenty of blokes out there in need of those beauties: the health service missed a trick there. A couple of those instead of a sick note would soon shift the layabouts. Might get the waiter to bag me up a portion, hand 'em out myself. What d'you reckon?' he asked, while summoning the waiter with a wave and a smile.

'I reckon...' Sal began.

Ray, red-faced and animated, jumped in. 'Might land me one of them knighthoods for services rendered.'

'More likely a straight-jacket,' chuckled Sal. 'And don't go embarrassing that poor lad, else we'll be barred before we've even started.'

The girls tittered behind their hands. Ray's upbeat mood, rare as they knew it to be, had in itself been a tonic. Presently, with the table cleared and coffee poured, the waiter explained about the fortune cookies he'd placed in a small wicker basket.

'Don't you want one, Ray?' Ruby asked.

Ray held a cookie to his nose and sniffed. 'What, and lose teeth. They're as stale as ...' The slightest pressure saw the cookie crumble in his hand. He picked out the oblong strip of paper. 'This like them jokes you get in Christmas crackers?'

'No, it's your fortune,' said Sal shaking her head. 'Just read the blimming thing,' she teased.

Ray reluctantly read aloud. 'He who rests on laurels gets thorn in backside.' He crushed and flicked the paper across the table. 'In my line of work. Huh! Are you kidding? What a load of tripe.'

'It doesn't have to relate to work,' said Sal.

'OK, Gypsy Rose Lee, what's your take on it then?'

'Who's to say? But I'd hang onto those prawn balls if I were you,' suggested Sal, struggling to keep her serious head on. 'You may need a little extra oomph yourself one day.'

Chapter 43

Jimmy slumped into the armchair, exhausted. His father, George, lay stretched out on the settee, eyes glued to the television set in the corner of the room; his balding head glistening like a newly waxed car.

'It's hotter than a ruddy furnace in here, Pa,' Jimmy complained, pushing his palm up into his damp hair. A thin smoky downdraft, drifted out from beneath the chimney and rose up to the ceiling. 'I think it's time we got a gas fire. At least we'd be able to turn the ruddy thing down.'

George, without looking away from the screen, asked, 'What's got your goat son? It's not like you to complain.'

'That's because I don't normally bear witness to you roasting yourself.' Jimmy knew full well that his father, a one-time stalwart of the merchant navy, now suffered through the winter months from the cold, and crippling pain of arthritic joints. Any fall in temperature called for Siberian measures and another shovel of coal onto an already roaring fire.

Gorge sat up, pushed his feet into slippers and grunted, 'Beats me. You left here all cock-a-hoop and waltz back in looking like a bulldog with a splinter up its arse. What's going on?'

'Yeah, cheers for that. Ignore me. I'm just bushed.'

'I get it, son. I do. Playing snooker down the youth club is a killer: more knackering than a day's work.'

Father and son locked eyes for a brief moment before Jimmy reacted. 'You taking the mick?' His cheeks lifted slightly.

'Me? Don't be daft!' George snatched up the newspaper beside him, rolled it into a makeshift truncheon, and stood up. 'Last chance. You tell me what's turned my boy into this miserable festering doppelganger, or I'll knock it out of yer.'

Jimmy hugged his knees to his chest as George swiped the newspaper back and forth. 'Get off me old timer,' he laughed. 'My love life's no business of yours.'

George threw the paper onto the fire and the flames licked high into the chimney. 'Ah, so now we're talking. Ruby? Right?'

Content that his father had backed off, Jimmy unfolded himself and shuffled forward. 'Listen, pa, I've got no idea what's happening,' he said, opening the buttons of his polo shirt. 'One minute life's the best ever, then, quick as a flash, it's not.'

George pondered his son's dilemma. His knowing chuckle was brief. 'There's no rule book where women are concerned. They're a complicated business, and anyone who says otherwise is a bigger liar than that Profumo bloke.'

'Fat lot of use that is.'

'Thing is, every single one of 'em is different. Ain't that the truth,' said George, as a reminder to himself. 'Get yourself out there. You know what I'm saying. I'm telling you now, once a ring is on that finger your wings aren't clipped, son, they're fucking mangled.'

'Says you, chomping at the bit to get hitched up with Sal.'

'Yeah, well, my wings are truly knackered, and these dodgy pins are headed the same way.' He slapped his legs for effect. 'My arm around a good woman would

270

help keep me stable, vertical,' was as far as George's lovey-dovey lingo would allow.

'Like those wooden crutches they dish out in casualty you mean?'

'OK, smart-arse. You got me there. But just so's you know, I think the world of Sal.'

'I know you do Pa. I know. I'm just ribbing.'

With no let up from the stifling heat of their small, first floor flat, Jimmy hauled himself out of the chair. He walked to the street door and out onto the balcony, where he peered over the safety wall. A sudden cheer went up from the pub on the corner, followed by bursts of laughter. George, struggling into a rug-thick jumper, followed his son onto the landing area. 'Sounds like they're having a bit of a knees-up. Fancy a swift half before closing? My shout.'

Jimmy puffed out rings of ghostly breath. 'Nah, not in the mood, Pa. I just want this day over with.'

George placed a hand between Jimmy's shoulder blades. 'Come on son. Cheer up. There's plenty out there interested. That Sally Army girl yesterday for instance, singing with that group on the corner: you saw her, red hair, cute bonnet. Nearly bashed a bloody hole through that tambourine whenever you looked her way.'

'Oh, give over.'

'Or that one round the block? Nice, pretty little thing, unusual laugh. Unique, yeah that's the word. Lots to be said for unique.'

'Like blown eardrums you mean? Thanks, but no thanks.'

'Shame that, cos I've already put a good word in with the mother.'

Jimmy gave his father a gentle shove. 'You better not have?'

'Nah, tempted though.'

271

With an early start ahead of them, both George and Jimmy decided to call it a day and made a beeline for their rooms. Jimmy stretched out on his bed. His transistor radio balanced against the black vinyl headboard as its tinny sound filled his ears. The lyrics of 'Dizzy' by Tommy Roe, mirrored his feelings exactly. As much as he preferred the up-coming reggae beat, he couldn't close his ears to the words he'd wished he had written himself. All had been well until that kiss, which he didn't mind admitting, curled his toes.

Jimmy grappled with the emptiness left by Ruby's sudden withdrawal. They barely spoke anymore. When he did catch her attention, she was suddenly busy, flitting between the Cafe and the stall in a blur of colour and determination. How many times had he rehearsed conversations in his mind, imagining witty remarks that would make Ruby laugh.

Maybe he'd misread the signs? Could she still be nursing a broken heart over that Billy character? His head was a tangled mess of hope and confusion. Just catching sight of her was like sunshine splicing through his now boring existence. He rolled over onto his stomach. Should he confront her? What if he pushes too hard and the fragile thread between them snaps. He flipped himself back over. What then? A loud 'Ugh,' filled the room, and the transistor clattered to the floor.

'All OK in there?' called George.

'Terrific, pa.' Jimmy's heart hung in the balance, torn between the agony of longing, and the potential heartbreak of letting go completely.

Chapter 44

Ray bypassed the Elephant & Castle and walked along St George's Road towards the war museum, referred to locally as Bedlam. As a lad he'd linked the name Bedlam to the state of war. It had been his old dad who'd put him straight some years later. He'd explained that the museum building had been part of the Bethlem psychiatric hospital, and that such institutions were known as Bedlam, due to the chaos, imagined or otherwise, behind closed doors.

It was a bit of a trek, especially today, with the wind blowing a gale and what felt like ten tonnes of grit piercing his eyeballs. Ray enjoyed his own company and walking helped to clear his head, or at least it did. Finding time for such luxuries these past years had been nigh-on impossible. Every blasted thing needed sorting pronto. A week on from the funerals and Ray had yet to shake off his sombre mood. Life at times seemed like a never-ending slog. Thoughts of his old man haunted him lately too. The poor bloke, stick thin, had slaved his whole life to put food on the table; never once complained, just waded through and got the job done. Ray missed him, even now, all these years later.

Once inside the museum, Ray unbuttoned his reefer jacket and weaved his way through the main viewing area. The Mark 4 tank drew a jostling crowd, everyone nudging for prime position. Standing firm and within touching distance, Ray still found it hard to believe that his father, a mere teenager at the time, had been in command of such a monster machine. He could only imagine the nightmares seen through the narrow look-out slots. Ray's understanding of the conflict endured by the tank regiment came from his book collection, since his father refused to talk about his time in combat. But he'd spoken volumes about the Mark 4 itself. He knew the position of every nut, bolt and inch of track. Ray senior and his seven-man crew owed their lives to the tank, affectionately known as Big Battling Bertha. Fear Naught, their motto, Ray had happily adopted for himself.

Raised voices from a group of nearby schoolboys broke Ray's train of thought. The ring leader, a cocky lad, took pleasure in taunting the female guide the minute she mentioned one of the tank's two prototypes, Big Willie. A crimson blanket crept up her neck and set her cheeks aflame. Ray expected tears any minute, as she riffled through pages looking for something less reactive for her young charges. The class teacher, helpful as a hedgehog in a condom factory, conveniently turned a deaf ear. Ray's focus returned to the boy. He understood the lad's mind-set. His fifteen-year-old self would have reacted the same way. Today however, he had one aim in mind, to stop the rot and save the woman from a possible fainting fit.

He edged towards her, noted the name on her badge and stepped forward. 'Leah here,' Ray gestured, 'needs a quick break.' Still glowing with embarrassment, she reluctantly moved aside, clutching the creased itinerary that Ray assured her he had no need of.

Fixing the lad with a don't-push-it, stare, Ray spoke about the first prototype, Little Willie, with emphasis on each syllable. A sudden wave of sniggers rose and faded, giving way to a flurry of hands and a deluge of questions. Ray, in his element, barely stopped for breath. Presently, the once disruptive pupil raised an arm.

'Why'd they call it a tank?' he asked.

Pleased that the boy's interest had finally been captured, Ray explained. 'Top secret projects were exactly that, top secret. No country in the world had this type of machinery. Even serving soldiers during exercise, who'd seen it rumble by were kept in the dark. During the early stages it was passed off as a water carrier, which is how the name tank came about.'

The boy was on a roll, his hand constantly jigging in the air. Ray had won him over, and felt proud as punch with himself for resisting his initial impulse to boot the kid out the door. With the session winding down, Leah accepted Ray's offer of a lunchtime drink at a local pub. With drinks in hand, they settled at a table closest to the large open fire. The crackle from flaming logs, filling the air with a sweet earthy scent, reminded Ray of winter evenings long ago. A time when, together with his sister, they would search out weird and wonderful shapes and faces in the burning wood.

Leah gave a polite cough before speaking. 'Thank you so much Ray for helping out. I'd literally been thrown to the wolves. Staff shortages you see, and when they told me I'd have to, well, you saw for yourself I was out of my depth, and those boys! Good gracious, what a handful. Teachers are a breed apart, aren't they just?' She paused for a sip of pineapple juice. 'I'm mostly back-room staff, organising group visits, meetings and cataloguing etcetera. Which I much prefer.'

Ray grinned at the nervous chatter emanating from across the polished wood table. The woman held him captive. He'd never understood the term 'smiling eyes' until now, and he was stoked that Leah's were trained on him. He studied her features, likening himself to a toff at an art gallery, taking in the lines, the curves, the symmetry.

The woman was damn well perfect. Her complexion, minus its earlier scarlet tone, had a smooth, ivory quality to it. He noticed too that her dark, up-styled hair remained almost perfect, in spite of the weather. However, the wispy fringe had gone awry and he fought the urge to reach over and smooth it back into position.

Leah was a class act. He fancied she had a look of Audrey Hepburn about her, in that iconic Tiffany's photo. A little older perhaps? He ran a finger along the inside of his shirt collar, before undoing the top button. At risk of turning into a bumbling idiot, Ray removed himself from the situation, albeit briefly. He stood at the bar and ordered peanuts, all the while watching her reflection in the mirror beyond the optics.

Sitting back down, he opened the packet and placed them within reach for both to share.

'Are you from around these parts?' asked Ray.

'Oxford originally, but my parents moved to Lambeth when I was a child. So yes, this has always been home to me.'

'You don't sound local, if you don't mind me saying?'

'That's parents for you,' she grinned. 'Mine were pretty strict on grammar, both being teachers. Ps and Qs were gospel too!'

'Mine were sticklers as well,' said Ray, straight-faced. 'Pints and Quarts mainly.'

Her laughter, not forced or grating like some, was a much-needed tonic. It occurred to him that anyone capable of dragging an ounce of humour from his sorry arse had to be some kind of special.

'I have to say, you were a natural with the boys, Ray, and with your level of knowledge you'd be an asset to the museum. Is it something you'd consider on a voluntary basis? I know they'd be happy to have you on board.'

Being openly appreciated had a good feel about it. Maybe Leah's idea wasn't too far-fetched? Luca would always take on extra hours. It was doable, at a push.

Suddenly, Sal's voice loomed large in his head. *Volunteer? What, a grumpy old fart like you? And tight as a knot to boot. Never!*

Sal knew him better than anyone. Time and again, much to his chagrin, she would try to jolly him out of the miseries, as she called it. As for volunteering, she'd laugh herself silly at the thought of him grafting for zilch. Under normal circumstances he would have laughed loudest. After-all, he'd earned his grumpy old fart moniker, put the hours in. Leopard and spots came to mind, making him fidget in his chair. It all suddenly seemed like too much hassle.

'It would take a lot of juggling, Leah. Nice name by the way.' A slight pink blush appeared above her neckline. Jesus, whatever possessed him to say that? He stood up and downed the remains of his bitter. 'Look, I best be shooting off. I'm glad to have helped out, and it's a tempting offer,' Ray continued as Leah got up from her chair. 'Not sure it'll fit with my regular job though. I'll have to get back to you on it.'

Standing face to face, he hesitated. Did he shake her hand or chance a kiss? A stirring in his groin dictated the latter. The moment Ray moved forward; Leah reached for his hand.

'It's been so lovely to meet you, Ray, and thank you again for coming to my rescue. I hope to see you soon.'

He followed her to the door. 'I'll walk you back if you like since I'm heading that way?'

'There's no need, really. I've a few errands to pick up.'

Ray watched her set off in the opposite direction, her black fitted coat hugging her curves. Some twenty-five yards along the road, unable to resist another look, he glanced back, only to find Leah doing the same.

'Damn.'

As soon as the Elephant came into view, Ray cut through the back streets and into The Lane, making a bee-line for the warmth of the Cafe. Non market days saw the street like any other, uncluttered, clean and surprisingly quiet. Ray stepped into the Cafe and smoothed back his hair. With only two chairs occupied and no sign of Sal, he hovered by the counter. An old regular, sitting slumped in the corner, jerked herself upright and cuffed the dribble from her chin. 'You'll have a bloody long wait,' she warned. 'Sal's hiding out in the kitchen,' she pointed. 'Thinks we can't hear her caterwauling along to the wireless. Had to put myself asleep just to escape the racket.'

Sal appeared and was greeted by two serious faces. She looked from one to the other. 'What? Did I miss something?'

'I hear you're auditioning for that talent show, Opportunity Knocks,' said Ray. 'Nellie here thinks you need more practice.'

'Is that right? Having the time to waste would be a fine thing. Now, what're you after, Ray? I've got an oven needs cleaning.'

'Rustle us up a couple of rolls, girl. I'm that starved I could eat a...'

Sal cut him off by leaping into mother hen mode. 'What's cheered you up? You had a face on earlier that would've put the wind-up Old Nick, and look at you, all spruced up,' her eyes little more than slits. 'If I didn't know better, I'd say you'd got a woman in tow.'

'Leave it out. I've had a mooch around Bedlam as it happens. Roped myself in to chatting with a bunch of schoolboys. I've been asked back on a voluntary basis.'

Sal's eyes rounded. 'You? A volunteer! Wonders will never cease. You'll be telling me next that you snatched their hand off.'

Ray understood his sister's reaction. He expected as much, but felt a bit miffed nonetheless.

'Well?' prompted Sal.

'Well nothing. What's with the questions anyway?'

'Pardon me for showing interest. I'll fix them rolls and fetch them over. Shall I?'

'Thanks, girl.'

Sal stopped in her tracks. 'Blimey. That's a first! You've not had another bump on the head?'

'Ps and Qs Sal. Don't cost a penny. Right? It's what you've been banging on about for yonks. Well, think yourself lucky that someone's finally taken notice. Now, about them rolls.'

Sal, too stunned to think straight, could do no more than mumble. 'Right you are Ray. Right you are.'

Chapter 45

The morning had got off to a bad start. Not only had Ray overslept, he'd also mislaid a would-be supplier's details, the one he was supposed to meet in twenty short minutes; and to make matters worse, the tea caddy had little more than a teaspoon of dust at the bottom. A clear oversight on Sal's part. As much as he enjoyed an occasional mug of Camp coffee, the bitter chicory taste first thing made him shudder. Adding more milk allowed him to down half a mug full in one hit.

A loud knock at the street door was excuse enough to tip the remainder into the sink, splattering the front of his shirt. His voice boomed along the passage. 'Hold up, I'll be there in a tick.' With a damp dishcloth he rubbed at the stains, and cursed the wet patch that had soaked through to his vest.

Glancing at his reflection in the mirror, Ray rolled his eyes; the neighbour's cat had dragged off better looking specimens. The person on the other side of the door continued to knock. With his patience wearing thin, he shouted a final time. 'Hold your hair on. Said I'm coming, didn't I?'

He stared moronically at the willowy blonde gracing his doorstep. For several seconds neither spoke. Had time allowed, he would happily have cancelled the whole day just to stand and chat, but the moment he saw the thin folder tucked beneath her arm, something twigged. Hawkeye, from the market, had warned about dodgy characters in the area, turning up at random and worming their way in. Ray couldn't remember specifics. He often tuned out when the old boy slipped into windbag mode, now he wished he'd paid more attention. Either way it made no odds. No one was getting a foot inside his gaff. As for the girl, any forthcoming niceties on Ray's part quickly fell away.

'Listen, darling, if you're peddling religion or some other save-my-arse cause, you'll do better to try a different door. I've a million and one things need doing, so if you don't mind.' he stepped back in order to close the door.

The woman placed her free hand on the blue painted woodwork. 'Please don't. You have no idea how long it's taken me to pluck up the courage to be here today.'

He would have had to be blind not to notice the tears on the brink of smudging her tasteful makeup. Despite his hard-line attitude, he wasn't about to slam the door in her face. 'Okay, five minutes. This had better be good.'

'I'm guessing you must be William?'

Ray harrumphed mockingly. 'You knock my door, take a guess at my name and expect me to fall in like a boy scout?'

'Can we talk inside?'

Ray's head lolled back in surprise. 'You're kidding me, right? It's a risky decision on your part, sweetheart. Didn't your parents teach you anything?' Ray could hear his pals down the pub, ribbing him rotten for passing up such an offer. 'I think we're about done here, don't you?'

The girl continued to hold his gaze. Ray decided she'd either forgotten her practised lines or was too scared to deliver them. 'Listen, I don't have time for this. Go waste someone else's...'

'I think you could be my father.'

Ray drew on all his reserves to remain upright. Everything internal seemed to combust and liquefy and gush towards the pit of his stomach, and there wasn't a thing he could do to stop it. A sickly, empty sensation filled the space between, bringing him close to collapse. Images of his baby daughter as she was some twenty-two years ago floated before his eyes.

'I know this has come as a shock. Please can I come inside now?'

'You know nothing of the sort.' Ray raised his palm towards her. 'Don't come any closer. Just go,' his voice gentle but firm. 'I've no idea what game you're playing, or who's put you up to this, but it stops now. And just so's you know, I did have a daughter. She died ...'

His voice faded to little more than the mutterings of a broken man. He pushed the door shut and toppled backwards onto the stairs where he sat, cradling his head in his hands. When he eventually looked up, the shadow, once visible through the opaque glass panel, had gone.

Ray barely registered the ringing of the telephone, and made no attempt to silence the loud trill echoing through the house. Eventually the caller hung up, leaving Ray alone with his thoughts.

He'd lost count of the times he'd tried visualising his daughter through her younger years, from a giggling, grubby kneed toddler, to a feisty teenager blessed with the cheek of the devil, just like her father. Without doubt, he'd have been a willing pushover, a slave to her every whim. He pulled the photo from his wallet, a copy from the framed original housed in his room alongside a flute vase of silk daffodils. His right hand held the picture with a feather-light touch so as not to further damage the worn print. His left hand, wound tight as a screw, showed white knuckles close to bursting through the surface.

Ray's thoughts darkened. Some evil bastard was winding him up, having a laugh at his expense. He'd be first to admit that he'd pissed a lot of people off in his time, but nothing to warrant such a low-level backlash. His money would have been on Mickey, but with him out of the picture, it could be almost anyone. Names and faces cartwheeled through his head as a band of pain burrowed deep into his forehead.

His thoughts returned to the young woman. There was something about her, something that unsettled him. He knew a panicky kid when he saw one. He'd seen a similar look the first time he clapped eyes on Ruby. Similar but by no means the same. The blonde appeared more fragile somehow, if such a thing were possible. She certainly didn't seem the type to have drummed up something so vicious. Most likely she'd been roped in against her will. The bozo behind the stunt would pay dearly for his cowardly actions. He would seek him out. However long it took. Whatever the cost.

*

Come late afternoon, Sal found herself clock watching. What she wouldn't give to lock up and head off early. With two remaining customers showing no sign of leaving and Pam restocking the cutlery rack, Sal chalked up 'meat pudding' on the menu board ready for tomorrow, while keeping a discreet watch on the lone female whose face remained tilted towards the wall. The young woman appeared to be stuck in position. Sal could not fathom why. She wondered if some budding Picasso had left a crude masterpiece? It wouldn't be the first time. Yet nothing had been defaced, as far as she could tell. Sal didn't recognise the girl, If nothing else, she would have remembered that gorgeous fair hair, trailing down the back of her burgundy corduroy coat, which had a definite look of quality about it. On the pretence of checking the condiments, Sal ambled over and shook the salt pot.

'Oh dear, I see you've let your tea go cold.' said Sal, reaching for the cup. 'Let me fetch you another?'

A slim pale hand quickly covered Sal's. 'No, please don't worry, but thank you. I'm just about to make a move.'

Sal did worry. Troubled souls often found their way to her door, and this one clearly needed a shoulder. She sat down at the table and introduced herself. 'Listen lovey, tell me to go away if you want, but whatever's bothering you won't seem half as bad if shared. What d'you say? How about we have ourselves a little chat?'

The young woman shifted in her seat. 'I appreciate your kindness but talking will only set me off again. I'm just about holding myself together as it is.'

'Well, you know what they say? Better out than in. Besides which, I'm a dab hand with a spot of foundation. Trust me. My skills with a pan-stick are second to none.' Sal lengthened her neck and posed side-on, revealing the remains of a tanned line smeared along her jowls. 'Not just a pretty face, eh?' The girl softened, as Sal knew she would.

Having poured her heart out, the young woman reached into her folder. 'This is the earliest photo I have,' her voice heavy with regret. 'My turning up really upset him. Silly really, but I imagined it so differently.'

Sal took the picture. 'Do you have a photo of your dad?'

'Afraid not. I do recall Mum talking about her childhood, and how the market was the hub of the community. So I decided it would be a good place to start.'

'You think he works close by?'

'I can only hope. I'd planned to wander through again on the off chance. Needless to say, I chickened out.'

Sal's heart bled for the girl. Her thoughts also took on the father's predicament. Shock, as well she knew, had

284

many guises. 'A letter might be the way forward?' she suggested. 'Give it time to sink in. It's a lot to take on board, after all. What d'you reckon?'

'I honestly don't know. I'm in two minds. This morning, I walked away, yet here I am, hanging on. I'm not looking for a handout or to become a burden. I just want to know my dad.'

'You're one brave girl, I'll give you that. I'm sure it'll come right in the end. You'll see.'

The photo of a child, harnessed in a Silver Cross pram with a fringed canopy, was slightly out of focus. However, there was no disputing the backdrop. The sight of the old Wells Way library combined with the washhouse took Sal back to her younger years. Two small stone plaques depicting mermaids and set above the main door were the cause of boss-eyed kids, according to her mother. *Ogling bare titties guarantees a sticky plaster being slapped on your glasses*, she'd warned.

'My old mum was a real tonic,' said Sal. 'She snapped me out the doldrums on many occasions. She once admitted sneaking into that library, reading all manner of saucy stories then popping next door for a quick dunk. A makeshift confessional she called it.'

'My mother didn't hold with religion, except for the obvious ceremonies.'

'Good Lord, duck, neither did mine. But she adopted some weird ideas down the years.' A sense of relief enveloped Sal. Her anecdote had helped raise the girl's sagging spirit, just as she hoped. To hear her laugh was on a par with the glorious aroma of freshly baked bread. Heavenly.

'Not sure what I expected, visiting those places. There're no memories attached of course.' She produced a second photo. 'This grand old church is where my parents married.'

'It's such a great building,' remarked Sal. 'Us kids spent hours playing around those enormous pillars. Typical gadabouts we were. Knew all the best hangouts.' A sudden rush of deja-vu triggered a memory.

'What did you say your father's name was?' she asked.

'Oh, I'm sorry, but I don't think I did. It's William. William Raymond Jarsdale to be precise.'

Come five o/clock, Sal locked the cafe door and flipped the sign to closed. With her brain whirring away like a circular saw, how on earth could she focus on balancing the books? But with the accounts due tomorrow, she'd no choice but to soldier on. In between erasing silly mistakes, she rang home. No answer. No Ray. No Ruby either to relay a message. Where in the world was her brother when needed?

Chapter 46

After last night's drinking session at The Thomas A Beckett, Ray's get up and go had buggered off long before the alarm sounded. He groaned feebly on lifting his head off the pillow, yet still managed to crawl from his bed, snatch up the underlined note from Sal, and arrive at the lock-up before his sister and Ruby even stirred.

Reaching middle-age came with unexpected benefits, as he'd discovered last night. Alcohol worked it's magic faster, costing less of his hard-earned dosh to bring about that often coveted, who-gives-a-fuck feeling. The downside being, his numbed brain's temporary struggle to communicate more than two words, 'never again.'

A nipper with a tin drum, lodged within Ray's head, bashed out a painful cadence. Feeling fragile, groggy, and a good deal older than his years, Ray needed company that would ease him into the day. What he didn't need was the sulky teenager he'd been lumped with, whose face, longer than a prison stretch, was almost identical to his own. His concentration span, a big fat zero, guaranteed mistakes would be made, merchandise lost and tempers flared, like last week's fireworks. Sal's note, 'We need to talk. Urgent!' was quickly thrust back into his pocket.

'How come Luca didn't work today?' asked Ruby. 'He always does Tuesdays.' She blew warm breath into her hands.

'Because, nose-ache, he wanted the day off. Should we have checked with you first?'

'Pardon me for asking. No need to jump down my throat.'

These past months he had seen a change in Ruby. The mousey little character had morphed into a more confident, gutsy little madam, quick to stand her ground. He liked to think he had had a hand in that. On days like today though, her backchat was as welcome as an earwig in his Y-fronts.

'Stick some gloves on if you're that cold.'

'Tried that. No good. Everything slips through me fingers.'

Losing patience and unable to resist, Ray tossed in a grenade. 'Bit like that phantom boyfriend you had.'

'He was no such thing, and you know it,' she snapped back.

The constant day-long backbiting was helping no one, least of all him. They were both ticked off for different reasons and both flexing a stubborn streak. The one thing experience had taught him was that the fairer sex could hold a sulk until doomsday. With only a few hours trading left and for the sake of his wallet, someone needed to turn things around. Peace-maker had never been a role he hankered after. People either sorted themselves out or they didn't. He had enough grief of his own to contend with. By mid-afternoon, to protect his sanity, he swapped his like-it-or-lump-it attitude for a different tack. He would speak with Sal tonight about yesterday's visitor. Meanwhile, a closer step to middle ground with Ruby would benefit them both, and hopefully shift his thoughts along a less damaging route. With the bulk of the day already behind them, he jumped in feet first.

'Look, let's start again, shall we? Pretend like we're best friends, having a blast while freezing our bits off.'

Ray nudged her gently off-balance time after time until she responded with something other than a dirty look. Acting the idiot while cold stone sober had its rewards. He could call a halt before making a complete prat of himself.

'Stop it. People are staring,' Ruby whinged, trying to maintain her scowl.

'What's that you're saying? I'm your best mate in the whole world?'

'Yes, all right. Now give over, you're showing me up.'

'Right answer, darling. You've secured yourself a stay of execution.'

Much to Ray's relief, his mood finally lifted and the last hours of trading sailed by without a hitch. The pair were busy packing up when Hawkeye called over.

''Ere, Ray. Hope I didn't drop you in it by giving that posh bird your address? Urgent family matter she reckoned. All very formal. I was in two minds about it, but she looked harmless enough.'

'I wondered who the Good Samaritan was. Cheers for that,' he answered sarcastically. 'As it happens, she got the wrong bloke. More's the pity,' he added, faking a grin.

'Should have sent her back to me then. Right little cracker that one.'

'Who's he on about?' asked Ruby.

'Blimey girl, you don't miss a trick. Just get them bags packed up.'

Ruby watched Hawkeye's attempt to juggle manky fruit, which ended as mush at his feet.

'Why's he always wearing that eyepatch? Think he's some sort of pirate or what?'

'War wound. Shrapnel. Poor sod lost his eye.'

'Oh gawd. Now I feel really bad.'

'Forget it. He wouldn't take offence. He's heard it all before. And anyway, they fitted him with a glass one.

Half the time he forgets to put the thing in, so shoves the patch on just in case.'

'Bloody hell,' she shuddered. 'He's lucky he hasn't lost it.'

'He's come close, especially down the pub. Been known to slip it in a woman's lager. It's a miracle it's still in one piece. That eye's been around the block in more ways than one. He'll let you have a butchers if you want? He's got no problem showing it off.'

Ruby cringed. 'Leave it out!'

Later, With the barrow back in the lock-up, Ruby shot off towards home while Ray stopped by the Cafe. The place had emptied out and all surfaces wiped clean of fag-ash and crumbs, ready for the morning. With no Sal in sight, Ray turned to Pam, busy washing down the counter.

'She's in the kitchen. Shall I give her a shout?' she asked.

'No need, I'll catch her later.'

The kitchen door opened and Sal came into view, followed by her female companion.

Ray took one look at the cosy duo and grunted. 'What the hell's going on?' he fumed. A raging heat tore through his body as once again he came face to face with the mystery woman from yesterday. He made a grab for the door.

'Hold up,' said Sal. 'We need to have words before you disappear.'

'Is that right? Well, you two plod on and fill your boots. I want no part in it, but cheers for the offer,' he grimaced and turned his back as if to leave.

'Please stay. I won't keep you long. I promise.'

The gentle pleading in the young woman's voice prompted him to hesitate.

He glanced across his shoulder. She had a delicate, classy air about her. Not the sort to knowingly court trouble, he surmised. But what did he know? He'd thought the same of Ruth Ellis, the last woman hanged at Holloway prison. Credit where it's due, this blonde was persistent, he'd give her that, and polite too! *Sal should take a leaf out of her book,* he thought. His sister's unexpected bossy manner had taken him by surprise, his back now well and truly up.

Sal was a magnet for constant gripes and hard knock stories. He knew that as well as every other sod. She only had herself to blame though. He'd told her over and again, *don't be so bloody gullible, they'll wear you down,* but did she listen to him? Of course not, and trying to protect the silly mare was like pushing treacle up a hill. All the same, taking her frustrations out on him was bang out of order. He'd be having words of his own, later.

Sal motioned towards Pam. 'I'll finish up here, love. You get yourself home.' Pam didn't need telling twice. The second the door closed behind her, Sal secured the lock. 'Let's just sit down and talk this through, Ray. Like adults.'

Ray remained by the counter, his jaw clenched and weight shifting constantly from one foot to the other.

'Heaven's above, Ray, what's to lose? Let's just sit and talk. You might be surprised by what Pearl here has to say.'

Ray froze momentarily at the mention of her name. Whoever she was, she had clearly done her homework, he decided. Besides which, the name itself, although rare, was hardly unique.

'That's a matter of opinion,' he grumbled, edging towards a chair. Instinct was his trusted fail-safe. He never questioned the urge to bolt. Not once. Why then did he allow a ripple of doubt to hold him back? It irked him to know he'd likely pay over the odds for ignoring his intuition.

The girl's voice carried a slight tremble. 'I had no idea you knew each other!'

'Don't look so worried,' said Sal reassuringly. 'We don't bite, as a rule,' she added for Ray's benefit. 'This handsome creature is my brother.'

Not a fan of being discussed within earshot, Ray interjected. 'Give it a rest, Sal. So, big on reincarnation are they in the USA?' His question directed at Pearl.

Two fine lines appeared between the girl's brows. 'I don't understand?'

'Let me put you straight then. My precious baby daughter died in America, days before her third birthday. So forgive me for not playing along. Perhaps now you can understand why your little charade won't work?'

'I did live in the States, it's true.'

'No one would guess from your accent. Bit of a slip up there I'd say.' He watched her closely. His memory was busy conjuring up similarities. She did resemble his ex. Didn't she? The high cheek bones, the full lips ...

'Look, I know this is difficult for you,' said Pearl.

'You have no idea, princess,' Ray cut in.

'Please, just give me chance to explain.'

'Floors yours. The sooner we get this over the better.'

'I've lived here from eight years old, just up the road in fact. I was in America, as I've mentioned. My father, um stepfather,' she corrected, 'was not a man to be crossed. One night he ordered us into his truck, Mum and me, and drove us miles from our remote farmhouse and dumped us on the edge of a town. We'd nothing but the clothes on our backs. Mum worked all hours for the fare to bring us back to England. I don't know the history between you two, but I do know that Mum sacrificed so much for me. I didn't know a single thing about you until Mum died a year ago. She kept a box of paperwork, which I discovered when sorting her belongings. No one was more shocked than me to find these photos and certificates.' She slid the buff-coloured folder across the tabletop towards Ray. 'When I came to your house, you told me your daughter had died?'

Ray laid the contents out in front of him, He swallowed hard. 'I had a letter. Whooping cough, it read.' His voice faltered. He glanced at Sal for back-up.

'Yes, I can vouch for that,' Sal put in, before sloping off to give her nose a good blow. Seconds later she was back in her chair.

Ray detected hairline cracks undermining his hardened exterior.

'I truly have no idea why or how that came about,' said Pearl. 'But it is beginning to make sense. Do take a look at what I found. If afterwards you want nothing to do with me, then I won't bother you again. Mum did leave a note. It's amongst those papers,' she indicated. You might want to read it. I think it refers to the letter you mentioned?' Ray unfolded the distinctive blue airmail writing paper.

My beautiful girl.

I have carried a secret for the longest time. A secret too shameful to share. At the risk of losing you, I kept quiet, but the time has come to put the record straight. As painful and confusing as it is, what I tell you now will make for a brighter future. It breaks my heart to deliver such news in this way, and you've every right to hate me. I know I don't deserve forgiveness, but maybe one day you'll see things differently?

As a young married mum, I was silly enough to fall for the charms of an American soldier. With my head lodged in the clouds, he offered me the stars. The world he described was beyond magical, (although the reality was anything but). One freezing fog-blurred morning I bundled you up and left London for the States. Bruce, who hopefully you won't remember too well, wasn't your real daddy. Your father was a lovely man and I am truly sorry for keeping you two apart. Many years ago, under Bruce's watchful eye, I was forced to write a letter. My heart broke knowing the pain it would bring, but believe me when I say I had no choice! The contents of the letter I am too ashamed to repeat, but once written there was no way back.

The documents in this box contain information about your father. Go and find him my darling girl. He loved you so much. He will protect you through this life like no other. I realised many years ago that I'd made the biggest mistake by walking out on my one true love. In the months that followed it quickly dawned on me, that Walworth had its own wealth of stars, only I was too blind to notice. Make a wonderful life for yourself my darling.

Your loving Mum xx

Still seated, Pearl struggled out of her coat and draped it over the chair back. The sight of the brooch, pinned to her jumper, brought a lump to Ray's throat, while Sal's hand flew to her chest as if to steady her heartbeat.

'Goodness me,' she exclaimed. 'The girl likes daffodils, Ray.'

A smile crept across Pearl's face. 'Yes, they're my favourite. Sunshine on sticks, I call them. Apparently, as a toddler I used to push my nose into the little trumpet.'

'And giggle till the cows came home,' said Ray, finishing her sentence.

Ray's chair grated backwards. Every known emotion poured in, merged and spiralled through his system. He'd no idea if he was on his head or his backside, whether to laugh, cry or mess himself. Everything was out of synch, and beyond his control. Like a doddery old-timer he forced himself up and out of the chair. His marshmallow knees would give out any minute. If he crumbled, she'd be gone, he'd convinced himself. She'd brush him off. See him as a liability; a noose around her pretty slender neck. He couldn't lose her. Not again. The child who had danced through his dreams stood before him, just as anxious, just as uncertain and just as beautiful. With no confidence in remaining upright, his words, tender as a dew-kissed petal, tumbled out, 'Come give your dad a hug. Please.'

Her piercing blue eyes, the exact shade as his own, brimmed with tears. Ray wrapped his arms around her, and with her face firm against his pounding chest, they melted into each other and cried.

Chapter 47

Within yards of home, Ruby froze. A figure, partially hidden in the doorway, set her heart thumping. With minimal street lamps working, the shadowy outline was hard to determine, appearing blacker than night itself. She crossed to the other side of the street, her feet barely moving. Dimmed yellow lights from behind drawn curtains offered little comfort. She wished she had hung back, waited for Ray and Sal as usual. Her thoughts diverted to Mickey. She knew she was being daft, but with the memory of his death still raw as a sliced finger, her senses remained on full alert. A shrill voice cut through her thoughts.

'About bloody time,' called Ellen from the doorway. 'I'm frozen stiff! Me poor nipples could double as coat hooks.'

Ruby beamed and raced into her sister's arms. Ellen had been the last person she'd expected to see. 'I'd no chance of recognising you in that getup,' she said, surprised. Ellen's black maxi coat with its deep collar reminded Ruby of the Dracula character skulking through the mist.

'Hardly recognised myself.' She laughed. 'It fell off the back of a lorry. You after it then?' she asked.

'You must be kidding! I'd have chucked it back,' Ruby laughed.

The sisters had a special bond, finding humour where others found only misery.

'Is anyone home?' asked Ellen.

'Not yet. Sal's off somewhere with George, and Ray's, well, who knows?'

'Good. Cos what I've got to say is for your ears only. Listen, I've been stood here forever,' she continued, checking her watch. 'Steve's picking me up by the library in half hour and I've loads to tell yer.'

Ruby, turned the key in the lock. 'You should have rung last night. I'd have made sure I was here when you turned up. You want a cuppa?'

'Gawd, no. I could plaster a wall with the coating on my tongue.' Ellen unbuttoned her coat and hurled it over the banister.

The girls rushed into the sitting room where Ruby turned the dial on the gas fire and waited for the click to signify ignition. Ellen immediately slipped off her shoes, dived into the nearside chair and offered her feet up to the pale blue flames. 'We hadn't planned to come. It was all last minute. Steve's mum had a funny turn. He's there now, checking on her.'

'Nothing serious?' asked Ruby concerned.

'Hope not. Doctor reckons she's diabetic. The woman's got more chance of shacking up with Elvis than giving up chocolate. Anyway, it gave me chance to nip to Chaucer, see Mum and all. Thanks for the address by the way. I was chuffed to bits when my neighbour said you'd rung.'

'The block's a bit of a dump, but they've got the flat looking nice,'

'Yeah, they've done all right. Oh, and as for Daisy,' Ellen teased. 'She was sat in the stairway holding hands with some goofy kid.'

'That'll be the boyfriend, Bunter.'

'I thought she called him Billy?'

'Same difference,' smiled Ruby.

Consciously aware that time was ticking, Ruby chivvied Ellen along. 'Come on, out with it. Must be dead serious to risk your nipples dropping off,' she teased.

Ellen shifted restlessly in her chair, and fussed with the ribbed edging of her chunky monochrome jumper. Ruby wondered about the news, and knew it would not be good. Ellen rarely held back. Tell it as it is and to hell with the consequences was a rule she lived by. Ruby knew her sister was struggling to find words that would soften the blow. The seemingly endless wait had her wincing from a bitten and bleeding fingernail. Despite her anxiety, she refused to push Ellen further. For every second she wasn't privy to the news, her world would remain relatively normal.

'Get your finger out your mouth. You'll get another whitlow at this rate,' Ellen warned. 'Hope your Sal's a dab hand with bread poultices, cos by the state of that nail you'll soon be needing one.'

Ruby folded her arms, keeping her hands out of sight. 'Is that why you're here, to keep me in check?'

'Not exactly. I've got some news. I take it you haven't spoken to Aunt Grace lately?'

Guilt shifted Ruby's gaze away from that of her sister's. Many times she had come close to making that call, but a reason not to always presented itself. 'I keep putting it off,' she admitted. 'But only in case he answers,' she added forcibly. 'Just hearing his voice turns my stomach. I really don't like that man.'

'Well, no need to worry. He won't be answering again, since he's no longer there.'

'I don't get it,' Ruby frowned. 'Oh, no, he's buggered off and left her, hasn't he?'

'That's one way of putting it.' A faint smile played on Ellen's lips. 'He's been banged up.'

'What? Prison?'

298

'The very same. He's been remanded. Just walked in off the street. Told the cops' all about his sleazy self.'

'No way!' Ruby shook her head. It doesn't make sense. Why would he do that?'

'I think he may have been persuaded.'

'Meaning what? Oh, please don't tell me you had a hand in it?'

'As if,' said Ellen. 'OK, so I knocked him off his bike, but that's it. I'd hardly punch two barrels out of him with my bare hands. Would I? No,' she answered herself. 'Whoever got to him had other plans. Prison for one. A taste of his own medicine if you get my meaning.' She grinned. 'Grace's neighbour Jean was there when I phoned. Turns out some blokes jumped him a couple of weeks beforehand. He ended up in hospital. Pretty bad by all accounts.'

'No!' murmured Ruby, finding it hard to take in.

'I'm telling you straight. The cops gave up looking for his missing fingers. Lost a few, so Jean reckons.'

The sudden acid burn in Ruby's throat triggered a gagging motion. Ellen rushed to the kitchenette, filled a beaker with water and encouraged her sister to take small sips. Ruby drank without taking breath and placed the empty vessel down on the hearth.

'I knew I shouldn't have opened my mouth.'

Ruby shook her head. 'No, you did right. I need to know what's going on. But what about Grace? Is she OK?'

'Yeah, Jean's organised everything, a cleaner, shopping, it's all sorted.'

'I meant, how'd she take it?'

'Devastated, as you'd expect. Typical Grace though: blames herself, her blindness. The police reassured her best they could. Between you and me, Jean says he was a spiteful son-of-a-bitch behind closed doors.'

Ruby's heart sank. 'Poor Grace. I had no idea,' she mumbled. Ruby had experience of her uncle sounding off, but it took a cowardly bully to beat a defenceless woman. A caring, gentle soul living her life like the rest of them, behind a painted smile. Ruby's words dripped with anger. 'I detest him so much.'

'Well, let's hope they nail him. Big time! The police searched the house,' she paused, wriggling her feet back into her shoes.

'And?' Ruby badgered. 'You can't leave me hanging, for Pete's sake!'

Ellen filled her lungs. 'Look, you're a mess. Maybe I've said too much already. I should go.' Placing her hands on the armrests, she had no sooner lifted her backside from the cushion when Ruby dropped to her knees in front of her.

'Maybe you should get it off your chest and be done with it.' Ruby held her sister's hands. 'Go on. Please.'

'They discovered a small bag.' She gulped. 'Polaroid prints.'

Ruby's mouth gaped in shock. Not a single word passed her lips.

'Yeah, that's how I felt when I heard. About time he got his comeuppance.'

'Will they question you?' Ruby asked.

'Shouldn't think so. I doubt for a minute he'd mention family. Sad truth is he'll likely get off. No one talks about this sort of thing. It's brushed under the mat. In all honesty, Rube, who'd put their child through those sorts of questions?' She stroked Ruby's cheek. 'I'm just grateful that he didn't get his grubby mitts on you. Don't think I could have lived with that.'

'He wouldn't have dared, not with you looking out for me.' She turned away, afraid that her expression would betray her.

Presently, out of sight in the kitchenette, Ruby lit the gas beneath the kettle. Tea was furthest from her thoughts, but it provided an excuse for time-out. One thing she did need was space. The space to bury her face in the backdoor curtain and release a torrent of silent tears. No questions asked.

*

George and Sal sat in the empty public bar of The Bedford Arms. Its ancient furniture and maroon flocked wallpaper were dingy in the extreme. One stop short of a mausoleum. Convenience was its main draw, for those seeking undisturbed thinking time. Other than a glass of Dutch courage, it offered little else by way of stimulus.

'So, what's with the love-birds, Sal? One minute my boy is all singing and dancing and driving me doolally and the next it's like some maudlin misfit has taken him over. Don't mind telling you, love, I'm that worried. I mean, it's not in his character to be so down in the mouth. You know my Jimmy, he's a bright spark.' He supped his beer. 'I reckon your Ruby's stringing him along, messing with him. One thing I do know is that he loves the bones of that girl. But I won't see him hurt, Sal. Not by her. Not by anyone.'

'Listen to yourself, George. They're just kids for heaven's sake. Give them a chance. Look, I'm not talking from experience, but that doesn't mean I walk around with my eyes shut. I've seen it a thousand times over. The more you put your foot down, warn them off, the more they'll do the opposite. He won't thank you for interfering.'

George stared into his beer, contemplating the froth. He caught the gist of what Sal said. His own thoughts ran along similar lines. She was a smart woman, spoke a lot of sense, and he valued her input. The one glaring

301

difference being, that he knew first hand from the boy's perspective how it felt to be taken for a mug. Things like that take some getting over. Oh yeah, his sixteen-year-old self-had laughed it off for the benefit of his mates, plenty more fish and all that malarky. But inside it does things to a lad: rips a gaping hole in a fragile confidence and plugs it with self-doubt.

'I hear what you're saying, I do. But it grieves me to see my boy so churned up when he's been through so much already. Look, you know her better than anyone, help me out here, girl. That's all I'm asking.'

Sal rubbed the back of his hand and his table tapping ceased.

'You know me, George. I won't break a confidence. But what I will say is this: Ruby's had a difficult time herself of late. It's a crying shame what that girl and her family have been through. But she's a good kid and I trust her like me own flesh and blood. Just give them space. That's all you can do.'

Chapter 48

Ruby fought to keep her emotions in check. Everything conspired against her. Little things that normally went unnoticed now riled her like ants on a free-for-all rampage. Not only did Ellen's revelations still dominate, but the stupid telly was on the blink, and her rotten monthly cramps had come way too early. But the final straw was being propped in the corner like a posable hat stand, with the portable television ariel glued to her hand. She realised her feelings toward Ray were unjustified. She'd have to be unconscious not to notice the positive change in him. His usual snappy wisecracks and grumpy-git character had, on occasions, been replaced with a grin so blinding that she suspected lockjaw.

It's OK for him, she thought, *shouting his orders like some trumped up sergeant major.* 'That's it! I've had enough,' she protested. 'I'm dropping it now, whether you like it or not.'

'Wait up,' Ray pleaded. 'It's nearly there, look!' Ghostly faces emerged through the snowy blizzard that filled the television screen.

'You said that ages ago.' Ruby moved away from the set. 'Here, you sort it.' She thrust the ariel into Ray's hand. She wished she'd followed Sal's lead and plumped for an earlier night.

Ray tossed the small metal structure aside. 'Bloody waste of time.'

'Thanks a lot.'

'Didn't mean you. Daft mare. I'll tell you what though,' he started, but his words were lost when the TV suddenly blasted out the national anthem. They both scrambled for the off switch. The circular metallic dial dropped into Ruby's palm. She straightened up, and with poker face intact, she offered it to Ray. Try as she might to hold the laughter at bay, it bubbled up and spilled out. She moved across to the settee and perched on the cushion's edge.

'Come on then, out with it. It's obvious something's bothering yer.'

'Don't know what you mean', said Ruby.

'OK. I'm not about to twist your arm, but I'm here if you change your mind.' He circled the room pulling plugs from sockets, a precursor to turning in for the night. It was a habit he'd picked up from his old man, and found difficult to shake. The moment the last plug hit the linoleum; Ruby spoke up.

'Actually, there is something.'

Ray sat down next to her, side-on.

'Do you remember my uncle turning up at the stall?'

'You mean the beady-eyed slimeball? I never forget a face darling.'

'I've just heard that he's been remanded.'

'On what charge? Oh, let me guess.'

Ruby couldn't bring herself to say the words. She glanced at the TV, willing it into life again to save her embarrassment.

'I knew the bloke was a bad lot the minute I clapped eyes on him,' said Ray. 'Good riddance is what I say.'

'The thing is, he got beat up just weeks before he handed himself in.'

'Nothing less than his kind deserves. Maybe a good whack jarred his conscience?'

'Doubt it,' said Ruby. 'He hasn't got one.'

'Well, there you go. So, what's the big deal?'

'They cut him, pretty bad,' she grimaced. 'He lost fingers.'

'Good for them. That'll teach the old git. Daresay he'll think twice in future. If he survives that long.'

'You don't seem shocked.'

'Why would I be? Listen, If I'd have been working the bolt cutters, he'd have lost a lot more than fingers. Believe me.'

'Bolt cutters?' Ruby's stomach somersaulted at the very idea. 'But they weren't even mentioned.'

'The thing is,' he stopped to organise his thoughts. 'It stands to reason, doesn't it. Tools of the trade, girl. Oh, come on, you've seen the newspapers. I'm not telling you anything you don't already know.' With no retort from Ruby, Ray continued. 'There's plenty out there with scores to settle. No one in their right mind would try it on with a table knife. Blunt as arseholes them things. Wouldn't cut your throat, let alone bone.'

A shiver ran the length of Ruby's spine. She despised her uncle, and always would. Nevertheless, the image now lodged in her head was not one she wanted. 'D'you reckon he'll get sent down?'

'Depends on the evidence. Be a damn shame if he doesn't though. They'd welcome his sort with open arms, if you get my drift.'

The conversation stalled. The ticking of the mantel clock appeared to dominate the room. She appreciated Ray's take on the situation. She could rely on him to be up front with her, which is what she wanted, after all. What she didn't want, were the nightmare graphics that would haunt her in the days to come. As if picking up on her thoughts, Ray reconsidered his response.

'Listen, who am I to say what went on? You know me, forever the pessimist.' He forced a chuckle. Realising his humour was wasted, he tried again.

'You heard of Chinese whispers?'

'Course.'

'I reckon that's what's happened here. People like a bit of drama. They change things to suit, till you end up with something so ridiculous it's laughable. Chances are the bloke was legless, kissed the pavement and smashed his bottles of stout. Simple as that. It happens to the best of us.'

'You don't believe that for a minute.'

'Anything's possible is all I'm saying.' Ray sprang to his feet. 'That's me done. I'm off upstairs.' He stopped unexpectedly at the sitting room door, and placed his ear to the woodwork. In his quietest voice he asked, 'Do you hear that?'

Ruby concentrated, hoping they hadn't woken Sal. She shook her head.

'It's me bed calling me.' He laughed at his own wit. 'All right for you with a day off tomorrow, but some of us have to work.'

The man was completely crackers, Ruby decided. She knew his game-plan was to leave her with a smile, and much to her surprise, it worked.

Chapter 49

The palatial, red brick building with its wealth of overly long sash windows, each section housing eight small panes of glass, made Ruby stop and check her scribbled directions. The East Street librarian had encouraged her to write down the details during her last visit. If it wasn't for the two navy-blue lamps, hung either side of the main door, she'd have turned, retraced her steps, and headed back to Sal's. Ruby decided that the grand building appeared more suited to Lord and Lady Whats-A-Name, than police interview rooms and stark cold cells.

Seated in the foyer, Ruby's fingers dug into the course blue fabric, as she fought the urge to head back towards the door. Such places gave her the creeps, made her feel guilty even though she'd done nothing wrong. Her constant fidgeting had the man seated alongside, moaning loudly. 'Quit with the moving. You're making me fucking seasick.'

The moment Ruby decided to leave, her name was called.

She looked away when sharing particular memories, even though the police officers' kid gloves approach made her feel easier for the first time in her own skin. She was able to give information that would stand up in court, if necessary, to bring about a conviction. She had made a stand, alone, something she never dreamt she'd have the guts to do. She would show Uncle Tom how she'd changed from that scared little girl he'd turned her into. Justice would be done. She had every confidence in that. An odd sensation came to the fore, a feeling of pride. Something that had never touched her life before. From this moment on she would walk tall, leave the past behind where it belonged and go forward into a brighter future.

By early-afternoon the ordeal was over. She had offloaded the guilt, the trauma and the self-loathing. All the sordid details were now deposited into a manila box file by the police.

Ruby walked the maze of white painted corridors and exited the building. She stood awhile on the lower step, re-buttoning her coat, eyes partly closed against the chill wind that greeted her. Only then did the enormity of the past hours hit home. Although her heart-rate had eventually found its natural rhythm, the cogs in her brain were free-wheeling, throwing everything at her. Remembered sentences were dissected, re-jigged and thrown back in the mix. Had she said too little? Too much? All manner of questions vied for space in an already crowded arena. She couldn't decide if the heels of her hands, pressed firm against her temples, eased the building pressure, the headache. Either way, standing there like someone about to implode was not a good look. She tucked her straggly hair inside her coat, sucked in a breath and moved on.

Although the clouds were finally shifting, the weak winter sun, barely visible, offered no respite from the freezing temperature that had already seeped into her bones. She shivered. As a child she would cheekily add that quivering brrr sound for her mother's benefit. Kate would steer her frozen nipper into the nearest cafe. *Let's pop in for a warm*, her mother would say, and they'd sit awhile with their hands crowded around a shared mug of tea.

Ruby smiled inwardly at the memory. She could see her mother's face, the love that lifted her cheeks with a ready smile, the tenderness in those pale blue eyes. The way her chin tilted when she giggled, and she did giggle, often at the silliest of things too. Ruby, somehow, had always known that her mother protected them, her babies, from the daily struggles, the hardships. Hardships that would have seen a lesser person crumble.

With the tables turned, Ruby and her sister would now protect their mother at all costs. They would shield her from the heartbreak, the truth of those summers spent in Bromley.

The bus appeared ahead of schedule. If she didn't move her backside, she'd miss the thing altogether and have to wait however long for the next. She ran, her small shoulder bag bashing against her hip, while waving frantically to catch the driver's attention, unaware that the queue ahead was twelve deep. A child, blessed with Shirley Temple curls and spring-loaded shoes, bounced and waved back from a near side seat.

Much to Ruby's annoyance, the driver ignored her sprinting alongside. She, however, had caught the discreet turn of his head as he sailed by. 'Miserable sod,' she fumed. Spotting the queue, she slowed down, caught her breath, and thought of all the names she'd consider calling him if she weren't so desperate to get home. The bus eventually stopped, and minutes later she climbed aboard. She took the stairs to the upper deck and flopped down in the front seat. With hands cupped to her mouth, short bursts of white breath did little to ease her tingling fingertips.

Ray elbowed his way into her thoughts, *bolt-cutters, tools of the trade*. Those same words kept her awake half the night. The other thing he'd mentioned had impact enough to drag her early from her bed that very morning. *Depends on the evidence.* Any ideas of a lazy day were soon forgotten. Uncle Tom was guilty. She knew it. Her sister knew it, so did the people who had scared him enough to force his hand to surrender himself for his own safety.

Ruby understood that if he pleaded guilty, she wouldn't have to attend court; the WPC had assured her. She could do no more than wait for that telephone call, a call that she prayed would bring tears of relief; the other option was simply too frightening to consider.

Chapter 50

Sal felt as though she had been put though the mangle. Her mood, flat as a bum note, did not go unnoticed. If one more customer ribbed her about having more hump than a camel, she would not be responsible for her actions. She never thought she'd see the day when her manner reflected that of a sulky teenager. Her heart went out to all the mothers. No wonder the poor things were on their knees.

Despite giving herself a good talking to, she could not snap out of it. Her face ached from the exaggerated smiles she felt forced to deliver. What the hell had got into her? *Get your glad rags ready*, George had instructed less than a week beforehand. *We're off up west, next Monday, for a date that will blow your socks off, Sal.* His grin, so big, it practically swallowed up his face. He laughingly ignored Sal's badgering for more details. *Give us a hint, George. I mean, what the hell do I wear*? He refused to budge, insisting she would do him proud whatever she chose.

Sal had visualised her so-called Sunday best, hanging moth eaten in the wardrobe. With Pam ever willing to hold the fort, Sal had hopped on the bus to Peckham High Street. After much dilly-dallying she settled on a smart two piece, a dress and longline jacket. The navy and cream design, more classic than modern, suited her to a tee, and with her hair set in the local salon she hardly recognised herself.

The morning, after the secret event, arrived with a bevy of starving workers crying out for their fry-up breakfast. By mid-morning Pam could hold her tongue no longer. 'Beats me,' she said, to no one in particular as she placed pink iced buns onto a plate. 'Some people are born kill-joys.'

Sal, continuing to fill the over-sized teapot, piped up. 'Meaning?'

'Stands to reason, doesn't it,' Pam nagged. 'Yesterday you could have passed for a Duchess, or so I've heard, in the company of royalty no less. We're all jealous and itching to know the ins and outs. Am I right or what?' she bellowed, directing her question to the customers, who cheered in response. 'And here you are, acting like you've been slapped in the face with a kipper. Don't keep us in suspenders, Sal,' she begged.

'It's suspense,' Sal corrected, trying to disguise a yawn.

'I know what the flipping word is! I'm just trying to cheer you up.'

'But who told you? I didn't even know myself until last night,' Sal wheedled.

Pam laughed wittingly. 'A little bird. Actually, it was a big bird, too damned excited to keep his surprise to himself. Bless him.'

Last night's event had knocked the stuffing out of Sal. She wanted to share the excitement that had her close to swooning on more than one occasion, but where did she start? What she actually needed was to close her eyes and drift off. She hadn't slept a blessed wink.

'Take no notice of me. I'm beat, that's all,' said Sal, reaching into the drawer below the counter. She lifted the glossy programme from her cloth carrier and handed it to Pam. She still couldn't believe her luck, and frequently pinched herself. The London Palladium had been furthest from her thoughts. At best she imagined

George taking her to an upmarket restaurant, where she'd likely show herself up by using the wrong cutlery. She hated surprises. They played havoc with her nerves.

'Blimey Sal.' Pam flicked hungrily through the glossy pages. 'I'd have given anything to be in your shoes. All these famous faces.'

'I'll treat you to the pictures, darling,' winked a saucy feller on his way to the yard.

'On your bike, cheapskate. It's Royal Variety or nothing,' Pam called out, drooling over a picture of Tom Jones.

Sal, under pressure for minute details, found herself once again stepping into the auditorium. 'The whole place was decked out in red and gold,' she offered dreamily. 'I felt like a kid sneaking into a fairytale, half expecting to be turfed out on my ear if caught. The gold carved pillars took my breath, and the carpets! Well, don't even get me started on them. I'd have been happy just sat there taking in the surroundings, never mind the constant stream of turns.'

Pam's concentration slipped. 'Carpets.' she frowned. 'To hell with the carpets, what about the Queen, the acts?'

'I did catch sight of the Queen's tiara. As for the acts, it's all in there,' Sal indicated. 'I've re-lived every single minute and then some, all night long, and my head is fit to burst.'

'Must have cost George an arm and a leg. He's clearly out to impress,' Pam remarked. With no answer forthcoming, she prattled on. 'You've got a good one there, Sal. My last excuse for a bloke was a tight git. He wouldn't give you the dripping from his nose.'

Sal ignored the comment, poured herself a cup of coffee and found a quiet corner.

The evening had been perfect. A feast for the eyes George had called it, and Sal could not have agreed

313

more. However, during the taxi ride home a sudden change occurred in his manner that she couldn't quite fathom. She wondered if the half-pint in the backstreet pub had anything to do with it? Warm beer played havoc with his indigestion. He'd admitted that himself. Didn't stop him polishing off every last drop though. His usual non-stop chatter drifted out of the taxi window along with his cigarette smoke, while awkward silences sat between them.

When the black cab pulled up outside her house, George had stepped out and held the door open. A beam of light from next door's window, reflected off the perspiration trickling in rivulets down his face. Taking her arm, he walked Sal to the door.

You sure you're okay, George? You're not sickening for something, are you? She'd asked

No Sal, but I'm in such a mess.

Fearful that he was about to collapse, Sal unlocked the street door and ushered him along the passage. *Sit yourself down there.* She'd gestured towards the settee. *I'll ring the doctor, see if he'll come and check you over.*

George struggled back to his feet. *There's no need for that. he protested. It's me ticker,* he said, loosening his tie. *I've been wanting to tell you for ages.*

Good Lord, you daft sod. Fancy keeping something like that to yourself. Does Jimmy know? Let me call an ambulance?

Stop fussing, woman, and sit down. I'm not about to kick the bucket, although some might prefer I did. It's just, well, I've been getting myself in a right two and eight lately. And it's all your doing.

What on earth are you going on about? What's this got to do with any...? Her words trailed off as the penny finally dropped.

George stood up and took her hands in his. *Sal, I can't stop thinking about you girl. Me hearts like one of them jumping jack firework thingies, sparking off like a dodgy connection.*

A nervous giggle rose in Sal's throat, which she coughed to disguise it. Feeling flustered, she'd attempted to play down his advances. *Warm beer has got a lot to answer for. Best I put the kettle on, water down the effects.* She stood up and turned towards the kitchen.

George reached for her arm. *Don't dash off. Hear me out, love. Please.* He lowered himself down onto one knee.

Saints alive! What's got into you? You're acting like a schoolboy.

That's exactly it, Sal. That's exactly how you make me feel. Although I might need a hand to get back up again, he'd added, with a sly grin. *Anyway, while I'm down here, I was about to ask...*

The answer's no, George, she'd interrupted. *It might surprise you to know, but I've already been proposed to.* Sal walked past him and into the kitchen.

Well, of all the... he grumbled, trying to lever himself off the floor. His dodgy knee cracked and creaked, gave way and flipped him onto his side.

Sal's head moved back and forth from behind the kitchen door. With a tea towel pressed hard against her mouth, she barely remained upright. Her body convulsed in a bid to stop her head exploding with laughter.

Well, I'd never have thought it of you, Sal. Seeing someone behind my back, he ranted. *I'll knock his fecking block off, so help me I will.*

Sal could hold back no longer. She poked her head through the opening. *It was you. You silly oaf.*

He scrambled to his feet. *Well, I'm glad you think it's funny. Hang on a minute. What'd you mean it's me?*

You asked me back in the summer. Sal stepped back into the room. *I'm guessing you don't remember? You'd had a skinful as I recall.'*

Oh, right, well, so I'm still in with a chance then? He'd rubbed his palm across his chin. *Hold up, didn't you turn me down?*

Sal took off down the passage with George following close behind. She opened the street door. *I believe my answer was that I'd think it over.*

Well, I can live with that, not indefinitely, mind. So, why not make an old man happy and give me an answer tonight?

Not tonight, George. I'm still thinking about it.

What the...

Sal closed the door behind him. *See you tomorrow*, she'd called, before drawing the curtain along the wire. She laughed her way back to the kitchen, lit the gas beneath the kettle and made herself a strong tea.

Pam bought Sal back to the present with a loud, 'Ahem. Apologies for interrupting your extended break, Duchess,' she said in a farcical hoity toity manner, 'but the gentleman at the counter is requesting your presence.'

Laughing off Pam's interpretation of a toff, Sal walked over to where George stood patiently waiting. His winning smile told her all she needed to know. The man was here for one reason alone. An answer.

Chapter 51

Ray's day got off to a good start. A lead on some quality supplies had turned up trumps. Deal done. Things were looking up all round, and he couldn't be happier. He headed home earlier than expected, with time enough to grab a bite and spruce himself up for an afternoon at the museum. It was a rarity to have the gaff to himself. No females fussing or bending his ear. Just to hear himself think was a blessing. He raided the larder and munched his way through cheese and crackers. With a coffee cooling on the draining board, he grabbed his shaving pouch from the windowsill, popped the small tarnished mirror against the tiled splashback and lathered up. Silver flecked stubble disappeared with each stroke of the razor. He doused himself with Old Spice, avoiding the specks of tissue dotted about his chin. Chuffed with the profile of the forty something teenager, he nodded his approval. 'Not bad, even if I do say so myself,' he said aloud, knowing full well that no one else would offer such praise.

For decades he had trudged a mundane path, going through the motions, work, pub and bed, with an occasional fling to break the monotony. Living like a monk after his excuse of a marriage was never on the cards. He enjoyed women's company, when on his terms. No strings, no hearts and flowers and definitely no pressure. Fortunately for him, his past acquaintances were like-minded. His lifestyle was not dissimilar to his drinking buddies. They did what they did to get by, same as everyone else. End of. It certainly didn't warrant discussion. He hadn't recognised the rut that held him knee-deep, until Leah. She had thrown him a life-line, dragged his unprotesting arse along a different path. She'd rescued him, he realised, and what did that say about him, oblivious to the fact that he even needed saving! No point losing sleep over wasted years, he told himself. He had lugged his size nines along the slow lane long enough. A remembered slogan from the TV slapped a smile on his face. He moved closer to the mirror. 'Full steam ahead, boyo. You've got yourself a tiger in the tank.'

Dressed in new grey Chinos, a crisp white shirt and V-neck pullover, Ray buttoned his refer jacket and headed towards the museum. Sal had often chipped in about his lack of so-called style, calling him a slovenly sod, her words wrapped in a half smile to lessen the blow. He'd kept many gents' outfitters solvent, back in the day. But now, spending dough on fancy togs to work the market was like tossing fivers down a drain, he'd argued. Who the hell would be interested in him anyway, a middle-aged lump with the beginnings of a flabby tyre just visible above his belt? Oh, he'd warranted second looks alright, when distracted and short changing someone. Even then, they'd bore into him, with their die-now-you-cheating-bastard stares, with not a single mention of his newly pressed Fred Perry shirt.

A passer-by broke Ray's train of thought. 'Ere Guv, you got the time?'

A moment's realisation struck Ray head-on. 'It'll be my own fault if I don't,' he said, quickening his pace.

Leah, in her black pencil skirt, pale peach blouse and low heels, greeted Ray as he entered the main display area. He loved the way her hair was loosely piled on top, not lacquered to perfection but natural, with wavy strands that shifted when she moved. Dark, soft hair splayed across a pillow, he wished, that moved like silk through his fingers just the way it had done in his dreams.

'Are you OK?' asked Leah, her fingers skimming his elbow. 'You seem miles away.'

'I, yeah, I was for a second,' he wavered. 'You fancy nipping back to that little Italian place when we've finished here? The one by the station, with the cosy booths and proper coffee?'

'You must have read my mind. I skipped breakfast and I'm ravenous.'

Ray enjoyed their visits to the restaurant cum sandwich bar, where they were now on first name terms with the staff. It was a far cry from the greasy spoons he'd normally use, where private conversations were anything but. Italian food though? All that garlic and spaghetti and sauce spattered shirt fronts, no chance. A slice of beef between two freshly baked doorsteps and heavy on the horseradish suited him just fine.

Leah continued. 'The under manager instructed that I take you through to the back office as soon as you arrive,' she said, a little concerned. 'Any idea what he wants?'

Ray shook his head. 'Nah. He phoned home, managed to catch Sal, and left a brief message. I reckon he's after giving me the elbow.'

'I doubt that. You're brilliant with the kids and he would know that already.' Leah held a hand to her mouth. 'I shouldn't be saying this, but he's a prickly character and very punctilious at times.' She quickly scanned the room. 'I know he hasn't been here these past weeks, but he does have spies who report back.'

Ray wanted nothing more than to sweep Leah up in his arms. He loved the way she slipped in those fancy words that totally stumped him. Just as well he was savvy enough to recognise a warning, whatever the disguise.

'Thanks for the heads up.'

Leah left him at the door leading to a narrow corridor, giving his hand a good luck squeeze.

Thirty minutes later, Ray emerged, limbs intact. He strolled over to the glass display units where Leah stood patiently waiting.

'And?' she urged, reading nothing in his stoic expression.

Ray played it for all it was worth. 'It's as I thought,' he replied glumly. 'The man wants change, and guess who's top of his hit list?'

'No, there must be some mistake. He can't possibly mean for you to leave. You are such an asset, Ray. I've heard nothing but praise for you. Would it help if I had a word?'

Leah's offer stunned Ray into silence. This beautiful wisp of a woman, ready to stand his corner had completely bowled him over. Trying to keep his rising passion under wraps proved difficult. He altered his stance. Even so, the urge to kiss her sweet mouth was strong enough for him to fluff his words. 'I, err, did I tell you, you are one attractive lady.'

Leah blushed and tapped him playfully on the chest. 'Stop it. Be serious for once.'

'I've never been more serious in my life! Look, about the meeting, I was just stringing you along. The boss man has only offered me paid work. Part-time, as and when. He reckons my knowledge about tanks is beyond valuable. Get that! Who'd have thought it? I told him I'd mull it over and get back to him.'

'I am so pleased for you, Ray. I hope you can make it work with your other commitments. On a selfish note, having you here more often will certainly make my shifts more interesting.'

Ray's life had been turned on its head. All the promises he had made decades beforehand no longer applied. From day one he had fallen hard. And if Leah's responses during the past weeks were anything to go by, she clearly felt the same. Saucy minx couldn't keep her hands off him. Not that he was complaining, mind. The mere thought of her touch had his heart pumping like a jack hammer. He had to be the luckiest man alive. Oh, he wasn't so naive as to think that people wouldn't have their little digs. He could hear them now, *Get him with his bit of posh - Must need her eyes tested -* If it made their lives all the sweeter, they could say what the hell they wanted, so long as he didn't hear them.

Later, with the sandwich bar practically to themselves, Ray topped up their glasses with the remains of the wine.

'Been meaning to say, Leah's a good name, unusual, can't say I've come across it before.'

'Oh, it isn't my full name. I was actually christened Cecelia.' She paused to compose herself. 'It caused me such grief at school. Some boys, girls too for that matter, would shout my name with an exaggerated stutter.' Leah sipped her wine and placed the glass back on the table. 'So, the moment I left school I tried out different variations and after a few years settled on the latter part only, with a slight change of spelling.'

'Kids can be total prats at times. Excuse my French,' Ray apologised. Thinking about his own name and the bunter jibes he suffered for being a bit on the chubby side. He recalled those early years when his mother's suet puddings were too hard to resist. His mouth watered. He could almost taste the sickly-sweet syrup, thick as an oil slick, covering the doughy mound,

'You know what, I reckon we're kindred spirits, you and me. I don't go by my proper name either. They named me William, but everyone knows me as Ray.'

'Ray definitely suits you, although William is a good name too. Why did you change it?'

'It might be OK for some, but not me. Anyway, that's a story for another day. Listen, are we still on for tomorrow? Sal's itching to meet you. To be honest she's doing my head in, so the sooner we get it over with the better.'

'Goodness, no pressure then. She laughed, half-heartedly. 'I, yes, Ray. I'm looking forward to it.'

'It'll be fine,' Ray reassured her. 'Sal's a good old stick, though she'd have me strung up for calling her old.' He joked. 'Salt of the earth is Sal. Everyone loves her, and I reckon you two will be ganging up on me in no time.'

Leah relaxed into the padded backrest. 'Sounds like it could be a fun evening, and from all that you've told me I feel as though I know Sal already.'

It'll be a laugh a minute if they turn up and Sal has her feet soaking in a bowl, thought Ray. *I'll brain the woman. So help me, I will.*

Chapter 52

Ruby finally accepted that Billy Beaufoy was a lost cause. Ellen had called her a dozy cow, said he wasn't worth the bother, and that stewing over some jumped-up copper nob had turned her into a damp squid.

Escaping to her room for some time alone, she curled up on the bed. The sound from the telly filtered up through the floorboards. The distinct voice of Benny Hill together with Ray's raucous outbursts had Ruby burying her head beneath the pillow.

It didn't seem that long ago that Billy moved into the area and started at her primary school. She first noticed him at the swimming baths during their six weeks of freedom. He marched along the highest diving board and with arms stretched out in front he dove straight off the end. The loud slap noise that made her gasp was a belly flop, according to her brother, Gary, who knew absolutely everything. Some kids cried because it hurt so much. Billy never did. He climbed back up that ladder and jumped off again.

Later, through secondary school, he would single her out, flirt outrageously until she resembled a beetroot, then laugh it off with his mates. She always fobbed it off, convinced herself that she was too sensitive, too shy and too bleeding pathetic for her own good. If she was serious about Billy she would need to change to fit with his idea of a girlfriend. The reality being, she'd have more luck joining the next space program than joining the slapper brigade.

She had brought it on herself. Saying that Billy was her boyfriend was more a slip of the tongue than an outright lie. He had been a friend, after all. She could hardly take it back though; admit she had made a mistake. She'd hoped that people would simply forget, allow the topic to fizzle out, like hand held sparklers.

When Jimmy mentioned he'd seen Billy at the market with the girls, her stomach had plummeted. She managed to act surprised and dismiss it as of no importance; even suggested they might be his cousins. Everyone knew the Beaufoy clan were a sizeable bunch. Jimmy had rabbited on about how Billy was bad news and not to be trusted. She'd snapped back at him, said things she'd regretted and shrugged off his concerns.

Out of embarrassment, she'd made no mention that Billy had stopped to voice his opinion about the eviction, and in front of strangers too! The shame of it had shredded her heart. His true colours, bright as neon, were close to blinding. He'd dug deeper still. Tried to worm out every heart-wrenching detail. What the hell was wrong with him? Couldn't he see beyond his gloating? At that moment in time, she detested both him and herself. For the first time ever, she wanted him gone, wished she'd never laid eyes on the ratbag. As for the two painted dolls hanging off his arms, they were welcome to him.

She had sensed Ray close by taking note and ready to step in if necessary. She was pleased he stayed back. To have him fight her battle in public would just about destroy her. Re-living the moment she'd let rip brought a tinge of exhilaration, all to quickly overshadowed by the shock of hearing herself spouting off. *Sod off back to sea and take your crabs with you.* she'd said. Her words, delivered like a smack to the face, came from nowhere, and stunned the trio into silence. The look on their faces, Rays too! Picture. Bloody. Perfect.

Ray had slipped a protective arm around her shoulder. *Couldn't have said it better myself. I knew you had it in you.* He'd paused. *Just one thing though, crabs?*

The girls!

Course. Just checking. In a bid to bolster her further, he'd added, *I'm dead proud of yer, and what's more, Billy's a poxy name anyway. Never could stand it myself. Puts me in mind of that Bunter kid.*

You should have mentioned it before. I'd have dumped him sooner.

In spite of being pleased that she'd actually turned a corner, she was nowhere close to happy. Everything was such a mess. She'd no one to blame but herself. Didn't even know if Jimmy would ever speak to her again. She'd mistook his negative digs about Billy as jealousy.

Only later did she realise he'd been looking out for her, because he cared, because that's what real mates did. Then the funfair happened. Their first proper date since making up, and she'd ruined that too! Kissing was supposed to feel good, and it did, but it also scared her.

A loud, quick-fire hammering forced her upright. She would never understand Ray's need to bash the ceiling with a broom handle, when his voice carried easily enough.

'Oi, misery cods, kettle's on if you fancy a cuppa?' he yelled.

She could hear him chuckling away, knowing full well she'd be struggling back into her skin. Buttoning up a thick Aran cardigan, Ruby made her way downstairs. Her thoughts concentrated on Jimmy. She had been a complete wally. The sooner she told him that, the sooner they could get things back on track. Fingers crossed that it wasn't too late.

The banging of the door knocker startled the pair. Ruby shoulders lifted at Ray's unspoken question.

People calling round, especially after nine, thought Ruby, checking the clock, *usually spelt trouble.*

She could hear Ray's voice but couldn't grasp the conversation. Close to finishing her tea, Ruby looked up as the sitting room door opened. She stood up, struggling to remember what she may or may not have done, as Ray stepped aside, allowing the WPC to show herself. Ruby's face fell. She could neither move or speak. Something terrible had happened. She knew it. Could feel it.

'I was passing and saw the light. Come sit yourself down, Ruby. I'd like a word in private,' The officer cast a cursory glance at Ray, who promptly disappeared upstairs.

Several minutes later, Ruby closed the street door behind the WPC. With her back to the door her body dropped into a crouched position. Ray bounded down the stairs, coaxed the girl upright and back to the settee.

'Family all OK?'

Ruby nodded.

'That's a weight lifted,' he said, breathing easier. 'So, what's brought the Old Bill to my door? Don't tell me you've nobbled that Bunter bloke? I know he had it coming but...'

'It's Uncle Tom. He's pleaded guilty.'

'Even better! Blimey girl, you should be dancing, whooping it up, not sitting there with a face like a stiff.'

'It's a shock all the same.'

'Yeah, I get what you're saying. I'm just trying to jolly you - hold on, something doesn't fit. How'd the police know where you live?'

Ruby faced him. Her vacant stare giving nothing away. 'I told them.' She swallowed. 'When I gave a statement.'

Ray stared back at her. His blank features mirroring her own. Presently, he wrapped his arms around the girl and hugged her close. 'Takes balls to do what you've done. I know grown men with less. I couldn't be prouder than if you were my own daughter.'

'No one knows about the statement, Ray. 'Cept you.'

'Mum's the word then, girl. Mum's the word.'

Chapter 53

Ray's day at the museum could not have gone better. Working part-time, he was now a recognised member of the team. His interaction with the school kids filled him with a sense of pride. Spending time helping to educate young minds gave him real purpose and a feeling of joy that he'd never experienced from flogging handbags. More and more he handed over the reins to his now partner, Luca. Ray had never imagined himself anything other than a trader. Leah had been the instigator. She'd opened his eyes, plied his shrivelled heart with balm and de-railed his life, setting him on a different course. A course he was eager to explore.

Later that evening, Leah's steps shortened as they approached the house. 'Daft as it sounds, Ray, I'm feeling nervous. Maybe I should have brought flowers, chocolates even?'

'You women are born worry mongers. Listen, I know Sal. She'll be run ragged, sorting stuff that doesn't need sorting, like arranging nibbles in funny patterns on doilies that no one will even notice.'

The moment Ray opened the street door, the warm, enticing aroma of home baking fired up his gastric juices. Sal was on form, out to impress, and he could not have been happier. Guiding Leah into what he considered the heart of the house, he zeroed in on the coffee table, bowed, he reasoned, beneath the weight of a hungry man's heaven. He stared like a kid in a tuck shop, his lips already moistened, ready to dive in. 'What, no plum duff, Sal?' Surprised that his sarcastic humour died a quick death, Ray peeled his gaze from the sausage rolls and vol-au-vents and honed in on the ladies.

Sal and Leah had stopped short of each other; the corners of their mouth's gradually lifting in unison, as they recognised each other from the bus stop.

'Bowler hat,' exclaimed Leah.

'Pidgeon poo,' Sal countered.

'What the f...' groaned Ray, his brow a network of lines. 'Did I miss something or is 'Thick' my middle name?'

The women tittered and embraced. 'We'll tell you later,' said Sal, stepping back. 'Help yourself to nibbles while I fetch the tea.'

The evening ticked along nicely, much to Ray's relief. Contentment, a word not of his choosing, suddenly sparked up in his head. It had never really figured in his life as such. Strewth, a few weeks back he wasn't even sure what the word meant. He did now though. He felt it. It was there every time Leah slipped her hand in his. It soared like an ocean wave whenever the school kids sulked about leaving the museum, and it was in the smile of his daughter. 'I am one lucky git,' he told himself.

Ruby and Pearl arrived much later, albeit unexpectedly. Despite a six-year age gap, their friendship had grown over the past weeks, helped along by their passion for trendy clothes. Ruby had jumped at Pearl's offer of a trip to Carnaby Street and the Kings Road. Their excited chatter carried down the hallway and into the sitting room, where they were greeted by a trio of smiles.

Ray stood up. 'Come on in girls. Join the party,' he gestured, ready to make the introductions when Leah spoke.

'Ruby! Oh my goodness, it's so lovely to see you. I've been so worried.' She crossed the room to kiss the girl's cheek.

'No need,' said Ruby, similarly amazed at seeing Cecelia. 'Everything turned out fine as it goes.'

'Hold your horses.' Ray looked from one to the other. What's going on here? Sal, is this a wind-up?'

A peal of laughter brought everyone together. Ray spoke to Leah. 'Please tell me you haven't met this beauty in the doorway?' He cast a wink at Pearl. 'Before I embarrass myself by introducing yous.'

'No, Ray,' said Leah, holding back the laughter. 'The floor is yours.'

Ray squeezed between Pearl and Ruby and placed his arms around them both. 'This gorgeous blonde, who clearly takes after her old man in looks, is my daughter, Pearl.'

'We didn't mean to disturb you,' said Pearl, anxiously fiddling with her beaded necklace.

'What! My little sister hasn't mentioned that I'm already disturbed; even more so after this carry-on?' He chided Sal. 'You're slipping, girl.'

Sal huffed. 'I hope you realise what you're taking on, Leah? He's a soppy sod at the best of times.'

Ruby's chin practically hit the floor. 'Are you getting married, Cece...? She hesitated, 'Leah,' she corrected herself. 'Great name by the way.'

'Will you lot give over and let a man get a word in?' Satisfied that he'd got their attention, he started over. 'As I was saying, these two gems here, Leah, help keep me in check, stop me turning into a fuddy-duddy, especially Ruby here. Am I right, sunshine?'

Ruby flushed. 'Don't go dragging me into it. And anyway, some people are past helping,' she grinned.

Ray coiled a thin length of her hair around his finger and gave a gentle tug. 'Which reminds me, been meaning to say, we won't be needing you on Saturdays anymore.'

Ruby's face, frozen in disbelief, showed the exact reaction Ray had counted on. The girl looked to Sal and back again. 'Have you just sacked me?'

'Not exactly,' said Ray. At risk of being suffocated by the silence closing in on him, he decided to come clean. 'We'll still expect you to help out some weekdays and Sundays of course. But from next Saturday you'll be working at '*Fantastic*' that boutique place. I've had to pull some strings, mind. So don't go letting me down. 9am start. On the frigging dot!'

After her initial shock, Ruby flew between Sal and Ray in a frenzy of hugs and tears, before whisking Pearl upstairs to help sort out suitable outfits.

Sal shook her head. 'If you'd held out any longer, she'd have told you to get knotted. That's all the kids ever say these days. Sounds indecent to me, but what do I know?'

Leah took it upon herself to explain. 'It's a version of get lost, I'm told. With a touch more venom.'

'Well, there you go then, no big deal,' Ray put in. 'We're all speaking the same language after-all. Might start using it myself on the stall, now that Luca's brought in neck ties as a sideline.'

'You're nuts, Ray, stark raving bonkers. Have a word here, Leah. You'll be the one cutting him loose when they've strung him with his bleeding ties.'

'It's progress, Sal,' said Ray.

'What, being hung? I don't know what's got into you of late.' Sal stopped herself going any further. She did know the cause of his upbeat silliness. It was there in his face. Her brother was in love. She looked over at Leah. 'I've just one thing to say to you, Leah. Welcome to the mad house.'

Chapter 54

Sal's attention shifted between Ruby and a paying customer. 'Stone the crows, duck,' she sighed in Ruby's direction. 'You certainly pick your moments!' Snapping the till drawer shut and keeping her voice low, Sal continued. 'Haven't you two sorted it yet? Jimmy's got a face like a plank, so George tells me, and that don't bode well for business. And look at you! Just gis a minute,' she said hurriedly, stopping to bag up bread pudding for a regular. 'As I was saying, you've lost your spark. And all this moping about, like someone's just stepped on your budgie isn't helping.'

'Never had a budgie, Sal.'

Sal sighed, moved round to Ruby's side of the counter and clasped the girl's hands. 'You know what I mean, lovey. Now please, just go and talk to him.'

Ruby had walked towards Jimmy's stall several times already that week. Her steps followed the same stop-start pattern each time. Never had she been more thankful of strangers blocking her route. The closer she got, the slower her movement. Strands of white fur pulled from the trim of her purple coat fluttered to the ground; her courage tumbled alongside. Within yards, she froze. Had George seen her? She could certainly see him, scowling in her direction. Ruby imagined him striding across, his face in hers, warning her off. With nerves frayed, she'd bottled out and had dashed back the way she came.

'I'm scared, Sal. What if he refuses to listen, tells me to get lost?' A sudden panic widened her dewy eyes. 'And what about George? He hates the sight of me. I know he does.'

'Now you're being silly. George is a big softy, a teddy bear with one of them growler thingies that barely squeaks. But he does have a son he dotes on.' Sal fussed with Ruby's hair. 'Look, I'm not getting at you, and no one likes to admit being wrong. My old mum would say, *least said soonest mended*. She lived by that rule and saved umpteen ding-dongs from escalating. Sorry might be a small word,' she explained, holding her thumb and forefinger a fraction apart, 'but it has the greatest impact.'

Ruby knew that Sal would set her straight. Although the pep talk had yet to sink in or ease her worries. 'Us women get ourselves into some fixes, don't we?' Sal chuckled. 'Here's me fighting off George while you're preparing to...'

Ruby's shoulders dropped. 'Oh Sal, I'm so sorry. It completely skipped my mind. Is it all settled then, with George? Have you set a date?'

'A date?' exclaimed Sal, guiding Ruby towards the door. 'Whatever for? Me and George are fine as we are. He just needs a little more convincing.' She grinned. 'Besides, I'm too old for change, duck. Routines all up the wall would drive me bananas. See, I like my own space, time to myself or not as the mood takes me. Now, you toddle off and make amends. Oh, and don't be late for dinner, you're down for washing up.'

The Lane had quietened down. With the bulk of sales over, traders began packing up. Aware of George making space in the van, Ruby fidgeted at the stall's edge, in spite of the freezing temperature, a sudden heat enveloped her. She leaned in harder against the stall, praying that her legs would not give way. With no interest in the remaining trinkets strewn across the velvet cover, Ruby lifted the closest to hand, balancing the hollow cone shaped item across her palm. It put her in mind of a miniature foghorn. The narrow end had a definite curve, bent during packing, she guessed; not that she cared about some dodgy looking piece of tarnished silver. However, it allowed her time to get her thoughts together and voice her apology.

She sensed Jimmy watching her, but was too self-conscious to look up and meet his gaze head-on. Afraid that the hurt she caused would still be there, reflected back at her. What a mess she'd made of things. Ruby knew if she walked away now there would be no going back, but would an apology ever be enough?

'Dad says it's a gadget for old dogs,' said Jimmy, appearing at her side. Stepping closer still, he continued. 'You slip it on their doodah to stop wet patches on the mat.' Maintaining a straight face was harder than he imagined.

The item flew across the display faster than a catapulted conker and bounced off the pavement beyond the stall. 'You rot pot! I can't believe you let me touch that disgusting thing.' she screeched, rubbing her hand up and down her coat sleeve. 'If I catch the lurgy, it'll be down to you.' Her contorted features began to soften. 'And I thought you were my friend?'

Jimmy, bent double from laughing, peered up. Catching breath enough to reply. 'I've never stopped being your friend, Rube.'

'Then tell me truthfully. Was that thing really a dog's gadget?'

He grinned. 'Of course not. But it was so worth it. The look on your face was priceless. But if it makes you feel any better, I think I've busted my gut.'

'You'll get no sympathy from me. So what is it?'

'Ruptured appendix I reckon,' he moaned for effect.

'I'm talking about that thing,' she pointed. 'As well you know.'

'Ruby Denton,' he paused, finding it difficult to speak with a soppy grin on his face. 'I love you so much. And that little antique you've just trashed was a Victorian ear trumpet, and might well have set us up for life,' he exaggerated.

The implications of Jimmy's words sailed over Ruby's head. She had yet to make her apology, although thanks to Jimmy, the ice had quickly thawed. But her mind remained busy with questions about the strawberry blonde she had seen hanging around his stall. A girl, who reminded her of the Barbarella character from the film of the same name. Everything about the girl was oversized: her hair, her smile and her pointy boobs. Had Ruby been burdened with such bazoomas, as Daisy called them, she would live her life face down on the pavement. Several times now, Ruby had seen the girl cosying up to Jimmy, with him seemingly enjoying the attention. Maybe he had been dating her, as remarked on by Ray in one of his tactless moments. Whatever the truth, she had to know either way.

Jimmy and Ruby both spoke at the same time, and a tentative smile was shared between them.

'You first,' he said.

Ruby took a breath. 'I, um, I never meant to upset you,' she began, shifting her weight to the other foot. 'I've been such an idiot, acting like a complete flake.'

'Let's leave it there Rube,' he winked. The way I see it, we're as bad as each other.'

With questions remaining about Barbarella, Ruby needed to tread carefully. She could not afford to get it wrong again.

'I expect George is well down on stock now,' she prompted. 'I've watched you both fighting off customers this past week.'

'Have you now?' said Jimmy, surprised. 'Ray given you the push, has he?'

'I should be so lucky! I've been trying to catch up with you but you're always so stretched. I came by yesterday, but that girl with the hair got in first.' Noting Jimmy's puzzled frown, she added. 'Do we know her from school?' Ruby was safe in the knowledge that she had never seen her before, and had no wish to do so again. He had to know who she meant. Half The Lane's customers had had their eyes glued to the blonde's anatomy.

A look of recognition brightened Jimmy's face. 'Oh, you mean the one with the big...' He began to raise his hands when Ruby interrupted.

'Yes. big hair. Like I said.'

'Oh, yeah. She's been helping me with a personal matter.'

Ruby's heart dipped and a wave of misery washed through her. Jimmy's initial crime had been to warn her, save her from the likes of Billy Beaufoy, which she'd completely misread. Pushing him away had to be the dumbest thing she'd ever done. Worse still was to ignore him because of a kiss that turned her insides to mush. The last thing she needed was details about Barbarella, and the part she now played in Jimmy's life. Feeling as though her world had crumbled to dust, she started to walk away.

'Listen, I was that excited Rube,' he gushed, catching her by the arm. 'It's been torture keeping it to myself. That's part of the reason I've been avoiding you, didn't want to blurt it out and spoil the surprise.'

'And the other part?'

Jimmy had no sooner opened his mouth, when Ruby quickly added, 'It's Okay, I already know I'm the biggest clot.'

Jimmy shushed her. 'It wasn't all your doing, Rube. We both spoke out of turn. Now let me get on with what I'm trying to tell you. That girl you mentioned, she's the pools man's daughter. You know the bloke, ginger beard, wonky eye, goes round collecting all the dosh and coupons.'

'I didn't know you were into football?'

'I'm not. I mean I like a kick-about, but doing the pools is a different kind of skill. Gist of it is, her dad reckoned my spot the ball looked to be spot on. In his experience of course. Reckoned I could be rolling in it. I had plans to surprise you, big-time.'

The knots in Ruby's stomach began to unravel.

'His daughter suggested places I could take you. places that normally we'd never get to go.'

'She was helping you?'

'Yeah, straight up. What? You didn't think there was something else going on, did you?'

Ruby's head bowed. With no reply forthcoming he titled her chin up and kissed her gently on the mouth. A loud cheer went up around them.

'I told you before, I love you. You are the only girl for me, Rube.'

A fluttery feeling danced in her belly. All her doubts and nagging thoughts simply melted away. 'So, where are you taking me then?'

'You'd never have guessed in a million years,' he gushed. 'I had the Savoy booked, malady, with candles, champagne, the whole shebang. Only the best for the best.' Jimmy removed his woollen neck scarf and draped it over his forearm. 'At your service madam,' he bowed.

'Had?'

'Yeah. There's the rub,' he sighed, suddenly crestfallen. He looped the scarf around her neck. 'Had to cancel, didn't I. I was miles out on the coupon. Didn't win a bleeding sausage.'

His disappointment ran deep. 'Now I'm the one who's apologising, Rube. But I will take you there one day. I promise. Listen, I can't match that a la carte stuff, but I could rustle up a Vesta curry later. Dad's got stacks in the cupboard.'

Ruby tried to turn things around. 'Never mind the Savoy, we got posh-nosh right here on the doorstep.'

Jimmy's face without his trademark smile tugged at her heart. She felt responsible and would make amends as best she could. The idea of something comforting, familiar and local came to mind. Ruby grabbed his hand and dragged him away from the stall. His father, George, hollered in the background as the couple ran towards the top of The Lane. They swerved around the elderly sandwich board carrier, displaying the regular ominous message. *The end of the world is nigh.*

'Will be, mate' Jimmy assured him. 'If my dad catches up with us.'

'I know exactly where we should go,' Ruby beamed.

'It'd better be worth it, because dad will skin my arse with his hobnails when I get back.'

They came to a halt a few streets up, refilled their lungs and joined the short queue outside Arments.

'Pie, mash 'n' liquor!' remarked Jimmy. 'I'd never have guessed.'

'What's not to love?' asked Ruby. 'Food of the gods. Pure and simple. If it's good enough for them, it's good enough for us.'

'And worth every inch of skin from my backside.' Jimmy's smile returned. With his scarf still round Ruby's neck, he pulled the ends and drew her in.

Holding her tight in his arms, Ruby nuzzled into his shoulder.

'A girl after my own heart,' he whispered lovingly.

'You bet,' said Ruby. 'Spot on!'

The moment their lips touched, a loud hum, mimicking a police siren, filled the space around them. Ruby coloured up, pulled back and turned to face the ill-timed intruder.

'He your boyfriend now?' asked Daisy.

'Yes. What! Blimey, where'd you spring from? Are you on your own?' Ruby asked, quickly surveying the area.

''Scuse me, but I'm not a baby, Rube. I am allowed out.' Daisy huffed. Her back straightening, adding inches to her height. 'I followed yous from the market. Didn't know you could run so fast. Did you pinch something?'

Ruby gave a brief throaty laugh and peered directly at Jimmy to garner his response, but with his vision now trained rigidly elsewhere, she knew he too struggled to keep a straight face.

'I can't believe you asked that.' Ruby removed a loosened Betty Rubble clip from Daisy's hair and re-positioning it. 'Of course we didn't steal anything.'

Daisy sagged with relief. 'Well that's good, cos I'm done with running. Me legs feel like sponge already just chasing you here. So, you having pie 'n' mash then?'

'Um, that was the plan,' said Ruby.

'Still is,' Jimmy agreed.

'Well, lucky for me I showed up then. I've had nothing since me breakfast.' Daisy moved closer to the door. 'Best I wait in the warm. I'll save us a table,' she called as she weaved her way around the queue and disappeared inside. Moments later she rushed back and threw her arms around her big sister. 'I miss you so much Rube,' her words dampened by the folds of Ruby's jumper. 'I wish you didn't have to stay with Sal. I get scared sometimes, thinking that we'll lose each other again.'

'Now you listen to me.' With her hands resting against Daisy's cheeks, Ruby tilted her face upwards, 'That will never happen. I know exactly where you are, and as for me - everything I love is right here, in this little pocket of London, and I am not budging an inch.'

'Promise?'

'Cross me heart and hope to wotsit, as you would say.'

Daisy stepped backwards, her smile reaching her ears. 'Thanks Rube. I'd best get inside before someone pinches our table.' And with that she was gone.

'Blimey,' said Jimmy incredulously. When did the cheeky little imp become a mini tornado?'

'It's a long story.'

'Ah, but from what you've just said, unless you're fibbing,' Jimmy's eyes tapered, 'you're not going anywhere?'

Taking hold of his hand, Ruby laced her fingers through his. 'And I meant every word, but,' she hesitated. 'Tell you what, let's leave the past where it is. Out with the old and in with the new, that's what everyone'll be singing about in a few short weeks.' A sensation of butterflies swelled in her belly, bringing with it an excitement matched only by those childhood Christmas mornings, on waking to find a partially stuffed pillowcase hanging from the bed frame. 'Let's get ahead of the game. Let's start now.'

'No reason not to. Just don't expect me to start belting out Auld Lang Syne,' Jimmy quipped. 'Else I'll be wearing pie 'n' mash instead of tucking into it.'

Ruby laughed, and tugged on his hand. 'No you won't, but what a great idea. Come on, we'll sing together. Cheer everyone up. Let's do it as a dare.'

'You're flipping serious, aren't you? They'll think we're nuts, Rube. We haven't even had Christmas yet.'

'Oh, come on. It'll be a laugh.'

'For who? said Jimmy. 'We have to live here. Remember?'

Ruby pushed open the door. In between a fit of giggling, she spurred Jimmy on. 'I thought you liked a bet? Well, I bet you chicken out.'

They stood together in the open doorway. 'I will never live this down. You owe me Ruby Denton. Bigtime!'

They stepped across the threshold and into the crowded shop. The door behind them slowly juddered to a close ...

Printed in Great Britain
by Amazon